BE

Hebrew

PHRASE BOOK & DICTIONARY

Easy to use features

- Handy thematic colour coding
- Quick Reference Section—opposite page
- Tipping Guide—inside back cover
- Quick reply panels throughout

How best to use this phrase book

• We suggest that you start with the **Guide to pronunciation** (pp. 6-9), then go on to **Some basic expressions** (pp. 10-15). This gives you not only a minimum vocabulary, but also helps you get used to pronouncing the language. The phonetic transcription throughout the book enables you to pronounce every word correctly.

• Consult the **Contents** pages (3-5) for the section you need. In each chapter you'll find travel facts, hints and useful information. Simple phrases are followed by a list of words applicable to the situation.

• Separate, detailed contents lists are included at the beginning of the extensive **Eating out** and **Shopping guide** sections (Menus, p. 39, Shops and services, p. 97).

• If you want to find out how to say something in Hebrew, your fastest look-up is via the **Dictionary** section (pp. 164-189). This not only gives you the word, but is also cross-referenced to its use in a phrase on a specific page.

• If you wish to learn more about constructing sentences, check the **Basic grammar** (pp. 159-163).

• Note the **colour margins** are indexed in Hebrew and English to help both listener and speaker. And, in addition, there is also an **index in Hebrew** for the use of your listener.

• Throughout the book, this symbol ☛ suggests phrases your listener can use to answer you. If you still can't understand, hand this phrase book to the Hebrew-speaker to encourage pointing to an appropriate answer.

Library of Congress Catalog Card No. 73-2274
Second revised edition—2nd printing 1994 Printed in Switzerland

Contents

Travelling around 65

Sightseeing 80

Relaxing 86

Making friends 92

Shopping guide 97

Acknowledgements
We are particularly grateful to Josephine Bacon and Yochanan Kinory for their help in the preparation of this book.

Guide to pronunciation

The alphabet

Listed below are the characters of the Hebrew alphabet (capital letters do not exist). The left-hand column shows the handwritten characters, the middle column their printed form. Five characters (צ, פ, נ, מ, כ) take on a different form when they appear at the end of a word (shown beside them).

א	א	alef	ל	ל	lamed
בּ	בּ	bet	מ, ם	מ, ם	mem
ב	ב	vet	נ, ן	נ, ן	nun
ג	ג	gimel	ס	ס	samekh
ד	ד	dalet	ע	ע	ain
ה	ה	he	פּ	פּ	pe
ו	ו	vav	פ, ף	פ, ף	fe
ז	ז	zain	צ, ץ	צ, ץ	tzadi
ח	ח	ḥet	ק	ק	kof
ט	ט	tet	ר	ר	resh
י	י	yod	שׁ	שׁ	shin
כּ	כּ	kaf	שׂ	שׂ	sin
כ, ך	כ, ך	khaf	ת	ת	tav

This section and the next one are intended to make you familiar with the transcription system we have used, and to get you accustomed to the sounds of the language.

The sounds of Hebrew

Traditional Hebrew script is composed of consonants only and written from right to left. A system of vowel signs (dots and lines with the characters), used mainly in poetry, in liturgical writing and in texts for beginners—including this phrase book—ensures proper pronunciation.

The transcription we use gives an approximation of the sounds of the language as we would say them, written in our own latin alphabet as opposed to the traditional Hebrew alphabet. The phrases can be said quite easily once a few rules have been mastered: in this transcription, letters shown in bold print should be read with more stress (louder) than the others; all vowels must be pronounced distinctly; apart from **ey** and **ay**, there are no diphthongs in the transcription.

If you follow the indications below carefully, you should be able to make yourself understood. In addition, listening to native speakers and constant practice will help you to improve your accent.

Letter	Approximate pronunciation	Example	
א	accompanies vowel sign (see below) and is pronounced accordingly **a**, **e**, **i**, **o** or **u**	אָמַר	a**mar**
		אֶשְׁכּוֹלִית	eshko**lit**
		אִשָּׁה	i**sha**
		אוֹר	or
		אוּלְפָּן	ul**pan**
בּ	like **b** in **b**oy	בּוּל	bul
ב	like **v** in **v**ery	בָּבֶל	Ba**vel**
ג	like **g** in **g**old	גָּמָל	ga**mal**
ד	like **d** in **d**ay	דָּג	dag
ה	like **h** in **h**ail	הֶגֶה	**he**ge
ו	1) like **v** in **v**ery	וֶרֶד	**ve**red
	2) may also serve as a vowel and is then pronounced **o** or **u**	אוּלָם	u**lam**
		אוֹלָר	o**lar**
ז	like **z** in **z**eal	זֶמֶר	**ze**mer

ח	like **ch** in the Scottish **loch** (symbol used **ḥ**)	חַיָּט	ḥayat
ט	like **t** in **tip**	טַיָּס	tayas
י	1) like **y** in **yard**	יֶלֶד	yeled
	2) may also serve as a vowel and is then pronounced **i**	שִׁירָה	shira
כּ	like **k** in **kite**	כָּתַב	katav
כ / ך	like **ch** in the Scottish lo**ch**, (a "soft" כּ); symbol used **kh**	מִכְתָּב	mikhtav
		פָּרִיךְ	parikh
ל	like **l** in **let**	לָשׁוֹן	lashon
מ / ם	like **m** in co**m**e	מָלוֹן	malon
		מַיִם	mayim
נ / ן	like **n** in **n**ot	נַעֲרָה	naara
		שָׁעוֹן	shaon
ס	like **s** in **s**it	סוֹחֵר	soḥer
ע	accompanies vowel sign and is pronounced accordingly **a**, **e**, **i**, **o** or **u**	עָמַד	amad
		עֶזְרָה	ezra
		עִתּוֹן	iton
		עוֹרֵךְ־דִּין	orekh din
		עוּגָה	uga
פּ	like **p** in **p**ot	פַּרְדֵּס	pardes
פ / ף	(a "soft" פּ) like **f** in **f**it	קָפֶה	kafe
		עוֹף	of
צ / ץ	like **ts** in hi**ts** (symbol used **tz**)	צֶמֶר	tzemer
		נַעַץ	naatz
ק	like **k** in **k**ite	בֹּקֶר	boker
ר	a gargling **r** sound, like in the French word **r**ire	תַּפְרִיט	tafrit
שׁ	like **sh** in **sh**oulder	שֶׁמֶשׁ	shemesh
שׂ	like **s** in **s**it	שְׂמִיכָה	smikha
ת	like **t** in **t**ip	תּוֹדָה	toda

Note: The letters א ,ו ,י can also function as vowels depending on the vowel sign:

א	like **a**, **e**, **o**, **i** or **u**
ו	**o** or **u**
י	like **i**

Vowel signs

Vowel signs and dots occur mostly under the letter; sometimes inside or over it. They are pronounced **after** the letter that carries the sign, e.g.: פָּשׁוּט **pashut**.

The system of vowel signs is as follows:

אֲ/אָ/אַ	pronounced as **a** in bar (symbol used **a**)	סַפָּר	sapar
		אֲגַם	agam
אַי	pronounced as **igh** in h**igh** (symbol used **ay**)	חַי	ḥay
אֵי	pronounced as **ey** in th**ey**	אֵיפֹה	eyfo
אֶ/אֱ/אֵ	pronounced as **e** in net (symbol used **e**)	אֶרֶץ	eretz
		אֱמֶת	emet
		שֵׂכֶל	sekhel
אִ	pronounced as **ee** (symbol used **i**) in m**ee**t	רִבָּה	riba
		גִּיטָרָה	gitara
אֳ/אוֹ/אֹ	pronounced as **oo** in d**oo**r (symbol used **o**)	אֹהֶל	ohel
		שׁוֹטֵר	shoter
		אֳנִיָּה	oniya
אֻ/אוּ	pronounced as **oo** (symbol used **u**) in b**oo**t	לַחוּת	laḥut
		שֻׁלְחָן	shulḥan
אְ	1) sometimes pronounced like **e** in net	לְחַיִּים	leḥayim
	2) sometimes not pronounced and not transcribed	כְּלִי	kli

Some basic expressions

Yes.	כֵּן.	ken
No.	לֹא.	lo
Please.	בְּבַקָּשָׁה.	bevaka**sha**
Thank you.	תּוֹדָה.	to**da**
Thank you very much.	תּוֹדָה רַבָּה.	to**da** ra**ba**
That's all right/You're welcome.	עַל לֹא דָבָר/בְּבַקָּשָׁה.	al lo da**var**/bevaka**sha**

Greetings בְּרָכוֹת

Good morning.	בֹּקֶר טוֹב.	**bo**ker tov
Good afternoon.	שָׁלוֹם.	sha**lom**
Good evening.	עֶרֶב טוֹב.	**e**rev tov
Good night.	לַיְלָה טוֹב.	**lay**la tov
Goodbye.	שָׁלוֹם.	sha**lom**
See you later.	לְהִתְרָאוֹת.	lehitra**ot**
Hello/Hi!	שָׁלוֹם.	sha**lom**
This is Mr/Mrs/Miss ...	תַּכִּיר (תַּכִּירִי*) אֶת מַר/גְבֶרֶת/גְבֶרֶת...	ta**kir** (ta**ki**ri) et mar/g**ve**ret/g**ve**ret
How do you do? (Pleased to meet you.)	נָעִים מְאֹד.	na**im** me**od**
How are you?	מַה שְׁלוֹמְךָ (שְׁלוֹמֵךְ)?	ma shlom**kha** (shlo**mekh**)
Very well, thanks. And you?	טוֹב תּוֹדָה. וְאַתָּה (וְאַתְּ)?	tov **toda**. vea**ta** (ve**at**)
How's life?	אֵיךְ הָעִנְיָנִים?	eykh hainya**nim**
Fine.	בְּסֵדֶר.	be**se**der
I beg your pardon?	סְלִיחָה?	sli**ḥa**
Excuse me. (May I get past?)	סְלִיחָה.	sli**ḥa**
Sorry!	סְלִיחָה!	sli**ḥa**

---

*Verbs in Hebrew change their endings according to whether the subject of the sentence is a man or a woman. Where there is a difference, forms used by a woman speaker or to address a woman are given in parentheses. For more details, see GRAMMAR section.

Questions שְׁאֵלוֹת

Where?	אֵיפֹה?	**ey**fo
How?	אֵיךְ?	eykh
When?	מָתַי?	ma**tay**
What?	מָה?	ma
Why?	מַדּוּעַ?	ma**dua**
Who?	מִי?	mi
Which?	אֵיזֶה (אֵיזוֹ)?	**ey**ze (**ey**zo)
Where is ... ?	אֵיפֹה...?	**ey**fo
Where are ... ?	אֵיפֹה...?	**ey**fo
Where can I find/ get ... ?	אֵיפֹה אוּכַל לִמְצֹא/לְהַשִּׂיג...?	**ey**fo **ukhal** lim**tzo**/leha**sig**
How far?	זֶה רָחוֹק?	ze ra**ḥok**
How long?	כַּמָּה זְמַן זֶה לוֹקֵחַ?	**ka**ma zman ze lo**keaḥ**
How much/How many?	כַּמָּה?	**ka**ma
How much does this cost?	כַּמָּה זֶה עוֹלֶה?	**ka**ma ze **ole**
When does ... open/ close?	מָתַי פּוֹתְחִים/סוֹגְרִים אֶת ...?	ma**tay** poṭ**ḥim**/sog**rim** et
What do you call this/that in ... ?	אֵיךְ קוֹרְאִים לָזֶה בְּ...?	eykh kor**im** le**ze** be
What does this/that mean?	מָה זֹאת אוֹמֶרֶת?	ma zot o**meret**

Do you speak ... ? אַתָּה (אַתְּ) מְדַבֵּר (מְדַבֶּרֶת) ...?

Do you speak English?	אַתָּה (אַתְּ) מְדַבֵּר (מְדַבֶּרֶת) אַנְגְּלִית?	**ata** (at) meda**ber** (meda**beret**) ang**lit**
Does anyone here speak English?	מִישֶׁהוּ כָּאן מְדַבֵּר אַנְגְּלִית?	**mi**shehu kan meda**ber** ang**lit**
I don't speak (much) Hebrew.	אֵינֶנִּי מְדַבֵּר (מְדַבֶּרֶת) עִבְרִית (טוֹבָה).	ey**ne**ni meda**ber** (meda**beret**) iv**rit** (**tova**)
Could you speak more slowly?	אֶפְשָׁר לְדַבֵּר יוֹתֵר לְאַט?	ef**shar** leda**ber** yo**ter** leat
Could you repeat that?	תּוּכַל (תּוּכְלִי) לוֹמַר זֹאת שֵׁנִית?	tu**khal** (tukh**li**) lo**mar** zot she**nit**
Could you spell it?	תּוּכַל (תּוּכְלִי) לְאַיֵּת זֹאת?	tu**khal** (tukh**li**) lea**yet** zot

How do you pronounce this?	איך מבטאים את זה?	eykh mevat**im** et ze
Could you write it down, please?	תוכל (תוכלי) לכתוב זאת בבקשה?	tu**khal** (tukh**li**) likh**tov** zot bevaka**sha**
Can you translate this for me?	תוכל (תוכלי) לתרגם זאת בשבילי?	tu**khal** (tukh**li**) letar**gem** zot bishvi**li**
Can you translate this for us?	תוכל (תוכלי) לתרגם זאת בשבילנו?	tu**khal** (tukh**li**) letar**gem** zot bishvi**le**nu
Could you point to the ... in the book, please?	תוכל (תוכלי) להראות את ה... בספר, בבקשה?	tu**khal** (tukh**li**) leha**rot** et ha ... ba**se**fer bevaka**sha**
word	מלה	mi**la**
phrase	ביטוי	bi**tuy**
sentence	משפט	mish**pat**
Just a moment.	רק רגע.	rak **re**ga
I'll see if I can find it in this book.	אנסה למצא את זה בספר.	ana**se** lim**tzo** et ze ba**se**fer
I understand.	אני מבין (מבינה).	**ani** me**vin** (mevi**na**)
I don't understand.	אינני מבין (מבינה).	ey**ne**ni me**vin** (mevi**na**)
Do you understand?	אתה (את) מבין (מבינה)?	**ata** (at) me**vin** (mevi**na**)

Can/May ... ? אפשר/אוכל ...?

Can I have ... ?	אוכל לקבל ...?	u**khal** leka**bel**
Can we have ... ?	נוכל לקבל ...?	nu**khal** leka**bel**
Can you show me ... ?	תוכל (תוכלי) להראות לי ...?	tu**khal** (tukh**li**) leha**rot** li
I can't.	אינני יכול (יכולה).	ey**ne**ni ya**khol** (yekho**la**)
Can you tell me ... ?	תוכל (תוכלי) לומר לי ...?	tu**khal** (tukh**li**) lo**mar** li
Can you help me?	תוכל (תוכלי) לעזור לי?	tu**khal** (tukh**li**) laa**zor** li
Can I help you?	אוכל לעזור לך (לך)?	u**khal** laa**zor** le**kha** (lakh)
Can you direct me to ... ?	תוכל (תוכלי) להדריך אותי ל...?	tu**khal** (tukh**li**) lehad**rikh** o**ti** le

Do you want ... ? אתה (את) רוצה (רוצה)?

I'd like ...	אבקש ...	ava**kesh**
We'd like ...	נבקש ...	neva**kesh**
What do you want?	מה אתה (את) רוצה (רוצה)?	ma **ata** (at) **rotze** (rot**za**)

Could you give me ... ?	תּוּכַל (תּוּכְלִי) לָתֵת לִי ...?	tu**khal** (tukh**li**) la**tet** li
Could you bring me ... ?	תּוּכַל (תּוּכְלִי) לְהָבִיא לִי ...?	tu**khal** (tukh**li**) leha**vi** li
Could you show me ... ?	תּוּכַל (תּוּכְלִי) לְהַרְאוֹת לִי ...?	tu**khal** (tukh**li**) leha**rot** li
I'm looking for ...	אֲנִי מְחַפֵּשׂ (מְחַפֶּשֶׂת) ...	**ani** meḥa**pes** (meḥa**pes**et)
I'm searching for ...	אֲנִי מְחַפֵּשׂ (מְחַפֶּשֶׂת) ...	**ani** meḥa**pes** (meḥa**pes**et)
I'm hungry.	אֲנִי רָעֵב (רְעֵבָה).	**ani** ra**ev** (ree**va**)
I'm thirsty.	אֲנִי צָמֵא (צְמֵאָה).	**ani** tza**me** (tzme**a**)
I'm tired.	אֲנִי עָיֵף (עֲיֵפָה).	**ani** a**yef** (aye**fa**)
I'm lost.	תָּעִיתִי בַּדֶּרֶךְ.	ta**i**ti ba**de**rekh
It's important.	זֶה חָשׁוּב.	ze ḥa**shuv**
It's urgent.	זֶה דָּחוּף.	ze da**ḥuf**

It is/There is ... זֶה/יֵשׁ ...

It is ...	זֶה ...	ze
Is it ... ?	הַאִם זֶה ...?	ha**im** ze
It isn't ...	זֶה לֹא ...	ze lo
Here it is.	הִנֵּה זֶה.	hi**ne** ze
Here they are.	הִנֵּה הֵם.	hi**ne** hem
There it is.	זֶה שָׁם.	ze sham
There they are.	הֵם שָׁם.	hem sham
There is/There are ...	יֵשׁ ...	yesh
Is there/Are there ... ?	הַאִם יֵשׁ ...?	ha**im** yesh
There isn't/aren't ...	אֵין ...	eyn
There isn't/aren't any.	אֵין.	eyn

It's ... * זֶה ...

beautiful/ugly	יָפֶה (יָפָה)/מְכוֹעָר (מְכוֹעֶרֶת)	ya**fe** (ya**fa**)/mekho**ar** (mekho**e**ret)
better/worse	יוֹתֵר טוֹב (טוֹבָה)/יוֹתֵר גָּרוּעַ (גְּרוּעָה)	yo**ter** tov (to**va**)/yo**ter** ga**rua** (grua)
big/small	גָּדוֹל (גְּדוֹלָה)/קָטָן (קְטַנָּה)	ga**dol** (gdo**la**)/ka**tan** (kta**na**)
cheap/expensive	זוֹל (זוֹלָה)/יָקָר (יְקָרָה)	zol (zo**la**)/ya**kar** (yeka**ra**)
early/late	מוּקְדָּם (מוּקְדֶּמֶת)/מְאוּחָר (מְאוּחֶרֶת)	muk**dam** (muk**de**met)/meu**khar** (meu**khe**ret)

* Adjectives in Hebrew agree with the gender of the noun to which they refer. In this section adjectives referring to feminine nouns are in parentheses. See GRAMMAR section p.163.

easy/difficult	קַל (קַלָּה)/קָשֶׁה (קָשָׁה)	kal (ka**la**)/ka**she** (ka**sha**)
free (vacant)/ occupied	פָּנוּי (פְּנוּיָה)/תָּפוּס (תְּפוּסָה)	pa**nuy** (pnu**ya**)/ta**fus** (tfu**sa**)
full/empty	מָלֵא (מְלֵאָה)/רֵיק (רֵיקָה)	ma**le** (mle**a**)/rek (re**ka**)
good/bad	טוֹב (טוֹבָה)/רַע (רָעָה)	tov (to**va**)/ra (ra**a**)
heavy/light	כָּבֵד (כְּבֵדָה)/קַל (קַלָּה)	ka**ved** (kve**da**)/kal (ka**la**)
here/there	פֹּה/שָׁם	po/sham
hot/cold	חַם (חַמָּה)/קַר (קָרָה)	ḥam (ḥa**ma**)/kar (ka**ra**)
near/far	קָרוֹב (קְרוֹבָה)/רָחוֹק (רְחוֹקָה)	ka**rov** (kro**va**)/ra**ḥok** (reḥo**ka**)
next/last	הַבָּא (הַבָּאָה)/הָאַחֲרוֹן (הָאַחֲרוֹנָה)	ha**ba** (haba**a**)/haaḥa**ron** (haaḥaro**na**)
old/new	יָשָׁן (יְשָׁנָה)/חָדָשׁ (חֲדָשָׁה)	ya**shan** (yesha**na**)/ḥa**dash** (ḥada**sha**)
old/young	זָקֵן (זְקֵנָה)/צָעִיר (צְעִירָה)	za**ken** (zke**na**/tza**ir** (tzei**ra**)
open/shut	פָּתוּחַ (פְּתוּחָה)/סָגוּר (סְגוּרָה)	pa**tuaḥ** (ptu**ḥa**)/sa**gur** (sgu**ra**)
quick/slow	מָהִיר (מְהִירָה)/אִטִּי (אִטִּית)	ma**hir** (mehi**ra**)/i**ti** (i**tit**)
right/wrong	נָכוֹן (נְכוֹנָה)/לֹא נָכוֹן (לֹא נְכוֹנָה)	na**khon** (nekho**na**)/lo na**khon** (lo nekho**na**)

Quantities כַּמֻּיּוֹת

a little/a lot	קְצָת/הַרְבֵּה	ke**tzat**/har**be**
few/a few	כַּמָּה	ka**ma**
much	הַרְבֵּה	har**be**
many	הַרְבֵּה	har**be**
more/less (than)	יוֹתֵר/פָּחוֹת (מֵאֲשֶׁר)	**yo**ter/pa**ḥot** (mi)
enough/too much	מַסְפִּיק/יוֹתֵר מִדַּי	mas**pik**/**yo**ter mi**day**
some/any	קְצָת	ke**tzat**

A few more useful words עוֹד כַּמָּה מִלִּים שִׁמּוּשִׁיּוֹת

above	מֵעַל	me**al**
after	אַחֲרֵי	aḥa**rey**
and	וְ...	ve
at	בְּ...	be
before (time)	לִפְנֵי	lif**ney**
behind	מֵאֲחוֹרֵי	meaḥo**rey**
below	מִתַּחַת	mi**ta**ḥat
between	בֵּין	beyn

but	אֲבָל	a**val**
down	לְמַטָּה	le**ma**ta
downstairs	לְמַטָּה	le**ma**ta
during	בְּמֶשֶׁךְ	be**me**shekh
for	בִּשְׁבִיל	bish**vil**
from	מִ...	mi
in	בְּ...	be
inside	בִּפְנִים/בְּתוֹךְ	bif**nim**/be**tokh**
near	קָרוֹב	ka**rov**
never	אַף פַּעַם לֹא	af **paam** lo
next to	סָמוּךְ לְ...	sa**mukh** le
none	לֹא כלום	lo khlum
not	לֹא	lo
nothing	שׁוּם דָּבָר	shum da**var**
now	עַכְשָׁו	akh**shav**
on	עַל	al
only	רַק	rak
or	אוֹ	o
outside	בַּחוּץ	ba**ḥutz**
perhaps	אוּלַי	u**lay**
since	מֵאָז	me**az**
soon	בְּקָרוֹב	beka**rov**
then	אָז	az
through	דֶּרֶךְ	**de**rekh
to	לְ...	le
too (also)	גַּם	gam
towards	לִקְרַאת	lik**rat**
under	מִתַּחַת	mi**ta**ḥat
until	עַד	ad
up	לְמַעְלָה	le**ma**ala
upstairs	לְמַעְלָה	le**ma**ala
very	מְאֹד	me**od**
with	עִם	im
without	בְּלִי	bli
yet	אוּלָם/עֲדַיִן	u**lam**/a**da**yin

Arrival

Passport control בִּקֹּרֶת דַּרְכּוֹנִים

Whether you've arrived by ship or plane, you'll have to go through passport and customs formalities. If you plan to visit an Arab country at some future date, ask the immigration official to put the visa stamp on an immigration form rather than in your passport; most Middle Eastern countries do not accept passports bearing Israeli stamps. Your entry stamp is good for a stay of up to three months.
Note: Passports must be valid for a minimum of six months after the intended date of arrival. Visitor's passports are not acceptable.

Here's my passport.	הִנֵּה דַּרְכּוֹנִי.	hi**ne** darko**ni**
I'll be staying ...	אֶשָּׁאֵר ...	esha**er**
a few days	כַּמָּה יָמִים	ka**ma** ya**mim**
a week	שָׁבוּעַ	sha**vu**a
2 weeks	שְׁבוּעַיִים	shvu**a**yim
a month	חֹדֶשׁ	**ḥo**desh
I don't know yet.	עֲדַיִין אֵינֶנִּי יוֹדֵעַ (יוֹדַעַת).	a**da**yin ey**ne**ni yo**de**a (yo**da**at)
I'm here on holiday.	אֲנִי כָּאן בְּחוּפְשָׁה.	ani kan beḥuf**sha**
I'm here on business.	אֲנִי כָּאן לַעֲסָקִים.	ani kan leasa**kim**
I'm just passing through.	אֲנִי רַק בְּמַעֲבָר.	ani rak bemaa**var**

If things become difficult:

I'm sorry, I don't understand.	סְלִיחָה אֵינֶנִּי מֵבִין (מְבִינָה).	sli**ḥa** ey**ne**ni me**vin** (mevi**na**)
Does anyone here speak English?	מִישֶׁהוּ כָּאן מְדַבֵּר אַנְגְּלִית?	**mi**shehu kan meda**ber** ang**lit**

מֶכֶס
CUSTOMS

After collecting your baggage at the airport (נְמַל הַתְּעוּפָה—ne**mal** hateu**fa**) you have a choice: use the green exit if you have nothing to declare. Or leave via the red exit if you have items to declare (in excess of those allowed). Spot checks are, however, carried out, so be patient. *Note*: A deposit is charged on arrival for video and TV cameras and is returned upon departure.

The chart below shows what you can bring in duty-free:

Cigarettes	Cigars	Tobacco	Spirits	Wine
250 or	50 or	250 g.	1 l. and	2 l.

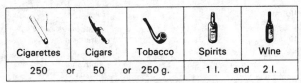

GOODS
to declare
טובין להצהרה
אין
טובין להצהרה
NOTHING
to declare

I have nothing to declare.	אֵין לִי דְּבָרִים לְהַצְהִיר.	eyn li dva**rim** lehatz**hir**
I have ...	יֵשׁ לִי ...	yesh li
a carton of cigarettes	קַרְטוֹן סִיגַרִיּוֹת	kar**ton** sigari**yot**
a bottle of whisky	בַּקְבּוּק וִיסְקִי	bak**buk** **vis**ki
It's for my personal use.	זֶה לְשִׁמּוּשִׁי הַפְּרָטִי.	ze leshimu**shi** hapra**ti**
It's a gift.	זוֹ מַתָּנָה.	zo mata**na**

דַּרְכּוֹן בְּבַקָּשָׁה.	Your passport, please.
יֵשׁ לְךָ (לָךְ) מַשֶּׁהוּ לְהַצְהִיר?	Do you have anything to declare?
נָא לִפְתּוֹחַ אֶת הַתִּיק הַזֶּה.	Please open this bag.
צָרִיךְ לְשַׁלֵּם מֶכֶס עַל זֶה.	You'll have to pay duty on this.
יֵשׁ לְךָ (לָךְ) עוֹד מִזְוָדוֹת?	Do you have any more luggage?

Baggage—Porter מִזְוָדוֹת—סַבָּל.

Porters are available but, generally speaking, you are left to your own devices unless you specifically request help (in which case, a tip is recommended). There are always plenty of trolleys in the baggage reclaim areas.

Porter!	סַבָּל!	sa**bal**
Please take (this/my) ...	בְּבַקָּשָׁה קַח אֶת הַ... (הַזֶּה/שֶׁלִּי).	bevaka**sha** kaḥ et ha ... (ha**ze**/she**li**)
luggage	יֵשׁ לְךָ (לָךְ) עוֹד מִזְוָדוֹת?	yesh le**kha** (lakh) od mizva**dot**
suitcase	מִזְוָדָה	mizva**da**
(travelling) bag	תִּיק (נְסִיעוֹת)	tik (nesi**ot**)
That one is mine.	זֶה שֶׁלִּי.	ze she**li**
Take this luggage ...	קַח אֶת הַחֲפָצִים הָאֵלֶּה ...	kaḥ et haḥafa**tzim** ha**e** le
to the bus	לָאוֹטוֹבּוּס	la**o**tobus
to the luggage lockers	לְתָאֵי שְׁמִירַת חֲפָצִים	leta**ey** shmi**rat** ḥafa**tzim**
to the taxi	לַמּוֹנִית	lamo**nit**
How much is that?	כַּמָּה זֶה?	**ka**ma ze
There's one piece missing.	אֶחָד חָסֵר.	e**ḥad** ḥa**ser**
Where are the luggage trolleys (carts)?	אֵיפֹה הָעֲגָלוֹת?	**ey**fo haaga**lot**

Changing money הַחֲלָפַת כֶּסֶף

You'll find a bank at the airport. If it's closed, don't worry. You'll be able to change money at your hotel.

Where's the nearest currency exchange office?	אֵיפֹה אוּכַל לְהַחֲלִיף מַטְבֵּעַ חוּץ בַּסְּבִיבָה?	**ey**fo **ukhal** lehaḥa**lif**mat**bea** ḥutz basvi**va**
Can you change these traveller's cheques (checks)?	תּוּכַל (תּוּכְלִי) לְהַחֲלִיף אֶת הַמַּחֲאוֹת הַנּוֹסְעִים הָאֵלֶּה?	tu**khal** (tukh**li**) lehaḥa**lif** et hamḥa**ot** hano**sim** ha**e**le
I want to change some dollars/pounds.	בִּרְצוֹנִי לְהַחֲלִיף דּוֹלָרִים/לִירוֹת שְׁטֶרְלִינְג.	birtzo**ni** lehaḥa**lif** dola**rim**/ li**rot** **ster**ling

BANK—CURRENCY, see page 129

| Can you change this into shekels | תּוּכַל (תּוּכְלִי) לְהַחֲלִיף אֶת זֶה לִשְׁקָלִים? | tukhal (tukhli) lehaḥalif et ze lishkalim |
| What's the exchange rate? | מַה הַשַּׁעַר? | ma hashaar |

Where is ... ? ‏אֵיפֹה ...?

Where is the ... ?	אֵיפֹה ...?	eyfo
booking office	אֶשְׁנָב הַכַּרְטִיסִים	eshnav hakartisim
duty (tax)-free shop	הַחֲנוּת לְלֹא מֶכֶס	haḥanut lelo mekhes
newsstand	דּוּכַן הָעִתּוֹנִים	dukhan haitonim
restaurant	הַמִּסְעָדָה	hamisada

How do I get to ... ?	אֵיךְ מַגִּיעִים לְ...?	eykh magiim le
Is there a bus into town?	יֵשׁ אוֹטוֹבּוּס הָעִירָה?	yesh otobus haira
Where can I get a taxi?	אֵיפֹה אוּכַל לְהַשִּׂיג מוֹנִית?	eyfo ukhal lehasig monit
Where can I hire (rent) a car?	אֵיפֹה אוּכַל לִשְׂכּוֹר מְכוֹנִית?	eyfo ukhal liskor mekhonit

Hotel reservation ‏הַזְמָנַת מָלוֹן

Do you have a hotel guide (directory)?	יֵשׁ לְךָ (לָךְ) רְשִׁימַת בָּתֵי מָלוֹן?	yesh lekha (lakh) reshimat batey malon
Could you reserve a room for me?	תּוּכַל (תּוּכְלִי) לְהַזְמִין לִי חֶדֶר?	tukhal (tukhli) lehazmin li ḥeder
in the centre	בַּמֶּרְכָּז	bamerkaz
near the railway station	לְיַד תַּחֲנַת הָרַכֶּבֶת	leyad taḥanat harakevet
a single room	חֶדֶר לְיָחִיד	ḥeder leyaḥid
a double room	חֶדֶר זוּגִי	ḥeder zugi
not too expensive	לֹא יָקָר מִדַּי	lo yakar miday
Where is the hotel/guesthouse?	אֵיפֹה הַמָּלוֹן/בֵּית הָאָרַחָה?	eyfo hamalon/beyt hahaaraḥa
Do you have a street map?	יֵשׁ לְךָ (לָךְ) מַפַּת רְחוֹבוֹת?	yesh lekha (lakh) mapat reḥovot

HOTEL/ACCOMMODATION, see page 22

Car hire (rental) שְׂכִירַת מְכוֹנִית

Local companies compete with the internationally known car hire firms, but it's best to reserve your car a day or more in advance.

In Israel, any current driving licence is normally sufficient, but it must be accompanied by an authorized translation if it's not in English or French. It is advisable to check the minimum age limit (which varies between over 21 and over 24 depending on the rental company), and you must have held a driving licence for at least one year. An International Driving Permit may also be useful. Many car rental firms will only accept payment via an international credit card.

I'd like to hire (rent) a car.	בִּרְצוֹנִי לִשְׂכּוֹר מְכוֹנִית	birtzo**ni** lis**kor** mekho**nit**
small	קְטַנָּה	kta**na**
medium-sized	בֵּינוֹנִית	beyno**nit**
large	גְּדוֹלָה	gdo**la**
automatic	אוֹטוֹמָטִית	oto**ma**tit
I'd like it for a day/a week.	הָיִיתִי רוֹצֶה (רוֹצָה) אוֹתָהּ לְיוֹם אֶחָד/לְשָׁבוּעַ.	ha**yi**ti ro**tze** (rot**za**) o**ta** le**yom** e**ḥad**/lesha**vu**a
What are the weekend arrangements?	מַה הַסִּדּוּרִים לְסוֹפְשָׁבוּעַ?	ma hasidu**rim** lesofsha**vu**a
Do you have any special rates?	יֵשׁ תַּעֲרִיפִים מְיוּחָדִים?	yesh taari**fim** meyuḥa**dim**
What's the charge per day/week?	מַה הַמְּחִיר לְיוֹם אֶחָד/לְשָׁבוּעַ?	ma hame**ḥir** le**yom** e**ḥad**/lesha**vu**a
Is mileage included?	זֶה כּוֹלֵל קִילוֹמֶטְרָז'?	ze ko**lel** kilomet**raj**
What's the charge per kilometre?	מַה הַמְּחִיר לְקִילוֹמֶטֶר?	ma hame**ḥir** lekilo**me**ter
I'd like to leave the car in ...	אוּכַל לְהַשְׁאִיר אֶת הַמְּכוֹנִית בְּ...?	u**khal** lehash**ir** et hamekho**nit** be
I'd like full insurance.	אֲבַקֵּשׁ בִּטּוּחַ מַקִּיף.	ava**kesh** bituaḥ ma**kif**
How much is the deposit?	כַּמָּה הַפִּקָּדוֹן?	**ka**ma hapika**don**
I have a credit card.	יֵשׁ לִי כַּרְטִיס אַשְׁרַאי.	yesh li kar**tis** ash**ray**
Here's my driving licence.	הִנֵּה רִשְׁיוֹן הַנְּהִיגָה שֶׁלִּי.	hi**ne** rish**yon** hanehi**ga** she**li**

CAR, see page 75

Taxi שֵׁרוּת

All taxis have meters. For any long-distance rides to other towns the fares are fixed. On arrival these fares are posted up in the taxi office at the airport.

Many taxi companies operate a *sherut* service in and between the main cities; some of them even operate on the sabbath. The word *sherut* means service; seats are sold on an individual basis with up to seven persons sharing the same cab. In the towns, the *sherut* follow the main bus routes.

Where can I get a taxi?	אֵיפֹה אוּכַל לְהַשִּׂיג מוֹנִית?	**ey**fo u**khal** leha**sig** mo**nit**
Where is the taxi rank (stand)?	אֵיפֹה עוֹמְדוֹת הַמּוֹנִיּוֹת?	**ey**fo om**dot** hamoni**yot**
Could you get me a taxi?	תּוּכַל (תּוּכְלִי) לְהַשִּׂיג לִי מוֹנִית בְּבַקָּשָׁה?	tu**khal** (tukh**li**) leha**sig** li mo**nit** bevaka**sha**
What's the fare to … ?	מָה הַמְּחִיר לְ...?	ma hameḥ**ir** le
How far is it to … ?	מָה הַמֶּרְחָק לְ...?	ma hamer**ḥak** le
Take me to …	סַע לְ...	sa le
this address	כְּתוֹבֶת הַזּוֹ	**kto**vet ha**zo**
the airport	שְׂדֵה הַתְּעוּפָה	sde hateu**fa**
the town centre	מֶרְכַּז הָעִיר	mer**kaz** ha**ir**
the … Hotel	מָלוֹן ...	ma**lon**
the railway station	תַּחֲנַת הָרַכֶּבֶת	taḥa**nat** hara**ke**vet
Turn … at the next corner.	פְּנֵה ... בַּפִּינָה הַבָּאָה.	pne … bapi**na** haba**a**
left/right	שְׂמֹאלָה/יְמִינָה	**smo**la/ye**mi**na
Go straight ahead.	סַע יָשָׁר.	sa ya**shar**
Please stop here.	עֲצוֹר כָּאן בְּבַקָּשָׁה.	**atzor** kan bevaka**sha**
I'm in a hurry.	אֲנִי מְמַהֵר (מְמַהֶרֶת).	**ani** mema**her** (mema**he**ret)
Could you drive more slowly?	תּוּכַל (תּוּכְלִי) לִנְסוֹעַ יוֹתֵר לְאַט?	tu**khal** (tukh**li**) lin**so**a yo**ter** le**at**
Could you help me carry my luggage?	תּוּכַל (תּוּכְלִי) לַעֲזוֹר לִי עִם הַמִּזְוָדוֹת?	tu**khal** (tukh**li**) laa**zor** li im hamizva**dot**
Could you wait for me?	תּוּכַל (תּוּכְלִי) לְחַכּוֹת לִי?	tu**khal** (tukh**li**) leḥa**kot** li
I'll be back in 10 minutes.	אֶחְזוֹר תּוֹךְ 10 דַּקּוֹת.	eḥ**zor** tokh **e**ser da**kot**

TIPPING, see inside back-cover

Hotel—Other accommodation

Early reservation and confirmation is essential in most major tourist centres during the high season. On major Jewish festivals, there is sometimes a supplement to pay.

אַכְסַנְיַת נוֹעַר (akhsani**yat no**ar) Youth hostel. These offer dormitory accommodation. Blankets are provided and sheets may be hired for a small additional charge. Most of them serve meals and all offer kitchen facilities. Group reservations must be made in advance.

אַכְסַנְיַת צַלְיָנִים (akhsani**yat** tzalya**nim**) Christian hospice. Available to Christians on a pilgrimage to the Holy Land. Bed and board is offered at reasonable prices, in hospices of various Christian denominations throughout the country.

בֵּית הַאֲרָחָה/קִבּוּץ (beyt haara**ḥa**/ki**bbutz**) Guesthouse. Many of Israel's *kibbutzim* (collective agricultural settlements) run their own guesthouses to allow outsiders to get an idea of their unique social structure. They're just as clean and comfortable as any hotel and offer complete privacy. Country-style food is usually served. Although there's no obligation to participate in communal activities, the administration may be able to arrange for you to spend your time in the fields if you're interested. Working holidays in *kibbutzim* can also be arranged in advance.

בֵּית הַבְרָאָה (beyt havra**a**) Health resort. Centred in the Sea of Galilee and Dead Sea areas, these offer a wide choice of accommodation and are equipped with all modern facilities. They provide a range of treatments for numerous ailments and conditions.

כְּפַר נֹפֶשׁ (kfar **no**fesh) Holiday village. Superb accommodation can be found at seaside holiday villages which are primarily geared to younger people, open-air life and informality. These villages tend to be open only during the summer months.

מָלוֹן (ma**lon**) Hotel. Israel offers a wide choice of hotel accommodation to suit all tastes and budgets, ranging from small, simple facilities to luxury five-star establishments. Prices vary according to grade and season.

מָלוֹן דִּירוֹת (me**lon** di**rot**)	Apartment hotel. These offer self-contained suites with their own living-room or lounge, bedroom, bathroom and kitchenette. Israeli-style full breakfast may be offered as an optional extra.
פֶּנְסְיוֹן (pensi**yon**)	There is a growing trend in bed and breakfast accommodation in Israel, most of which are *kibbutzim*, but there are also many in major tourist resorts. Some of these offer full board.
דִּירוֹת לְשֵׁרוּת עַצְמִי (di**rot** lesher**ut** atz**mi**)	Self-catering flats. This type of accomodation is gaining in popularity, though has not yet matched that existing in some other well-known tourist destinations.

Can you recommend a hotel/guesthouse?	תּוּכַל (תּוּכְלִי) לְהַמְלִיץ עַל מָלוֹן/בֵּית הָאֲרָחָה?	tu**khal** (tukh**li**) leham**litz** al ma**lon**/beyt haara**ḥa**
Are there any self-catering flats (apartments) vacant?	יֵשׁ דִּירוֹת לְשֵׁרוּת עַצְמִי?	yesh di**rot** lesher**ut** atz**mi**

Checking in—Reception נִכְנָסִים—קַבָּלָה

You should have no language difficulties in the luxury and first-class hotels, where most of the staff speak English.

My name is ...	שְׁמִי ...	shmi
I have a reservation.	יֵשׁ לִי הַזְמָנָה.	yesh li hazma**na**
We've reserved 2 rooms/an apartment.	הִזְמַנּוּ 2 חֲדָרִים/דִּירָה.	hiz**ma**nu shney ḥada**rim**/ dira
Here's the confirmation.	הִנֵּה הָאִשּׁוּר.	hi**ne** hai**shur**
Do you have any vacancies?	יֵשׁ לָכֶם חֲדָרִים?	yesh la**khem** ḥada**rim**
I'd like a ...	אֲבַקֵּשׁ ...	ava**kesh**
single room	חֶדֶר לְיָחִיד	**ḥe**der leya**ḥid**
double room	חֶדֶר זוּגִי	**ḥe**der zu**gi**
We'd like a room ...	נְבַקֵּשׁ חֶדֶר ...	neva**kesh ḥe**der
with twin beds	עִם שְׁתֵּי מִטּוֹת	im shtey mi**tot**
with a double bed	עִם מִטָּה זוּגִית	im mi**ta** zu**git**
with a bath	עִם אַמְבַּטְיָה	im am**bat**ya
with a shower	עִם מִקְלַחַת	im mik**la**ḥat
with a balcony	עִם מִרְפֶּסֶת	im mir**pe**set
with a view	עִם נוֹף	im nof
at the front	בַּחֲזִית	baḥa**zit**
at the back	מֵאָחוֹר	mea**ḥor**
It must be quiet.	הוּא חַיָּב לִהְיוֹת שָׁקֵט.	hu ḥa**yav** lih**yot** sha**ket**

CHECKING OUT, see page 31

Is there ...?	?... יֵשׁ	yesh
air conditioning	מִזּוּג אֲוִיר	mizug avir
a conference room	אוּלָם יְשִׁיבוֹת	ulam yeshivot
a laundry service	מִכְבָּסָה	mikhbasa
a private toilet	שֵׁרוּתִים פְּרָטִיִּים	sherutim pratiyim
a radio/television in the room	רַדְיוֹ/טֶלֶוִיזְיָה בַּחֶדֶר	radyo/televizya baḥeder
a swimming pool	בְּרֵיכַת שְׂחִיָּה	brekhat sḥiya
hot water	מַיִם חַמִּים	mayim ḥamim
room service	שֵׁרוּת חֲדָרִים	sherut ḥadarim
running water	מַיִם זוֹרְמִים	mayim zormim
Could you put an extra bed/a cot in the room?	תּוּכַל (תּוּכְלִי) לָשִׂים עוֹד מִטָּה/מִטָּה מִתְקַפֶּלֶת (לְתִינוֹק) בַּחֶדֶר?	tukhal (tukhli) lasim od mita/mita mitkapelet (letinok) baḥeder

How much? כַּמָּה?

What's the price ...?	?... מָה הַמְּחִיר	ma hameḥir
per day	לְיוֹם	leyom
per week	לְשָׁבוּעַ	leshavua
for bed and breakfast	עִם אֲרוּחַת בֹּקֶר	im aruḥat boker
excluding meals	בְּלִי אֲרוּחוֹת	bli aruḥot
for full board (A.P.)	לְפֶּנְסְיוֹן מָלֵא	lepensyon male
for half board (M.A.P.)	לַחֲצִי פֶּנְסְיוֹן	leḥatzi pensyon
Does that include ...?	?... זֶה כּוֹלֵל	ze kolel
breakfast	ארוחת בקר	aruḥat boker
service	[illegible]	sherut
value-added tax (VAT)*	מַס עֶרֶךְ מוּסָף (מָעָם)	mas erekh musaf (maam)
Is there any reduction for children?	[illegible]	yesh hanaḥa liladim
Do you charge for the baby?	צָרִיךְ לְשַׁלֵּם בִּשְׁבִיל הַתִּינוֹק?	tzarikh leshalem bishvil hatinok
That's too expensive.	זֶה יָקָר מִדַּי.	ze yakar miday
Do you have anything cheaper?	יֵשׁ מַשֶּׁהוּ יוֹתֵר זוֹל?	yesh mashehu yoter zol
Is electricity included?	זֶה כּוֹלֵל חַשְׁמַל?	ze kolel ḥashmal

How long? כַּמָּה זְמַן?

We'll be staying ...	... נִשָּׁאֵר	nishaer
overnight only	רַק לַיְלָה אֶחָד	rak layla eḥad
a few days	כַּמָּה יָמִים	kama yamim
a week (at least)	שָׁבוּעַ (לְפָחוֹת).	shavua (lefaḥot)
I don't know yet.	עוֹד לֹא בָּטוּחַ.	od lo batuaḥ

* Americans note: a type of sales tax.

NUMBERS, see page 147

Decision הַחְלָטָה

May I see the room?	אֶפְשָׁר לִרְאוֹת אֶת הַחֶדֶר?	ef**shar** li**rot** et ha**ḥe**der
That's fine. I'll take it.	זֶה בְּסֵדֶר. אֶקַּח אוֹתוֹ.	ze be**se**der. e**kaḥ** **o**to
No. I don't like it.	לֹא. הוּא לֹא מוֹצֵא חֵן בְּעֵינַי.	lo. hu lo mo**tze** ḥen beey**nay**
It's too …	הוּא יוֹתֵר מִדַּי …	hu yo**ter** mi**day**
cold/hot	קַר/חַם	kar/ḥam
dark/small	חָשׁוּךְ/קָטָן	ḥa**shukh**/ka**tan**
noisy	רוֹעֵשׁ	ro**esh**
I asked for a room with a bath.	בִּקַּשְׁתִּי חֶדֶר עִם אַמְבַּטְיָה.	bi**kash**ti **ḥe**der im am**bat**ya
Do you have anything … ?	יֵשׁ לָכֶם מַשֶּׁהוּ …?	yesh la**khem** **ma**shehu
better	יוֹתֵר טוֹב	yo**ter** tov
bigger	יוֹתֵר גָּדוֹל	yo**ter** ga**dol**
cheaper	יוֹתֵר זוֹל	yo**ter** zol
quieter	יוֹתֵר שָׁקֵט	yo**ter** sha**ket**
Do you have a room with a better view?	יֵשׁ לָכֶם חֶדֶר עִם נוֹף יוֹתֵר יָפֶה?	yesh la**khem** **ḥe**der im nof yo**ter** ya**fe**

Registration מַגִּיעִים

Upon arrival at a hotel or guesthouse you'll be asked to fill in a registration form (**to**fes).

שֵׁם מִשְׁפָּחָה/שֵׁם פְּרָטִי	Surname/First name
עִיר מְגוּרִים/רְחוֹב/מִסְפָּר	Home town/Street/Number
אֶזְרָחוּת/עִסּוּק	Nationality/Occupation
תַּאֲרִיךְ/מְקוֹם הוּלֶדֶת	Date/Place of birth
בָּא (בָּאָה) מ.../נוֹסֵעַ (נוֹסַעַת) ל...	Coming from … /Going to …
דַּרְכּוֹן	Passport number
עִיר/תַּאֲרִיךְ	Place/Date
חֲתִימָה	Signature

What does this mean?	מַה זֹּאת אוֹמֶרֶת?	ma zot o**me**ret

אֶפְשָׁר לִרְאוֹת אֶת דַּרְכּוֹנְךָ (דַּרְכּוֹנֵךְ) בְּבַקָּשָׁה?	May I see your passport, please?
תּוּכַל (תּוּכְלִי) לְמַלֵּא אֶת הַטּוֹפֶס, בְּבַקָּשָׁה?	Would you mind filling in this registration form?
נָא לַחְתּוֹם כַּאן.	Please sign here.
כַּמָּה זְמַן תִּשָּׁאֵר (תִּשָּׁאֲרִי)?	How long will you be staying?

What's my room number?	מַה מִסְפָּר הַחֶדֶר שֶׁלִּי?	ma mis**par** ha**ḥe**der she**li**
Will you have our luggage sent up?	תּוּכַל (תּוּכְלִי) לְהַעֲלוֹת אֶת הַמִּזְוָדוֹת שֶׁלָּנוּ?	tu**khal** (tukh**li**) lehaa**lot** et hamizva**dot** shela**nu**
Where can I park my car?	אֵיפֹה אוּכַל לְהַחֲנוֹת אֶת הַמְּכוֹנִית שֶׁלִּי?	**ey**fo u**khal** lehaḥa**not** et hamekho**nit** she**li**
Does the hotel have a garage?	יֵשׁ מוּסָךְ בַּמָּלוֹן?	yesh mu**sakh** bama**lon**
I'd like to leave this in the hotel safe.	אֲבַקֵּשׁ לִשְׁמוֹר זֹאת בְּכַסֶּפֶת הַמָּלוֹן.	ava**kesh** lish**mor** zot bekha**se**fet hama**lon**

Hotel staff עוֹבְדֵי הַמָּלוֹן

hall porter	שׁוֹעֵר	sho**er**
maid	חַדְרָנִית	ḥadra**nit**
manager	מְנַהֵל	mena**hel**
porter	סַבָּל	sa**bal**
receptionist	פְּקִיד (פְּקִידַת) קַבָּלָה	pe**kid** (peki**dat**) kaba**la**
switchboard operator	מֶרְכָּזָנִית	merkaza**nit**
waiter	מֶלְצַר	mel**tzar**
waitress	מֶלְצָרִית	meltza**rit**

Call the members of staff *Adoni* (for men) or *Geveret* (for women) when calling for service.

TELLING THE TIME, see page 153

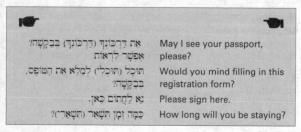

General requirements בַּקָּשׁוֹת כְּלָלִיּוֹת

The key to room ..., please.	הַמַּפְתֵּחַ לְחֶדֶר ..., בְּבַקָּשָׁה.	hamaf**te**aḥ le**ḥe**der ... bevaka**sha**
Could you wake me at ... please?	אֶפְשָׁר לְהַזְמִין הַשְׁכָּמָה לְ... בְּבַקָּשָׁה?	ef**shar** lehaz**min** hashka**ma** le ... bevaka**sha**
When is breakfast/ lunch/dinner served?	מָתַי מַגִּישִׁים אֲרוּחַת בֹּקֶר/אֲרוּחַת צָהֳרַיִם/אֲרוּחַת עֶרֶב?	ma**tay** magi**shim** aru**ḥat** **bo**ker/aru**ḥat** tzoho**ra**yim/ aru**ḥat** **e**rev
May we have breakfast in our room, please?	אֶפְשָׁר לֶאֱכוֹל אֲרוּחַת בֹּקֶר בַּחֶדֶר, בְּבַקָּשָׁה?	ef**shar** lee**khol** aru**ḥat** **bo**ker ba**ḥe**der bevaka**sha**
Is there a bath on this floor?	יֵשׁ אַמְבַּטְיָה בַּקּוֹמָה הַזּוֹ?	yesh am**bat**ya bako**ma** ha**zo**
What's the voltage?	מַה הַמֶּתַח?	ma ha**me**taḥ
Where's the shaver socket (outlet)?	אֵיפֹה הַשֶּׁקַע לִמְכוֹנַת הַגִּלּוּחַ?	**ey**fo ha**she**ka limkho**nat** hagi**lu**aḥ
Can you find me a ... ?	תּוּכַל (תּוּכְלִי) לִמְצֹא לִי ...?	tu**khal** (tukh**li**) lim**tzo** li
babysitter	שְׁמַרְטַף	shmar**taf**
secretary	מַזְכִּירָה	mazki**ra**
typewriter	מְכוֹנַת כְּתִיבָה	mekho**nat** kti**va**
May I have a/an/ some ... ?	אוּכַל לְקַבֵּל ...?	u**khal** leka**bel**
ashtray	מַאֲפֵרָה	maafe**ra**
bath towel	מַגֶּבֶת רַחֲצָה	ma**ge**vet raḥa**tza**
(extra) blanket	שְׂמִיכָה (נוֹסֶפֶת)	smi**kha** (no**se**fet)
envelopes	מַעֲטָפוֹת	maata**fot**
(more) hangers	(עוֹד) קוֹלָבִים	(od) kola**vim**
hot-water bottle	בַּקְבּוּק חַם	bak**buk** ḥam
ice cubes	קוּבִּיּוֹת קֶרַח	kubi**yot** **ke**raḥ
needle and thread	חוּט וָמַחַט	ḥut va**ma**ḥat
(extra) pillow	כַּר (נוֹסָף)	kar (no**saf**)
reading lamp	מְנוֹרַת לַיְלָה	meno**rat** **lay**la
soap	סַבּוֹן	sa**bon**
writing paper	נְיַר כְּתִיבָה	ne**yar** kti**va**
Where's the ... ?	אֵיפֹה ...?	**ey**fo
bathroom	חֲדַר הָאַמְבַּטְיָה	ḥa**dar** haam**bat**ya
dining-room	חֲדַר הָאֹכֶל	ḥa**dar** ha**o**khel
electricity meter	שְׁעוֹן חַשְׁמַל	she**on** ḥash**mal**
emergency exit	יְצִיאַת חֵרוּם	yetzi**at** ḥe**rum**
hairdresser's	מִסְפָּרָה	mispa**ra**
lift (elevator)	מַעֲלִית	maa**lit**
Where are the toilets?	אֵיפֹה הַשֵּׁרוּתִים?	**ey**fo hasheru**tim**

Telephone—Post (mail) טֶלֶפוֹן—דֹּאַר

Can you get me Haifa 123-45-67?	תּוּכַל (תּוּכְלִי) לְהַשִּׂיג לִי אֶת חֵיפָה 67 45 123?	tu**khal** (tukh**li**) leha**sig** li et ḥey**fa** a**ḥat** sht**a**yim sha**losh** ar**ba** ḥa**mesh** sesh **she**va
Do you have any stamps?	יֵשׁ לְךָ (לָךְ) בּוּלִים?	yesh le**kha** (lakh) bu**lim**
Would you post this for me, please?	תּוּכַל (תּוּכְלִי) לִשְׁלוֹחַ אֶת זֶה בִּשְׁבִילִי, בְּבַקָּשָׁה?	tu**khal** (tukh**li**) lish**loaḥ** et ze bishvi**li** bevaka**sha**
Are there any letters for me?	יֵשׁ מִכְתָּבִים בִּשְׁבִילִי?	yesh mikhta**vim** bishvi**li**
Are there any messages for me?	יֵשׁ הוֹדָעוֹת בִּשְׁבִילִי?	yesh hoda**ot** bishvi**li**
How much is my telephone bill?	כַּמָּה חֶשְׁבּוֹן הַטֶּלֶפוֹן שֶׁלִּי?	**ka**ma ḥesh**bon** hate**le**fon she**li**

Difficulties בְּעָיוֹת

The ... doesn't work.	הַ... לֹא פּוֹעֵל.	ha ... lo po**el**
air conditioning	מִזּוּג אֲוִיר	mi**zug** a**vir**
bidet	בִּידֶה	bi**de**
fan	מְאַוְרֵר	meav**rer**
heating	הַסָּקָה	hasa**ka**
light	תְּאוּרָה	teu**ra**
radio	רַדְיוֹ	**rad**yo
television	טֶלֶוִיזְיָה	tele**viz**ya
The tap (faucet) is dripping.	הַבֶּרֶז מְטַפְטֵף.	ha**be**rez metaf**tef**
There's no hot water.	אֵין מַיִם חַמִּים.	eyn **ma**yim ḥa**mim**
The washbasin is blocked.	הַכִּיּוֹר סָתוּם.	haki**yor** sa**tum**
The window is jammed.	הַחַלּוֹן נִתְקַע.	haḥa**lon** nit**ka**
The curtains are stuck.	הַוִּילוֹנוֹת תְּקוּעִים.	havilo**not** teku**im**
The bulb is burned out.	הַנּוּרָה נִשְׂרְפָה.	hanu**ra** nisre**fa**
My bed hasn't been made up.	הַמִּטָּה לֹא הוּצְעָה.	hami**ta** lo hu**tza**

BREAKFAST, see page 38

The ... is broken.	הַ... שָׁבוּר (שְׁבוּרָה).	ha ... sha**vur** (shvu**ra**)
blind	וִילוֹן	vi**lon**
lamp	מְנוֹרָה	meno**ra**
plug	תֶּקַע	**te**ka
shutter	תְּרִיס	tris
switch	מַפְסֵק	maf**sek**
Can you get it repaired?	תוּכַל (תוּכְלִי) לְתַקֵּן אוֹתוֹ?	tu**khal** (tukh**li**) leta**ken** o**to**

Laundry—Dry cleaner's מִכְבָּסָה—נִקּוּי יָבֵשׁ.

I'd like these clothes ...	אֲבַקֵּשׁ ... אֶת הַבְּגָדִים הָאֵלֶה.	ava**kesh** ... et habega**dim** haele
cleaned	לְנַקּוֹת	lena**kot**
ironed	לְגַהֵץ	lega**hetz**
pressed	לְגַהֵץ	lega**hetz**
washed	לְכַבֵּס	lekha**bes**
When will they be ready?	מָתַי הֵם יִהְיוּ מוּכָנִים?	ma**tay** hem yihi**yu** mukha**nim**
I need them ...	אֲנִי זָקוּק (זְקוּקָה) לָהֶם ...	ani za**kuk** (zeku**ka**) la**hem**
today	הַיּוֹם	ha**yom**
tonight	הָעֶרֶב	ha**e**rev
tomorrow	מָחָר	ma**ḥar**
before Friday	לְיוֹם שִׁשִּׁי	le**yom** shi**shi**
Can you ... this?	תוּכַל (תוּכְלִי) ... אֶת זֶה?	tu**khal** (tukh**li**) ... et ze
mend	לְתַקֵּן	leta**ken**
patch	לְהַטְלִיא	lehat**li**
stitch	לִתְפּוֹר	lit**por**
Can you sew on this button?	תוּכַל (תוּכְלִי) לִתְפּוֹר אֶת הַכַּפְתּוֹר הַזֶּה?	tu**khal** (tukh**li**) lit**por** et hakaf**tor** ha**ze**
Can you get this stain out?	תוּכַל (תוּכְלִי) לְהוֹצִיא אֶת הַכֶּתֶם הַזֶּה?	tu**khal** (tukh**li**) leho**tzi** et ha**ke**tem ha**ze**
Is my laundry ready?	הַכְּבִיסָה שֶׁלִּי מוּכָנָה?	hakvi**sa** she**li** mukha**na**
This isn't mine.	זֶה לֹא שֶׁלִּי.	ze lo she**li**
There's something missing.	מַשֶּׁהוּ חָסֵר.	**ma**shehu ḥa**ser**
There's a hole in this.	יֵשׁ בְּזֶה חוֹר.	yesh be**ze** ḥor

POST OFFICE AND TELEPHONE, see page 132

Hairdresser—Barber סָלוֹן/מִסְפָּרָה לְנָשִׁים—מִסְפָּרָה לִגְבָרִים.

Is there a hairdresser/ beauty salon in the hotel?	יֵשׁ בַּמָּלוֹן מִסְפָּרָה/מְכוֹן יוֹפִי?	yesh bama**lon** mispa**ra**/ me**khon yo**fi
Can I make an appointment for Thursday?	אֶפְשָׁר לְקַבֵּל תּוֹר לְיוֹם חֲמִישִׁי?	ef**shar** leka**bel** tor le**yom** ḥami**shi**
I'd like a cut and blow dry.	אֲבַקֵּשׁ תִּסְפֹּרֶת וְיִבּוּשׁ שֵׂעָר.	ava**kesh** tis**po**ret veyi**bush** se**ar**
I'd like a haircut, please.	תִּסְפֹּרֶת, בְּבַקָּשָׁה.	tis**po**ret bevaka**sha**
bleach	הַבְהָרָה	havha**ra**
blow-dry	יִבּוּשׁ עִם אֲוִיר	yi**bush** im a**vir**
colour rinse	שְׁטִיפַת צֶבַע	shti**fat tze**va
dye	צְבִיעָה	tzvi**a**
face pack	מַסֵּכַת פָּנִים	mase**khat** pa**nim**
hair gel	גֶ'ל שֵׂעָר	jel se**ar**
manicure	מָנִיקוּר	mani**kur**
permanent wave	סִלְסוּל תְּמִידִי	sil**sul** tmi**di**
setting lotion	מְיַצֵּב	meya**tzev**
shampoo and set	שַׁמְפּוּ וְסִדּוּר	sham**pu** vesi**dur**
with a fringe (bangs)	עִם פּוֹנִי	im **po**ni
I'd like a shampoo for . . . hair.	אֲבַקֵּשׁ שַׁמְפּוּ לְשֵׂעָר ...	ava**kesh** sham**pu** lese**ar**
normal/dry/greasy (oily)	רָגִיל/יָבֵשׁ/שָׁמֵן	ra**gil**/ya**vesh**/sha**men**
Do you have a colour chart?	אֶפְשָׁר לִרְאוֹת קָטָלוֹג צְבָעִים?	ef**shar** li**rot** kata**log** tzva**im**
Don't cut it too short.	נָא לֹא לְקַצֵּר יוֹתֵר מִדַּי.	na lo leka**tzer** yo**ter** mi**day**
A little more off the . . .	אֶפְשָׁר לְהוֹרִיד עוֹד קְצָת ...	ef**shar** leho**rid** od ktzat
back	מֵאָחוֹר	mea**ḥor**
neck	בָּעֹרֶף	ba**o**ref
sides	בַּצְּדָדִים	batzda**dim**
top	לְמַעְלָה	le**ma**la
I don't want any hairspray.	בְּלִי סְפְּרֵיי.	bli sprey
I'd like a shave.	גִּלּוּחַ, בְּבַקָּשָׁה.	gi**luaḥ** bevaka**sha**

DAYS OF THE WEEK, see page 151

Would you trim my ..., please?	בְּבַקָּשָׁה רַק לְיַשֵּׁר לִי אֶת הַ...	bevaka**sha** rak leya**sher** li et ha
beard	זָקָן	za**kan**
moustache	שָׂפָם	sa**fam**
sideboards (sideburns)	פֵּאוֹת	pe**ot**

Checking out עוֹזְבִים

May I have my bill, please?	אֶפְשָׁר לְקַבֵּל אֶת הַחֶשְׁבּוֹן בְּבַקָּשָׁה?	ef**shar** leka**bel** et haḥesh**bon** bevaka**sha**
I'm leaving early in the morning.	אֲנִי עוֹזֵב (עוֹזֶבֶת) מוּקְדָם בַּבֹּקֶר.	**ani** **ozev** (**oze**vet) muk**dam** ba**bo**ker
Please have my bill ready.	אֲבַקֵּשׁ לְהָכִין אֶת הַחֶשְׁבּוֹן.	ava**kesh** leha**khin** et haḥesh**bon**
We'll be checking out around noon.	נַעֲזוֹב בַּצָּהֳרַיִם.	naa**zov** batzoho**ra**yim
I must leave at once.	אֲנִי חַיָּב (חַיֶּבֶת) לַעֲזוֹב מִיָּד.	**ani** ḥa**yav** (ḥa**ye**vet) laa**zov** mi**yad**
Is everything included?	זֶה כּוֹלֵל הַכֹּל?	ze ko**lel** ha**kol**
Can I pay by credit card?	אוּכַל לְשַׁלֵּם בְּכַרְטִיס אַשְׁרַאי?	u**khal** lesha**lem** bekar**tis** ash**ray**
I think there's a mistake in the bill.	כַּנִּרְאֶה יֵשׁ טָעוּת בַּחֶשְׁבּוֹן.	kanir**e** yesh ta**ut** baḥesh**bon**
Can you get us a taxi?	תּוּכַל (תּוּכְלִי) לְהַשִּׂיג לָנוּ מוֹנִית?	tu**khal** (tukh**li**) leha**sig** **la**nu mo**nit**
Could you have our luggage brought down?	אֶפְשָׁר לְהוֹרִיד אֶת הַמִּזְוָדוֹת שֶׁלָּנוּ, בְּבַקָּשָׁה?	ef**shar** leho**rid** et hamizva**dot** shela**nu** bevaka**sha**
Here's the forwarding address.	הִנֵּה הַכְּתֹבֶת לְהַעֲבָרַת דֹּאַר.	hi**ne** hak**to**vet shela**nu** lehaava**rat** **do**ar
You have my home address.	יֵשׁ לָכֶם הַכְּתֹבֶת שֶׁלִּי בַּבַּיִת.	yesh la**khem** hak**to**vet sheli ba**ba**yit
It's been a very enjoyable stay.	הָיָה מְאֹד נָעִים.	ha**ya** me**od** na**im**

TIPPING, see inside back cover

Camping קֶמְפִּינְג/מַחֲנָאוּת

As a result of its special climate, Israel is a favourable country for camping. There are numerous camping sites, all with excellent facilities, including showers and washrooms, electricity, restaurants, stores, telephones, camp-fire areas as well as bus connections. All have swimming facilities either on site or within easy access.

Is there a camp site near here?	יֵשׁ בַּסְּבִיבָה חַנְיוֹן?	yesh basviva ḥanyon
Can we camp here?	אֶפְשָׁר לַעֲשׂוֹת פֹּה קֶמְפִּינְג?	efshar laasot po kemping
Do you have room for a tent/caravan (trailer)?	יֵשׁ מָקוֹם לְאֹהֶל/לְקָרָוָן?	yesh makom leohel/ lekaravan
What's the charge ... ?	מַה הַמְּחִיר ...?	ma hameḥir
per day	לְיוֹם	leyom
per person	לְאִישׁ	leish
for a car	לִמְכוֹנִית	limkhonit
for a tent	לְאֹהֶל	leohel
for a caravan (trailer)	לְקָרָוָן	lekaravan
Is VAT included?	זֶה כּוֹלֵל מַעַם?	ze kolel maam
Is there/Are there (a) ... ?	יֵשׁ ...?	yesh
drinking water	מֵי שְׁתִיָּה	mey shtiya
electricity	חַשְׁמָל	ḥashmal
playground	מִגְרָשׁ מִשְׂחָקִים	migrash misḥakim
restaurant	מִסְעָדָה	misada
shopping facilities	חֲנוּיוֹת	ḥanuyot
swimming pool	בְּרֵיכַת שְׂחִיָּה	brekhat sḥiya
Where are the showers/toilets?	אֵיפֹה הַמִּקְלָחוֹת/הַשֵּׁרוּתִים?	eyfo hamiklaḥot/ hasherutim
Where can I get butane gas?	אֵיפֹה אוּכַל לְהַשִּׂיג גַּז בִּשּׁוּל?	eyfo ukhal lehasig gaz bishul
Is there a youth hostel near here?	יֵשׁ אַכְסַנְיַת נוֹעַר בַּסְּבִיבָה?	yesh akhsaniyat noar basviva

Eating out

There are many different kinds of eating and drinking places in Israel.

בֵּית קָפֶה
(beyt ka**fe**)

Coffee house. The coffee house is a favourite Israeli haunt. Your drinks will generally be cheaper at the counter. Food isn't normally served, except for cakes, biscuits and sandwiches. There may be several kinds of coffee available.

מִילְק בַּר
(milk bar)

Milk bar. Milk shakes and ice cream are served.

מִסְעָדָה
(misa**da**)

Restaurant. These are classified according to the standard of cuisine and service. Three forks in a circle indicates outstanding quality – it is the equivalent of four stars. Three forks alone is the equivalent of three stars, two forks of two stars and one fork of one star.

סְטֵיקִיָּה
(steki**ya**)

Steak house. Snack shop with a few tables, where light dishes such as *humus, tehina* and salads can be had. Grilled steaks, often served in *pita*, are also served.

קִיוֹסְק
(ki**yosk**)

Kiosk. Stands serving fresh fruit juice, cold beverages and *gazoz*, a fruit syrup with carbonated water.

פָּלָפֶל
(falafel)

Small stand or shop where you can buy Israel's most popular snack. *Falafel* is the equivalent of the American hot dog or the British fish and chips. It's basically small balls of ground chick peas, fried and served in *pita* bread.

Meal times זְמַנֵּי אֲרוּחוֹת

Breakfast (aru**hat bo**ker) is usually eaten between 7 and 9 am; elevenses (aru**hat e**ser), often a snack or sandwiches, are quite popular, eaten between 10.00 and 11.00 am; lunch (aru**hat** **tzohora**yim) is generally taken between 12 noon and 2.00 pm; an afternoon snack (aru**hat ar**ba), sometimes coffee and cakes, may be eaten between 3.00 and 5.00 pm, while supper/dinner (aru**hat e**rev) is usually between 7.00 and 9.00 pm, earlier during the week and later on Friday evening, depending on the time of year (always after sundown, which is when the Sabbath starts). Many restaurants serve meals all day, though some close between 3.00 pm and 6.00 pm.

Israeli cuisine הַמִּטְבָּח הַיִשְׂרְאֵלִי

Israeli food is very tasty and offers a wide range of specialities. It is generally either Middle Eastern (referred to in Hebrew as Oriental), or based on Eastern and Central European cooking (referred to as Ashkenazi), or it can be a mixture of the two, with some dishes originating from North Africa as well as contributions from other Mediterranean countries, for example Greece.

Truly Israeli foods are usually based on fruits and vegetables, which are plentiful all year round. Typical dishes include grated carrot salad and mixed salad of tomatoes and cucumbers. Dairy products and poultry also feature strongly. Red meat is considered a luxury as it is expensive.

Almost all Jewish restaurants in Jerusalem, and most outside it, observe Jewish *kashrut* (dietary) laws. The only animals eaten are those which both chew the cud and have a cloven hoof. Thus, rabbit, pork products, shellfish and fish without true scales are forbidden, as is the mixing of dairy and meat products in any one meal; kitchens are required to have separate preparation areas and separate sinks for milk and meat products. Although game would normally be allowed, any meat that is not ritually slaughtered is not kosher, so in practice it is not available for those who eat kosher food.

Any food that is neither meat nor milk is called *parve*. Most kosher restaurants serve either exclusively meat or exclusively non-meat dishes (fish is not considered meat) to overcome this problem. Foreign restaurants are mainly to be found in the larger cities, e.g. Jerusalem, Tel Aviv and Haifa, and non-kosher food and restaurant meals are generally available in most parts of Israel. Arab restaurants generally do not serve pork or alcohol.

What would you like?	מַה אֶפְשָׁר לְהַצִּיעַ לְךָ (לָךְ)?
I recommend this.	אֲנִי מַמְלִיץ (מַמְלִיצָה) עַל זֶה.
What would you like to drink?	מַה תִּרְצֶה (תִּרְצִי) לִשְׁתּוֹת?
We don't have ...	אֵין לָנוּ ...
Would you like ...?	הַאִם תִּרְצֶה (תִּרְצִי) ...?

Hungry? רָעֵב (רְעֵבָה)?

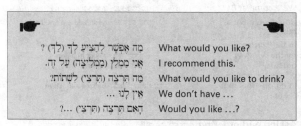

I'm hungry/I'm thirsty.	אֲנִי רָעֵב (רְעֵבָה)/אֲנִי צָמֵא (צְמֵאָה).	**ani raev** (**reeva**)/**ani tzame** (**tzmea**)
Can you recommend a good restaurant?	הַאִם תּוּכַל (תּוּכְלִי) לְהַמְלִיץ עַל מִסְעָדָה טוֹבָה?	**haim tukhal** (**tukhli**) leham**litz** al misa**da** tova
Can you recommend a kosher restaurant?	הַאִם תּוּכַל (תּוּכְלִי) לְהַמְלִיץ עַל מִסְעָדָה כְּשֵׁרָה?	**haim tukhal** (**tukhli**) leham**litz** al misa**da** kshe**ra**
Is this restaurant dairy?	זוֹ מִסְעָדָה חֲלָבִית?	zo misa**da** ḥala**vit**
Does this restaurant serve meat dishes?	זוֹ מִסְעָדָה בְּשָׂרִית?	zo misa**da** besa**rit**
Are there any inexpensive restaurants around here?	יֵשׁ בַּסְּבִיבָה מִסְעָדוֹת זוֹלוֹת?	yesh basvi**va** misa**dot** zo**lot**

| Are there any kosher restaurants around here? | יֵשׁ בַּסְּבִיבָה מִסְעָדוֹת כְּשֵׁרוֹת? | yesh basviva misadot ksherot |

If you want to be sure of getting a table in a well-known restaurant, it is advisable to book in advance.

I'd like to reserve a table for 4.	אֲבַקֵּשׁ לְהַזְמִין שֻׁלְחָן לְאַרְבָּעָה.	avakesh lehazmin shulḥan learbaa
We'll come at 8.	נָבוֹא בִּשְׁמוֹנֶה.	navo bishmone
Could we have a table ...?	יֵשׁ לָכֶם שֻׁלְחָן ...?	yesh lakhem shulḥan
in the corner	בַּפִּנָּה	bapina
by the window	לְיַד הַחַלּוֹן	leyad haḥalon
outside	בַּחוּץ	baḥutz
on the terrace	עַל הַמִּרְפֶּסֶת	al hamirpeset
in a non-smoking area	בָּאֵזוֹר לְלֹא עִשּׁוּן	beezor lelo ishun

Asking and ordering בַּקָּשׁוֹת וְהַזְמָנוֹת

Waiter/Waitress!	מֶלְצַר/מֶלְצָרִית!	meltzar/meltzarit
I'd like something to eat/drink.	אֲבַקֵּשׁ מַשֶּׁהוּ לֶאֱכֹל/לִשְׁתּוֹת.	avakesh mashehu leekhol/lishtot
May I have the menu, please?	אֶפְשָׁר לְקַבֵּל אֶת הַתַּפְרִיט בְּבַקָּשָׁה?	efshar lekabel et hatafrit bevakasha
Do you have a set menu*/local dishes?	תַּפְרִיט קָבוּעַ/מַאֲכָלִים יֵשׁ לָכֶם מְקוֹמִיִּים?	yesh lakhem tafrit kavua/maakhalim mekomiyim
Do you serve Middle Eastern dishes?	יֵשׁ לָכֶם מַאֲכָלִים מִזְרָחִיִּים?	yesh lakhem maakhalim mizraḥiyim
What do you recommend?	מָה מוּמְלָץ?	ma mumlatz
Do you have anything ready quickly?	אֶפְשָׁר לְקַבֵּל מַשֶּׁהוּ מַהֵר?	efshar lekabel mashehu maher
I'm in a hurry.	אֲנִי מְמַהֵר (מְמַהֶרֶת).	ani memaher (memaheret)
I'd like to wash my hands.	אֲבַקֵּשׁ לִטֹּל יָדַיִם.	avakesh litol yadayim

* A set menu is a number of pre-chosen courses, usually cheaper than à la carte.

Could we have a/an ..., please?	נוּכַל לְקַבֵּל ..., בְּבַקָּשָׁה?	nu**khal** leka**bel** ... bevaka**sha**
ashtray	מַאֲפֵרָה	maafe**ra**
cup	סֵפֶל	**se**fel
fork	מַזְלֵג	maz**leg**
glass	כּוֹס	kos
knife	סַכִּין	sa**kin**
napkin (serviette)	מַפִּית	ma**pit**
plate	צַלַּחַת	tza**la**ḥat
spoon	כַּף	kaf
May I have some ...?	אֶפְשָׁר לְקַבֵּל ...?	ef**shar** leka**bel**
bread	לֶחֶם	**le**ḥem
butter	חֶמְאָה	ḥe**ma**
cholla (braided bread)	חַלָּה	ḥa**la**
hot pepper sauce	סְחוּג	sḥug
lemon	לִמּוֹן	li**mon**
oil	שֶׁמֶן	**she**men
pepper	פִּלְפֵּל	pil**pel**
salt	מֶלַח	**me**laḥ
seasoning	תַּבְלִינִים	tavli**nim**
sugar	סוּכָּר	su**kar**
vinegar	חֹמֶץ	**ḥo**metz

Special diet דיאטה מיוחדת

Hotels and restaurants can cater for visitors who have special dietary restrictions, including low-fat or low-salt diets, vegetarian meals, and so on. Here are some useful expressions for those with special requirements:

I'm on a diet.	אני בדיאטה.	**ani** bedi**e**ta
I'm vegetarian.	אני צמחוני (צמחונית).	**ani** tzimḥ**oni** (tzimḥ**onit**)
I only eat kosher food.	אני אוכל רק אוכל כשר.	**ani** **o**khel rak **o**khel ka**sher**
Is this parve?	זה פרוה?	ze **par**ve
I don't drink alcohol.	אינני שותה (שותה) אלכהול.	ey**ne**ni sho**te** (sho**ta**) alko**hol**
I don't eat meat.	אינני אוכל (אוכלת) בשר.	ey**ne**ni o**khel** (**okhe**let) ba**sar**
I mustn't eat food containing ...	אסור לי לאכול שום דבר המכיל ...	a**sur** li lee**khol** shum **da**var hame**khil**
flour/fat	קמח/שומן	**ke**maḥ/shu**man**
salt/sugar	מלח/סוכר	**me**laḥ/su**kar**
Do you have ... for diabetics?	יש לכם ... לחולי סכרת?	yesh la**khem** ... le**ḥo**ley sa**ke**ret
cakes	עוגות	u**got**
fruit juice	מיץ פירות	mitz pe**rot**
a special menu	תפריט מיוחד	taf**rit** meyu**ḥad**
Do you have any vegetarian dishes?	יש לכם מאכלים צמחוניים?	yesh la**khem** maakha**lim** tzimḥoni**yim**
Could I have cheese/fruit instead of dessert?	אוכל לקבל גבינה/פירות כמנה אחרונה?	u**khal** leka**bel** gvi**na**/pe**rot** kema**na** aḥa**ro**na
Can I have an artificial sweetener?	אוכל לקבל ממתיק מלאכותי?	u**khal** leka**bel** mam**tik** melakhu**ti**

And ...

I'd like some more.	אבקש עוד קצת.	ava**kesh** od ke**tzat**
Can I have more ..., please?	אוכל לקבל עוד ..., בבקשה?	u**khal** leka**bel** od ... bevaka**sha**
Just a small portion.	רק מנה קטנה.	rak **ma**na kta**na**
Nothing more, thanks.	מספיק תודה.	mas**pik** to**da**
Where are the toilets?	איפה השרותים?	**ey**fo hasheru**tim**

What's on the menu? מה בתפריט?

Under the headings below, you will find alphabetical lists of dishes that might be offered on an Israeli menu with their English equivalent. You can simply show the book to the waiter. If you want some fruit, for instance, let *him* point to what's available on the appropriate list. Use pages 36 and 37 for ordering in general.

Reading the menu הַתַּפְרִיט

In addition to various à la carte dishes, restaurants usually offer one or more set menus (תַּפְרִיט קָבוּעַ—taf**rit** ka**vu**a) or a dish of the day (מְיוּחָד לְהַיּוֹם—meyu**ḥad** leha**yom**) which provide a good meal at a fair price.

תּוֹסֶפֶת	...extra
הַזְמָנָה מְיוּחֶדֶת	Made to order
לִבְחִירָה	Of your choice
מַאֲכָלִים קָרִים	Cold dishes
תַּפְרִיט קָבוּעַ	Set menu of the day
הַטַּבָּח מַמְלִיץ..	The chef recommends...
מְיוּחָד לְהַיּוֹם	Dish of the day
מַאֲכָלִים מְיוּחָדִים	Specialities
בֵּיתִי	Home made
אָנוּ מַמְלִיצִים...	We recommend...
מְיוּחָד שֶׁלָּנוּ	Speciality of the house
מַאֲכָלִים מְקוֹמִיִּים	Local specialities

appetizers	מָנָה רִאשׁוֹנָה	ma**na** risho**na**
beer	בִּירָה	**bi**ra
beverages	מַשְׁקָאוֹת	mashka**ot**
burgers	הַמְבּוּרְגֶר	**ham**burger
chicken	עוֹף	of
desserts	קִנּוּחַ/מָנָה אַחֲרוֹנָה	kinuaḥ/ma**na** aḥaro**na**
egg dishes	מַאַכְלֵי בֵּיצִים	maakh**ley** bey**tzim**
entrées	מָנָה אֶמְצָעִית	ma**na** emtza**it**
fish	דָּגִים	da**gim**
fruit	פֵּירוֹת	pe**rot**
ice cream	גְּלִידָה	gli**da**
pasta	אִטְרִיּוֹת	itri**yot**
poultry	עוֹף	of
salads	סָלָטִים	sa**la**tim
seafood	מַאַכְלֵי יָם	maakh**ley** yam
snacks	חֲטִיפִים	ḥati**fim**
soups	מְרָקִים	mera**kim**
vegetables	יְרָקוֹת	yera**kot**
wine	יַיִן	**ya**yin

Breakfast אֲרוּחַת בֹּקֶר

Breakfast is a hearty meal and includes hard-boiled eggs, fresh vegetables such as tomatoes and green peppers, sour cream and yoghurt-type soured milks and even pickled herring. There is also *lakierda*, or pickled tuna, which is a Turkish speciality.

Israelis eat a vast range of soured milks with varying fat contents, ranging from sha**me**net ḥa**mu**tza (sour cream) to **le**ben (a low fat curdled milk). Other dairy foods of this type include eshel and low-fat curd cheese (gvi**na ra**za). Cereals are moderately common, and sometimes a semolina porridge or pudding is eaten.

I'd like breakfast, please.	אֲרוּחַת בֹּקֶר, בְּבַקָּשָׁה.	aru**ḥat bo**ker bevaka**sha**
I'll have a/an/ some ...	אֲבַקֵּשׁ ...	ava**kesh**
boiled egg	בֵּיצָה מְבוּשֶׁלֶת	bey**tza** mevu**she**let
soft/hard	רַכָּה/קָשָׁה	**ra**ka/**ka**sha
cereal	דְּגָנִים	dega**nim**
eggs	בֵּיצִים	bey**tzim**
fried eggs	בֵּיצָה מְטֻגֶּנֶת	bey**tza** metu**ge**net
scrambled eggs	בֵּיצָה מְקֻשְׁקֶשֶׁת	bey**tza** mekush**ke**shet
poached eggs	בֵּיצָה שְׁלוּקָה	bey**tza** shlu**ka**
eshel	אֶשֶׁל	**e**shel
fruit juice	מִיץ פֵּרוֹת	mitz pe**rot**
grapefruit	אֶשְׁכּוֹלִיּוֹת	eshkoli**yot**
orange	תַּפּוּזִים	tapu**zim**
jam	רִיבָּה	**ri**ba
lakierda	לָקֵרְדָּה	la**ker**da
leben	לֶבֶּן	**le**ben
marmalade	מַרְמֶלָדָה	marme**la**da
salad	סָלָט	sa**lat**
salt herring	דָּג מָלוּחַ	dag ma**lu**aḥ
schmaltz herring	הֶרִינְג	**shmaltz**
semolina porridge	דַּיְסָה סֹלֶת	**day**sat **so**let
toast	טוֹסְט	tost
yoghurt	יוֹגוּרְט	**yo**gurt
May I have some ...?	אֶפְשָׁר לְקַבֵּל ...?	ef**shar** leka**bel**
bread	לֶחֶם	**le**ḥem
butter	חֶמְאָה	ḥem**a**
(hot) chocolate	קָקָאוֹ (חַם)	ka**kao** (ḥam)

coffee	קָפֶה	ka**fe**
decaffeinated	נטול קָפְאִין	ne**tul** kafe**in**
black/with milk	שָׁחוֹר/בְּחָלָב	sha**ḥor**/beḥa**lav**
Turkish coffee	טוּרְקִי	tur**ki**
instant	נָמֵס	na**mes**
milky	הָפוּךְ	**hafukh**
honey	דְּבַשׁ	dvash
milk	חָלָב	ḥa**lav**
cold/hot	קַר/חַם	kar/ḥam
pepper	פִּלְפֵּל	pil**pel**
rolls	לַחְמָנִיּוֹת	laḥmani**yot**
salt	מֶלַח	**me**laḥ
tea	תֵּה	te
with milk	בְּחָלָב/עִם חָלָב	beḥa**lav**/im ḥa**lav**
with lemon	בְּלִמוֹן/עִם לִמוֹן	beli**mon**/im li**mon**
(hot) water	מַיִם (חַמִּים)	**ma**yim (ḥa**mim**)

Starters (Appetizers) מָנָה רִאשׁוֹנָה

It is quite common in Israel to have an appetizer. The most popular appetizer in oriental restaurants is humus (ground chick peas) with tahina (a liquid paste of ground sesame seeds) flavoured with garlic and cayenne pepper, and sprinkled with a dash of olive oil and a handful of parsley. Lemon wedges are usually served on the side. Ashkenazi appetizers include chopped liver and egg-and-onion. Other appetizers are avocado, melon, Turkish or Greek salad.

I'd like an appetizer.	אֲבַקֵּשׁ מָנָה רִאשׁוֹנָה.	ava**kesh** ma**na** rishona
What would you recommend?	? מָה מוּמְלָץ	ma mum**latz**

סָלָט	sa**lat**	salad
מֶלוֹן	me**lon**	melon
כָּבֵד קָצוּץ	ka**ved** katzutz	chopped liver
חומוס	**ḥu**mus	humus
טְחִינָה	t**ḥi**na	tahina
אַרְטִישׁוֹק	arti**shok**	artichoke
אֲבוֹקָדוֹ	avo**ka**do	avocado

שַׁקְשׁוּקָה (shak**shu**ka)	A very spicy dish of Tunisian origin, consisting of eggs scrambled with tomatoes and red peppers
בְּלִינְצֶס (**blin**zes)	Thin pancakes, rolled and stuffed with meat, vegetables or sweet cream cheese

Soups and stews מְרָקִים

Chicken soup is popular all over the Jewish world, from North Africa to Poland. It is always eaten with dumplings, noodles, or other additions. Bean soup and vegetable soups are popular in Israel in winter. In summer, cold borscht (beetroot soup) is drunk as a first course, and cold fruit soup is a popular dessert.

The most important stew in Israeli cuisine is the slow-cooked stew prepared before the Sabbath on Friday night and eaten on the Sabbath at lunchtime. It has various names, depending on the origin of the cook. The Israeli name is ḥa**min**, but it is also referred to as **cho**lent, fijo**ni**cas or dfina.

מְרָק עוֹף	me**rak** of	chicken soup
מְרָק עַגְבָנִיּוֹת	me**rak** agvani**yot**	tomato soup
מְרָק יְרָקוֹת	me**rak** yera**kot**	vegetable soup
מְרָק גּוּלָשׁ	me**rak gu**lash	goulash soup
מְרָק בָּשָׂר	me**rak** ba**sar**	beef soup
מְרָק אִטְרִיּוֹת	me**rak** itri**yot**	noodle soup
בּוֹרְשְׁט	borsht	beetroot soup

Main course מָנָה עִיקָּרִית

Fish and seafood דָּגִים וּמַאַכְלֵי יָם

Fish is a traditional Jewish dish, but only fish with scales. Shellfish, crustaceans and fish without true scales, such as shark and monkfish, are not kosher, although they can be found on the menu in non-kosher restaurants. In general, people of Middle Eastern origin prefer saltwater fish, and people of Eastern European origin prefer freshwater fish. Carp are raised commercially in Israel. They are most often eaten as gefilte fish (chopped and stuffed). The most easily available saltwater fish is frozen bakala (hake or cod), from the Atlantic. St. Peter's fish (am**nun**) is found in the Sea of Galilee.

I'd like some fish.	אֲבַקֵּשׁ דָּג.	ava**kesh** dag
What kind of seafood do you have?	אֵילוּ מַאַכְלֵי יָם יֵשׁ לָכֶם?	**e**lu maakh**ley** yam yesh la**khem**

אַמְנוּן	am**nun**	"St. Peter's fish"
בַּקָלָה	**ba**kala	cod
דָּג מָלוּחַ	dag ma**lu**ah	herring
טוּנָה	**tu**na	tunny, tuna
קַרְפִּיוֹן	karpi**yon**	carp
שְׁפְּרוֹטִים	**shpro**tim	sprats
גֶּפִילְטֶה פִישׁ	gefil**te** fish	stuffed fish

baked	אָפוּי	a**fuy**
fried	מְטוּגָן	metu**gan**
grilled	בְּגְרִיל	bi**gril**
marinated	כָּבוּשׁ	ka**vush**
poached	שָׁלוּק	sha**luk**
sautéed	מְטוּגָן	metu**gan**
smoked	מְעוּשָׁן	meu**shan**
steamed	מְאוּיָד	meu**yad**

Meat בָּשָׂר

Only animals which chew the cud and have cloven hooves are kosher and are traditionally eaten by Jews. In practice this means mostly beef and mutton, though even venison is kosher if ritually slaughtered. Food containing blood may not be eaten. Pork is forbidden to both Jews and Moslems, and is only widely available in Christian restaurants in and around Jerusalem, and in the north of the country, e.g. Nazareth. Meat, including the non-kosher variety, is very expensive. Offal is very popular, including heart, lung, liver, kidney and spleen.

I'd like some …	אֲבַקֵּשׁ ...	ava**kesh**
beef	בְּשַׂר בָּקָר	be**sar** ba**kar**
lamb	טָלֶה	**ta**le
veal	בְּשַׂר עֵגֶל	be**sar e**gel
chitterlings	מֵעַיִים	me**a**yim
chop/cutlet	צֶלַע	**tze**la
escalope	שְׁנִיצֶל	**shni**tzel
fillet	פִילֶה	**file**
kidneys	כְּלָיוֹת	kla**yot**
leg (of lamb)	שׁוֹק (כֶּבֶשׂ)	shok (**ke**ves)
meatballs	כַּדּוּרֵי בָּשָׂר	kadu**rey** ba**sar**
mutton	כֶּבֶשׂ	**ke**ves
oxtail	זְנַב פָּר	znav par
pot roast	בָּשָׂר צָלוּי	ba**sar** tza**luy**
saddle	אוּכָּף	u**kaf**
sausage	נַקְנִיק	nak**nik**
shank	שׁוֹק	shok
sirloin	בְּשַׂר וֶרֶד	bsar **ve**red
sweetbreads	בְּלוּטוֹת	balu**tot**
tongue	לָשׁוֹן	la**shon**
venison	בְּשַׂר צְבִי	tzvi

baked	אֲפוּיָה	afu**ya**
barbecued	בַּרְבֶּקְיוּ	**bar**bekyu
baked in greaseproof paper	אֲפוּיָה בִּנְיָר פֶּרְגָמֶנְט	afu**ya** bin**yar** perga**ment**
boiled	מְבוּשֶׁלֶת	mevu**she**let
braised	מְאוּדָּה	meu**da**
fried	מְטוּגֶנֶת	metu**ge**net
grilled	בְּגְרִיל	bi**gril**
roast	צְלוּיָה	tzlu**ya**
sautéed	מְטוּגֶנֶת	metu**ge**net
stewed	מְבוּשֶׁלֶת	mevu**she**let
very rare	נָא מְאֹד	na me**od**
underdone (rare)	נָא	na
medium	בֵּינוֹנִי	beyno**ni**
well-done	מְבוּשָׁל הֵיטֵב	mevu**shal** hey**tev**

Some meat specialities מַאֲכְלֵי בָּשָׂר

רֵיאוֹת	**re**ot	lungs
קְצִיצוֹת בָּשָׂר	ktzi**tzot** ba**sar**	chopped meat patties
קוּסְקוּס	**kus**kus	couscous
כָּבֵד	ka**ved**	liver

חַמִּין (**ḥamin**) — cholent: stuffed tripe, beef and beans; a traditional Jewish dish, especially for the Sabbath

שַׁשְׁלִיק (**shish**lik) — chunks of beef or lamb, grilled on a skewer

קְבָּב (ka**bab**) — spiced ground meat, grilled on a skewer

קְצִיצוֹת בָּשָׂר (ktzi**tzot** ba**sar**) — chopped meat patties

שׁוּאַרְמָה (shu**ar**ma) — small pieces of lamb or turkey cooked over an open flame on a vertical spit.

קִישְׁקֶע (**kish**ke) — home-made sausages

קְרֶפְּלַךְ (**krep**lakh) — ravioli or dumplings filled wih meat

Poultry עוֹף

Chicken is the main Israeli meat dish, and it takes many appetizing forms. Goose and duck are expensive. Smoked breast of goose, imported by French Jews, has become a delicacy. Israel exports a large quantity of *foie gras* to France, but it is not a popular dish locally.

chicken	עוֹף	of
breast/leg/wing	חָזֶה/רֶגֶל/כָּנָף	ḥaze/regel/kanaf
barbecued chicken	עוֹף בָּרְבֶּקְיוּ	of barbekyu
duck	בַּרְוָז	barvaz
duckling	בַּרְוָזוֹן	barvazon
goose	אַוָּז	avaz
partridge	חָגְלָה	ḥogla
pheasant	פַּסְיוֹן	pasyon
pigeon	יוֹנָה	yona
quail	שְׂלָו	slav
turkey	תַּרְנְגוֹל הֹדוּ	tarnegol hodu
woodcock	חַרְטוּמָן	ḥartuman

אַוָּז מְמוּלָּא	avaz memula	stuffed goose
שְׁנִיצֶל עוֹף	shnitzel of	chicken schnitzel
שְׁנִיצֶל הֹדוּ	shnitzel hodu	turkey schnitzel
עוֹף מְטוּגָן	of metugan	fried chicken

Potatoes תַּפּוּחֵי אֲדָמָה

Potatoes are a staple of the Israeli diet, especially among those of European origin; Jews of Middle Eastern origin prefer rice. *Latkes* are traditional at Chanukah, the mid-winter festival. *Kugel* is of Lithuanian origin and is often eaten with the Sabbath stew.

תַּפּוּדִים מְטוּגָנִים	tapudim metuganim	fried potatoes
לְבִיבוֹת	levivot	potato pancakes

לַטְקֶס (**lat**kes) — fried potato patties made from grated raw potato, sometimes with a little onion added.

קוּגֶל (**ku**gel) — a potato pudding made from raw grated potato baked in the oven

Rice and Noodles אֹרֶז וְאִטְרִיּוֹת

Rice is the staple of Jews from Iraq and Persia. It is even allowed on Passover in their case, although it is forbidden at that time to Ashkenazi Jews. Noodles are mentioned in the Talmud and so have been popular for a long time. Most people add them to chicken soup. People of Hungarian background eat them for breakfast, sprinkled with grated nuts or poppyseed.

פַּסְטָה	pasta	pasta
אִטְרִיּוֹת	itri**yot**	noodles
אֹרֶז	**o**rez	rice

Sauces רְטָבִים

Sauces do not feature greatly in Israeli cuisine, except for hot pepper sauce used as a condiment in oriental cooking.

סְחוּג	sḥug	hot pepper sauce

Vegetables and salads יְרָקוֹת וְסָלָטִים

artichokes (bottoms/ hearts)	(לְבָבוֹת) אַרְטִישׁוֹק	(leva**vot**) arti**shok**
asparagus (tips)	(חוּדֵי) אַסְפָּרָגוּס	(ḥu**dey**) aspa**ra**gus
aubergine (eggplant)	חָצִיל	**ḥatzil**
avocado	אָבוֹקָדוֹ	avo**ka**do
beans	שְׁעוּעִית	**sheuit**
green beans	שְׁעוּעִית יְרוּקָה	sheu**it** yeru**ka**
kidney beans	שְׁעוּעִית אֲדוּמָה	sheu**it** adu**ma**
wax beans	שְׁעוּעִית צְהוּבָּה	sheu**it** tzehu**ba**
beetroot	סֶלֶק	**se**lek
beets	סֶלֶק	**se**lek
broccoli	בְּרוֹקוֹלִי	**bro**koli
Brussels sprouts	כְּרוּב נִיצָּנִים	kruv nitza**nim**
cabbage	כְּרוּב	kruv
carrots	גֶּזֶר	**ge**zer
cauliflower	כְּרוּבִית	kru**vit**
celery	סֶלֶרִי	**se**leri
chestnuts	עַרְמוֹנִים	armo**nim**
corn	תִּירָס	**tiras**

courgette (zucchini)	קִשּׁוּא	ki**shu**
cucumber	מְלָפְפוֹן	melafe**fon**
endive (chicory)	עֹלֶשׁ	**o**lesh
fennel	שׁוּמָר	shu**mar**
gherkins	מְלָפְפוֹן חָמוּץ	melafe**fon** ḥa**mutz**
leeks	כְּרֵישָׁה	kri**sha**
lentils	עֲדָשִׁים	ada**shim**
lettuce	חַסָּה	**ḥa**sa
mixed vegetables	יְרָקוֹת מְעוֹרָבִים	yera**kot** meora**vim**
mushrooms	פִּטְרִיּוֹת	pitri**yot**
okra	בַּמְיָה	**bam**ya
onions	בָּצָל	ba**tzal**
peas	אֲפוּנָה	afu**na**
(sweet) peppers	פִּלְפֵּל (מָתוֹק)	pil**pel** (ma**tok**)
green/red	יָרוֹק/אָדוֹם	ya**rok**/a**dom**
potatoes	תַּפּוּחֵי אֲדָמָה	tapu**ḥey** ada**ma**
pumpkin	דְּלַעַת	dl**a**at
radishes	צְנוֹנִית	tzno**nit**
ratubaga	כָּלְרָבִּי	kol**ra**bi
spinach	תֶּרֶד	**te**red
squash	דְּלַעַת	dl**a**at
sweetcorn	תִּירָס	**ti**ras
sweet potatoes	בָּטָטָה	ba**ta**ta
tomatoes	עַגְבָנִיּוֹת	agvani**yot**
turnips	לֶפֶת	**le**fet
vegetable marrow	קִשּׁוּא	ki**shu**

Vegetables may be served. . .

boiled	מְבוּשָּׁלִים	mevusha**lim**
creamed	מוּקְרָמִים	mukra**mim**
diced	חֲתוּכִים	ḥatu**khim**
mashed	מְרוּסָקִים	merusa**kim**
oven-browned	מוּשְׁחָמִים	mushḥa**mim**
steamed	מְאוּיָדִים	meuya**dim**
stewed	מְבוּשָּׁלִים	mevusha**lim**
stuffed	מְמוּלָאִים	memula**im**

Herbs and spices תַּבְלִינִים

Horseradish is traditionally eaten on Passover to represent the "bitter herb", but is rare at other times of the year. Hot pepper and hot pepper mixtures, as well as coriander, are very popular among Israelis of North African descent, for example in salads and pickles. The latter also prefer tea flavoured with mint. Arab coffee is always served with cardamom; the Israelis put a whole pod in the coffee cup, the Arabs grind the cardamom seeds with the coffee.

aniseed	כַּמִּיָּה	kam**un**
basil	רֵיחָן	rey**ḥan**
bay leaf	עֲלֵי דַּפְנָה	al**ey** daf**na**
capers	צָלָף	tza**laf**
caraway	כַּרְוִיָּה	karvi**ya**
cardamom	הֵל	hel
chili	צִ׳ילִי	**chi**li
chives	בְּצַלְצַל	betzal**tzal**
cinnamon	קִנָּמוֹן	kina**mon**
clove	צִפֹּרֶן	tzi**po**ren
coriander	כּוּסְבָּרָה	kus**bara**
dill	שֶׁבֶת	**she**vet
garlic	שׁוּם	shum
ginger	זַנְגְּבִיל	**zang**vil
horseradish	צְנוֹן	tznon
marjoram	אֵזוֹבִית	ezo**vit**
mint	נַעֲנָע	**na**ana
mixed herbs	תַּבְלִינִים מְעוֹרָבִים	tavl**inim** meora**vim**
mustard	חַרְדָּל	ḥar**dal**
nutmeg	אֱגוֹז מוּסְקָט	e**goz** mus**kat**
oregano	אוֹרֶגָנוֹ	ore**ga**no
paprika	פַּפְּרִיקָה	**pap**rika
parsley	פֶּטְרוֹסִילְיָה	petro**si**liya
pepper	פִּלְפֵּל	pil**pel**
pickles	חֲמוּצִים	ḥamu**tzim**
pimiento	פִּלְפֵּל חָרִיף	pil**pel** ḥa**rif**
rosemary	רוֹזְמָרִין	rozma**rin**
saffron	כּוּרְכּוּם	kur**kum**
sage	מַרְוָה	mar**va**
salt	מֶלַח	**me**laḥ
shallot	שָׁלוֹט	sha**lot**
tarragon	טַרְגוֹן	**ta**ragon
thyme	קוֹרָנִית	kora**nit**
vanilla	וָנִיל	va**nil**
watercress	גַּרְגִּיר נְחָלִים	gar**gir** neḥa**lim**

Cheese גְּבִינָה

Cheese is popular in Israel, but as kosher law requires the separation of dairy products and meat, it is eaten mainly at breakfast. The most popular types are a cheddar-type cheese, often referred to as Anglo-Saxon cheese, heavily salted curd cheese, which is just known as "salty cheese" and *katchkeval* (a goats' cheese). Other cheeses (Limburger, smoked cheese, etc.), are copies of European types.

גְּבִינָה רָזָה	gv**ina** raza	low fat curd cheese
גְּבִינָה צְהוּבָּה	gv**ina** tzehu**ba**	hard, yellow cheese
גְּבִינַת עִזִּים	gv**inat** iz**im**	goats' cheese
גְּבִינָה מְלוּחָה	gv**ina** melu**ḥa**	salty cheese
גְּבִינָה לְבָנָה	gv**ina** leva**na**	type of cottage cheese
גְּבִינַת קַשְׁקָוָל	gv**inat** katshke**val**	katchkeval (goats' cheese)

Fruit and nuts

Do you have any fresh fruit?	יֵשׁ לָכֶם פֵּירוֹת טְרִיִּים?	yesh la**khem** pe**rot** tri**yim**
I'd like a (fresh) fruit cocktail.	אֲבַקֵּשׁ קוֹקְטֵיל פֵּירוֹת (טְרִיִּים).	ava**kesh** kok**teil** pe**rot** (tri**yim**)
almonds	שְׁקֵדִים	shke**dim**
apple	תַּפּוּחַ	ta**puaḥ**
apricots	מִשְׁמֵשׁ	mish**mesh**
banana	בָּנָנָה	ba**na**na
bilberries	אוּכְמָנִיּוֹת	ukhmani**yot**
blackcurrants	דֻּמְדְּמָנִיּוֹת שְׁחוֹרוֹת	dumdmani**yot** shḥo**rot**
blueberries	אוּכְמָנִיּוֹת	ukhmani**yot**
cherries	דּוּבְדְּבָנִים	duvdva**nim**
chestnuts	עַרְמוֹנִים	armo**nim**
coconut	אֱגוֹז קוֹקוֹס	e**goz** **ko**kos
dates	תְּמָרִים	tma**rim**
dried fruit	פֵּירוֹת מְיוּבָּשִׁים	pe**rot** meyuba**shim**
figs	תְּאֵנִים	te**enim**

gooseberries	דֻּמְדְּמָנִיּוֹת	dumdmani**yot**
grapefruit	אֶשְׁכּוֹלִיּוֹת	eshkoli**yot**
grapes	עֲנָבִים	ana**vim**
hazelnuts	לוּזִים אִלְסָרִים	lu**zim**, ilsa**rim**
lemon	לִמוֹן	li**mon**
lime	לַיִם	laim
melon	מֶלוֹן	me**lon**
nectarine	נֶקְטָרִין	nekta**rin**
orange	תַּפּוּז	ta**puz**
peach	אֲפַרְסֵק	afar**sek**
peanuts	בָּטְנִים	bot**nim**
pear	אַגָּס	a**gas**
pineapple	אֲנָנָס	ananas
plums	שְׁזִיפִים	shezi**fim**
prunes	שְׁזִיפִים מְיוּבָּשִׁים	shezi**fim** meyuba**shim**
quince	חַבּוּשׁ	ḥa**bush**
raisins	צִמּוּקִים	tzimu**kim**
raspberries	פֶּטֶל	**pe**tel
strawberries	תּוּת שָׂדֶה	tut sa**de**
sultanas	צִמּוּקֵי סוּלְטָנָה	tzimu**key** sul**ta**na
tangerine	מַנְדָּרִינָה	manda**ri**na
walnuts	אֱגוֹזֵי מֶלֶךְ	ego**zey** **me**lekh
watermelon	אֲבַטִּיחַ	avatiaḥ

לִפְתָּן	lif**tan**	compote
מְרַק פֵּירוֹת	me**rak** pe**rot**	fruit soup
סָלָט פֵּירוֹת	sa**lat** pe**rot**	fruit salad

Desserts—Pastries מָנָה אַחֲרוֹנָה/קִנּוּחַ—עוּגוֹת

I'd like a dessert, please.	מָנָה אַחֲרוֹנָה בְּבַקָּשָׁה.	ma**na** a**ḥ**aro**na** bevaka**sha**
What do you recommend?	מַה מוּמְלָץ	ma mum**latz**
Something light, please.	מַשֶּׁהוּ קַל בְּבַקָּשָׁה.	**ma**shehu kal bevaka**sha**
Just a small portion.	רַק מָנָה קְטַנָּה.	rak ma**na** kta**na**

שְׁטְרוּדֶל	sht**ru**del	Central European apple cake
קְרֶם קָרָמֶל	krem kara**mel**	caramel pudding
פַּשְׁטִידָה	pashti**da**	a sort of pie
פּוּדִינְג שׁוֹקוֹלָד	puding **sho**kolad	chocolate pudding
עוּגַת שׁוֹקוֹלָד	**ugat sho**kolad	chocolate cake
עוּגַת פֶּרֶג	**ugat pe**reg	poppyseed cake
עוּגַת גְּבִינָה	**ugat** gvi**na**	cheesecake
מְרַק פֵּירוֹת	me**rak** pe**rot**	fruit soup
לִפְתָּן	lif**tan**	compote
גְּלִידָה	gli**da**	ice cream

מוּחַלָבִּיָה (muḥala**bi**ya) — *Muhalabiya*: an aromatic pudding made from ground rice and perfumed with rose-water; it is eaten cold

סַחְלָבּ (**saḥ**lab) — *Sahlab*: a pudding made from the ground root of an orchid, usually mixed with corn-flour, and eaten hot in winter, sprinkled with coconut and ground cinnamon

Drinks מַשְׁקָאוֹת

Beer בִּירָה

Beer in Israel is either light or dark. Light beer is a type of lager or ale; dark beer is a malt beer with a sweetish taste and low alcohol content. Beer is served by the litre. There are few pubs, and bars are considered rather upmarket. Liquor licensing laws in Israel are minimal. Beer is served at every kiosk, restaurant and café at any time of day.

What would you like to drink?	מַה תִּרְצֶה (תִּרְצִי) לִשְׁתּוֹת?	ma **tirtze** (**tirtzi**) lish**tot**
I'd like a beer, please.	בִּירָה, בְּבַקָּשָׁה.	**bira** bevaka**sha**
Have a beer!	אוּלַי בִּירָה?	u**lay bira**
A bottle of lager, please.	בַּקְבּוּק לָגֶר, בְּבַקָּשָׁה.	bak**buk la**ger bevaka**sha**
malt beer	בִּירָה שְׁחוֹרָה	**bira** shḥ**ora**

Wine יַיִן

For strict Jews, wine has to be kosher. Very few wines are imported, and most of these are kosher. This means that they must be handled by Jews right from the grapes growing in the vineyard to the final pouring. Wine is always kosher for Passover, that is, the growing and fermentation process never involve contact with bread or other leaven, other than the natural yeasts in the grapes.

There are many local varieties of wine, from sweet red Alicante-types to dry champagne.

May I have the wine list?	אֶפְשָׁר לִרְאוֹת אֶת רְשִׁימַת הַיֵּינוֹת?	ef**shar** li**rot** et reshi**mat** hayey**not**
I'd like a ... of red wine/white wine.	אֲבַקֵּשׁ ... יַיִן אָדוֹם/יַיִן לָבָן.	ava**kesh** ... **yayin** a**dom**/ **ya**yin la**van**
a bottle	בַּקְבּוּק	bak**buk**
half a bottle	חֲצִי בַּקְבּוּק	**ḥatzi** bak**buk**
a carafe	קַנְקַן	kan**kan**
a small carafe	חֲצִי קַנְקַן	**ḥatzi** kan**kan**
a glass	כּוֹס	kos
How much is a bottle of champagne?	כַּמָּה עוֹלֶה בַּקְבּוּק שַׁמְפַּנְיָה?	**ka**ma **ole** bak**buk** sham**panya**
Bring me another bottle/glass of ..., please.	הָבֵא (הָבִיאִי) לִי עוֹד בַּקְבּוּק/כּוֹס ..., בְּבַקָּשָׁה.	ha**ve** (ha**vii**) li od bak**buk**/ kos ... bevaka**sha**

Where does this wine come from?	מֵאֵיפֹה הַיַּיִן הַזֶּה?	mee**y**fo ha**ya**yin haze

red	אָדוֹם	a**dom**
white	לָבָן	la**van**
rosé	רוֹזֶה	ro**ze**
sweet	מָתוֹק	ma**tok**
dry	יָבֵשׁ	ya**vesh**
sparkling	נְתָזִים	**net**azim
chilled	קַר	kar
at room temperature	בְּטֶמְפֶּרָטוּרַת הַחֶדֶר	betempera**tu**rat ha**ḥe**der

Other alcoholic drinks מַשְׁקָאוֹת חֲרִיפִים אֲחֵרִים

Israelis are not big consumers of alcoholic drinks. The only types of spirits made locally are vodka, brandy and *arak*, an aniseed-flavoured brandy. *Arak* turns a milky colour when water and ice are added, and it is mild and refreshing enough to be consumed with a meal. On its own, it is a delicious liqueur. *Golden Arak* is one of the preferred brands. Another popular liqueur is *Sabra*, a brandy-based liqueur flavoured with orange and chocolate. Whisky drinking tends to be an upper-class fashion, and cocktails are rare.

I'd like a/an ...	אֲבַקֵּשׁ ...	ava**kesh**
aperitif	אַפֵּרִיטִיב	aperi**tiv**
arak	עָרָק	**a**rak
brandy	בְּרֶנְדִי	**bren**di
cognac	קוֹנְיָאק	**kon**yak
gin	ג'ין	jin
liqueur	לִיקֶר	li**ker**
rum	רוּם	rum
vermouth	וֶרְמוּט	**ver**mut
vodka	ווֹדְקָה	**vod**ka
whisky	וִיסְקִי	**vis**ki

neat (straight)	לֹא מָהוּל	lo ma**hul**
on the rocks	עִם קֶרַח	im **keraḥ**
with a little water	עִם קְצָת מַיִם	im ke**tzat ma**yim
Give me a large gin and tonic, please.	תֵּן לִי גִ'ין גָּדוֹל וְטוֹנִיק בְּבַקָּשָׁה.	ten li jin ga**dol** ve**to**nik bevaka**sha**
Just a dash of soda, please.	רַק טִיפַּת סוֹדָה בְּבַקָּשָׁה.	rak ti**pat so**da bevaka**sha**

Nonalcoholic Drinks מַשְׁקָאוֹת קַלִּים

Fruit juices, especially orange and grapefruit juice, are the most popular soft drink. *Gazoz* is a drink made from a syrup with soda water added. Soda water is also drunk *au naturel*, as a thirst-quencher. Pep is a non-alcoholic malt beer. Both tea and coffee are drunk iced in summer.

apple juice	מִיץ תַּפּוּחִים	mitz tapu**ḥim**
(hot) chocolate	קָקָאוֹ (חַם)	ka**kao** (ḥam)
fruit juice	מִיץ פֵּירוֹת	mitz pe**rot**
grapefruit juice	מִיץ אֶשְׁכּוֹלִיּוֹת	mitz eshkoli**yot**
herb tea	תֵּה צְמָחִים	te ztma**ḥim**
lemon juice	מִיץ לִימוֹן	mitz li**mon**
lemonade	לִימוֹנָדָה	limo**nada**
milk	חָלָב	ḥa**lav**
milkshake	מִילְקְשֵׁייק	**milk**sheik
mineral water	מַיִם מִינֶרָלִיִּים	**ma**yim mine**ra**liyim
fizzy (carbonated)	תּוֹסְסִים	tose**sim**
still	לֹא תּוֹסְסִים	lo tose**sim**
orange juice	מִיץ תַּפּוּזִים	mitz tapu**zim**
orangeade	אוֹרַנְזָ'דָה	oran**ja**da

soda water	סוֹדָה	**so**da
tomato juice	מִיץ עַגְבָנִיּוֹת	mitz agvani**yot**
tonic water	טוֹנִיק	**to**nik

גַּזּוֹז (gazoz) — *Gazoz*: a syrup mixed with soda water

Hot beverages מַשְׁקָאוֹת חַמִּים

Both coffee and tea are drunk hot in winter and often cold or iced in summer. Turkish coffee is strong, thick and sweet. Arab coffee is flavoured with cardamom. Lemon tea is more popular than white tea, and is often flavoured with a sprig of mint.

I'd like a/an …	אֲבַקֵּשׁ ...	ava**kesh**
(hot) chocolate	קָקָאוֹ (חַם)	ka**kao** (ḥam)
coffee	קָפֶה	ka**fe**
with cream	עִם שַׁמֶּנֶת	im sha**me**net
with milk	בְּחָלָב	beḥa**lav**
black/decaffeinated coffee	שָׁחוֹר/נְטוּל קָפֶאִין	sha**ḥor**/ne**tul** kafe**in**
espresso coffee	אֶסְפְּרֶסוֹ	es**pre**so
mokka	מוֹקָה	**mo**ka
Turkish	עֲרָבִי	tur**ki**
instant	נָמֵס	na**mes**
milky	הָפוּךְ	**hafukh**
iced	קַר	kar
tea	תֵּה	te
cup of tea	כּוֹס תֵּה	kos te
with milk/lemon	בְּחָלָב/בְּלִימוֹן	beḥa**lav**/beli**mon**
with mint	עִם נַעְנַע	im **na**ana
iced tea	תֵּה קַר	te kar

Complaints תְּלוּנוֹת

There's a plate/glass missing.	חָסְרָה צַלַּחַת/כּוֹס.	ḥase**ra** tzala**ḥ**at/kos
I don't have a knife/fork/spoon.	אֵין לִי סַכִּין/מַזְלֵג/כַּף.	eyn li sa**kin**/maz**leg**/kaf

That's not what I ordered.	זֶה לֹא מַה שֶׁהִזְמַנְתִּי.	ze lo ma shehiz**man**ti
I asked for ...	בִּקַּשְׁתִּי ...	bi**kash**ti
There must be some mistake.	יֵשׁ פֹּה טָעוּת.	yesh po ta**ut**
May I change this?	אֶפְשָׁר לְהַחֲלִיף אֶת זֶה?	ef**shar** lehaḥa**lif** et ze
I asked for a small portion (for the child).	בִּקַּשְׁתִּי מָנָה קְטַנָּה (בִּשְׁבִיל הַיֶּלֶד/יַלְדָּה).	bi**kash**ti ma**na** kta**na** (bish**vil** ha**ye**led/hayal**da**)
The meat is ...	הַבָּשָׂר ...	haba**sar**
overdone	יוֹתֵר מִדַּי מְבוּשָּׁל	yo**ter** mi**day** mevu**shal**
underdone	פָּחוֹת מִדַּי מְבוּשָּׁל	pa**ḥot** mi**day** mevu**shal**
too rare	נָא מִדַּי	na mi**day**
too tough	קָשֶׁה מִדַּי	ka**she** mi**day**
This is too ...	זֶה יוֹתֵר מִדַּי ...	ze yo**ter** mi**day**
bitter/salty/sweet	מַר/מָלוּחַ/מָתוֹק	mar/ma**lu**aḥ/ma**tok**
I don't like this.	זֶה לֹא בְּסֵדֶר.	ze lo be**se**der
The food is cold.	הָאֹכֶל קַר.	ha**o**khel kar
This isn't fresh.	זֶה לֹא טָרִי.	ze lo ta**ri**
What's taking you so long?	לָמָּה זֶה לוֹקֵחַ כָּל כָּךְ הַרְבֵּה זְמַן?	**la**ma ze lo**ke**aḥ kol kakh har**be** zman
Have you forgotten our drinks?	שָׁכַחְתָּ (שָׁכַחַתְּ) אֶת הַשְּׁתִיָּה שֶׁלָּנוּ?	sha**khaḥ**ta (sha**khaḥt**) et hashti**ya** shel**a**nu
The wine doesn't taste right.	טַעַם הַיַּיִן לֹא בְּסֵדֶר.	**ta**am ha**ya**yin lo be**se**der
This isn't clean.	זֶה לֹא נָקִי.	ze lo na**ki**
Would you ask the head waiter to come over?	אֶפְשָׁר לְדַבֵּר עִם הַמֶּלְצַר הָרָאשִׁי?	ef**shar** leda**ber** im hamel**tzar** hara**shi**

The bill (check) הַחֶשְׁבּוֹן

Tipping is acceptable, 10 to 15 per cent being the standard rate. A tip in U.S. dollars is particularly appreciated. Payment by credit card are accepted in better establishments.

I'd like to pay.	אֲבַקֵּשׁ לְשַׁלֵּם.	ava**kesh** lesha**lem**
We'd like to pay separately.	אֲנַחְנוּ מְשַׁלְּמִים לְחוּד.	ana**ḥ**nu meshal**mim** le**ḥud**
I think there's a mistake in this bill.	יֵשׁ כַּנִּרְאֶה טָעוּת בַּחֶשְׁבּוֹן.	yesh kanir**e** ta**ut** baḥesh**bon**
What's this amount for?	בִּשְׁבִיל מַה הַסְּכוּם הַזֶּה?	bish**vil** ma has**khum** ha**ze**
Is service included?	זֶה כּוֹלֵל שֵׁרוּת?	ze ko**lel** she**rut**
Is the cover charge included?	זה כּוֹלֵל תַּשְׁלוּם מִינִימוּם?	[phonetics]
Is everything included?	זֶה כּוֹלֵל הַכֹּל?	ze ko**lel** ha**kol**
Do you accept traveller's cheques?	אַתֶּם מְקַבְּלִים הַמְחָאוֹת נוֹסְעִים?	a**tem** meka**blim** hamḥa**ot** no**sim**
Can I pay with this credit card?	אוּכַל לְשַׁלֵּם בְּכַרְטִיס הָאַשְׁרַאי הַזֶּה?	**ukhal** lesha**lem** bekhar**tis** haash**ray** ha**ze**
Please round it up to ...	עַגֵּל (עַגְּלִי) אֶת זֶה לְ...	**agel** (ag**li**) et ze le
Keep the change.	שְׁמֹר (שִׁמְרִי) אֶת הָעֹדֶף.	shmor (shim**ri**) et ha**o**def
That was delicious.	זֶה הָיָה מְצֻיָּן.	ze ha**ya** metzu**yan**
We enjoyed it, thank you.	נֶהֱנֵינוּ מְאֹד, תּוֹדָה.	nehe**ne**nu me**od** to**da**

כּוֹלֵל שֵׁרוּת
SERVICE INCLUDED

Snacks—Picnic חֲטִיפִים—פִּיקְנִיק

Snacks are popular and can be bought at kiosks, including kiosks and stands especially for *felafel*. Pizza bars which sell individual slices are gaining in popularity. You'll also find special kiosks that sell *shwarma*.

Give me two of these and one of those.	תֵּן (תְּנִי) לִי שְׁנַיִם מֵאֵלֶּה וְאֶחָד מִזֶּה.	ten (tni) li **shna**yim me**ele** vee**ḥad** mi**ze**
to the left/right	שְׂמֹאלָה/יָמִינָה	**smo**la/ya**mi**na

TIPPING, see inside back-cover

above/below	מֵעַל/מִתַּחַת	me**al**/mita**ḥ**at
It's to take away.	זֶה לָקַחַת.	ze la**ka**ḥat
I'd like a piece of cake.	אֲבַקֵּשׁ פְּרוּסַת עוּגָה.	ava**kesh** pru**sat** u**ga**
fried sausage	נַקְנִיק מְטוּגָן	nak**nik** metu**gan**
omelette	חֲבִיתָה	ḥavi**ta**
open sandwich with cheese	כָּרִיךְ פָּתוּחַ עִם גְּבִינָה	ka**rikh** patu**aḥ** im gvi**na**
potato salad	סָלָט תַּפּוּחֵי אֲדָמָה	sa**lat** tapu**ḥey** ada**ma**
sandwich	כָּרִיךְ	ka**rikh**

Here's a basic list of food and drink that might come in useful when shopping for a picnic.

I'd like a/an/some ...	אֲבַקֵּשׁ ...	ava**kesh**
apples	תַּפּוּחִים	tapu**ḥim**
bananas	בָּנָנוֹת	ba**na**not
biscuits (Br.)	בִּיסְקְוִיטִים	bisk**vi**tim
beer	בִּירָה	**bi**ra
bread	לֶחֶם	**le**ḥem
butter	חֶמְאָה	ḥem**a**
cheese	גְּבִינָה	gvi**na**
chips (Am.)	חֲטִיפִים	ḥati**fim**
chocolate bar	טַבְלַת שׁוֹקוֹלָד	tav**lat sho**kolad
coffee	קָפֶה	ka**fe**
cold cuts	בָּשָׂר קַר	ba**sar** kar
cookies	עוּגִיּוֹת	ugi**yot**
crisps	חֲטִיפִים	ḥati**fim**
eggs	בֵּיצִים	bey**tzim**
gherkins (pickles)	מְלָפְפוֹנִים כְּבוּשִׁים	melafe**fo**nim kvu**shim**

grapes	עֲנָבִים	ana**vim**
ice cream	גְּלִידָה	gli**da**
milk	חָלָב	ḥa**lav**
mustard	חַרְדָּל	ḥar**dal**
oranges	תַּפּוּזִים	tapu**zim**
pepper	פִּלְפֵּל	pil**pel**
roll	לַחְמָנִיָּה	laḥmani**ya**
salt	מֶלַח	**me**laḥ
sausage	נַקְנִיק	nak**nik**
soft drink	מַשְׁקֶה קַל	mash**ke** kal
sugar	סוּכָּר	su**kar**
tea bags	שַׂקִּיּוֹת תֵּה	saki**yot** te
yoghurt	יוֹגוּרְט	**yo**gurt

זֵיתִים	zey**tim**	olives
פִּיתָּה	**pi**ta	pita
טְחִינָה	te**ḥi**na	tahina
חוּמוּס	**ḥu**mus	humus

פְלָפֶל (fa**la**fel) — *Felafel* are ground chick peas shaped into balls and deep-fried; they are usually served in pita with salad and pickles

אֶשֶׁל (**e**shel) — Eshel is made from soured milk and is similar to yoghurt

כַּעַךְ (**bey**gel) — Bagels are ring-shaped rolls made from a yeast dough which is briefly boiled and then baked. In Israel, bagels are never made with egg dough and are never flavoured

בּוּרֶקָס (bu**re**kas) — *Bourekas* are triangular, savoury flakey pastries filled with salty curd cheese or spinach, sprinkled with sesame seeds and fried

שׁוּאַרְמָה (shu**ar**ma) — *Shwarma*, known in the UK as doner kebab, consists of small pieces of meat cooked over an open flame on a vertical spit. Traditionally, the meat should be lamb, but in Israel it is often turkey

Arab cooking

Appetizers, salads, soups

You'll find *falafel, humus* and *thina* (see p.61) in Arab restaurants as well as other appetizers that are nearly always served with Arab bread (*khubez arabi*). Try these preparations, too, with *khubez*::

تبوله (ta**bu**leh)	A salad of chopped tomatoes, lettuce, onions, mint leaves, cracked wheat and bread crumbs all marinated in salad dressing
فول مدمس (ful me**da**mes)	A dish of baked black beans seasoned with oil, lemon juice, caraway seeds
خيار باللبن (khi**ar** bi**la**ban)	Minced cucumbers in yoghurt, flavoured with garlic and ground mint leaves

Main dishes

Chicken, lamb and mutton are used in countless preparations virtually always accompanied by a dish of well-prepared rice. Fish may be ordered in coastal areas but shellfish is rarely found in restaurants. Like kosher law, that of the Moslem faith forbids eating pork.

منسف (**man**saf)	Seasoned, boiled rice garnished with boiled chunks of mutton, topped with a butter sauce; served on Arab bread
سفيحا (**sfi**ḥa)	A pastry crust garnished with seasoned minced mutton
مدفون (mad**fun**)	Layers of aubergines (eggplant), minced meat or chicken, onion, rice; baked with tomato sauce and grated cheese, flavoured with spices
سمكه حاره (**sa**make **ha**ra)	Marinated sea bass stuffed with fresh chili peppers, finely-minced onion, parsley, pomegranates, minced nuts; grilled

كباب (ka**bab**)	Chunks of lamb and/or mutton seasoned with parsley and ground pepper; charcoal grilled
مسخن (mu**sa**khan)	Grilled chicken, served on bread with oil, chili peppers, onions
كدره (**kid**reh)	Lamb chops baked with rice and butter
مقلوبه (mak**lu**beh)	Rice with meat and cauliflower or aubergines (eggplant)
كبّه (**kib**eh)	Minced mutton, cracked wheat, onion and nutmeg formed into a patty

You can order many types of vegetable, poultry or meat dishes stuffed with seasoned mutton or other minced meat, rice and a tomato or lemon sauce. Try some of these preparations:

كوسا محشي	**ku**sa **maḥ**shi	stuffed vegetable marrow (zucchini)
باذنجان محشي	batin**jan** **maḥ**shi	stuffed aubergine (eggplant)
بندوره محشي	ban**do**ra **maḥ**shi	stuffed tomatoes
ورق عنب محشي	**wa**rak **i**nab **maḥ**shi	stuffed vine leaves
حمام محشي	ḥa**man** **maḥ**shi	stuffed pigeons
دجاج محشي	d**jaj** **maḥ**shi	stuffed chicken
خاروف محشي	kha**ruf** **maḥ**shi	stuffed lamb

Desserts

Desserts are generally taken with a cup of coffee between meals and not so much as a last course. Arab desserts are usually very sweet, baked in melted butter and topped with a honey syrup. Among some of the popular sweet dishes are:

كنافه (ku**na**fa)	crushed almonds, pistachio or other nuts enclosed in a mesh of pastry fibres; fried in melted butter and topped with honey syrup
بقلاوة (bak**la**va)	crushed almonds, pistachios or other nuts wrapped in paper-thin layers of dough, baked in melted butter and topped with honey syrup

بسبوسه (basbuse)	semolina cake containing melted butter, crushed almonds, served in syrup
مهلبيه (muhalabieh)	rice pudding
كازان ديي (kazan dibi)	pudding with caramelized bottom, served with syrup

Beverages

While aperitifs and cocktails are largely unknown and wine is scarcely served in Arab restaurants, *bira* (beer) or *arak* (aniseed liqueur) may be ordered with a meal.

Only Arab or Turkish coffee (*kahve*) will be offered in Arab restaurants. You may order it *mazbut* (medium sweet) or *sukar ziadh* (sweet).

شاي	chay	tea
ختميه	khit**mieh**	bedouin tea (with herbs)
شراب	sha**rab**	syrup
جزوز	**gazoz**	fizzy (carbonated) water
جزوز لمون	**gazoz** la**mun**	lemon drink
جزوز برتقال	**gazoz** borto**kal**	orangeade, orange squash
حليب	ḥa**lib**	milk

Travelling around

Plane מָטוֹס

As with booking accommodation, it is essential to reserve and confirm flights as early as possible, particularly during peak season. There are a great number of highly experienced and recommended tour operators around that can cater for any taste. Most principal cities and some vacation resorts are served by domestic airlines.

Is there a flight to Eilat?	יֵשׁ טִיסָה לְאֵילַת?	yesh ti**sa** leey**lat**
Is it a direct flight?	זוֹ טִיסָה יְשִׁירָה?	zo ti**sa** yeshi**ra**
When's the next flight to Athens?	מָתַי הַטִּיסָה הַבָּאָה לְאַתּוּנָה?	ma**tay** hati**sa** haba**a** lea**tu**na
Is there a connection to Rome?	יֵשׁ מִשָּׁם קֶשֶׁר לְרוֹמָא?	yesh mi**sham ke**sher le**ro**ma
I'd like to book a ticket to Cairo.	אֲנִי רוֹצֶה (רוֹצָה) לְהַזְמִין טִיסָה לְקָהִיר.	**ani** rot**ze** (rot**za**) lehaz**min** ti**sa** leka**hir**
single (one-way)	בְּכִוּוּן אֶחָד	bekhi**vun** e**ḥad**
return (round trip)	הָלוֹךְ וָשׁוֹב	ha**lokh** va**shov**
business class	מַחְלֶקֶת עֲסָקִים	maḥ**le**ket asa**kim**
aisle seat	מוֹשָׁב בַּמַּעֲבָר	mo**shav** bamaa**var**
window seat	לְיַד הַחַלּוֹן	le**yad** haḥa**lon**
What time do we take off?	מָתַי הַהַמְרָאָה?	ma**tay** hahamra**a**
What time should I check in?	מָתַי צָרִיךְ לְהַגִּיעַ לִנְמַל הַתְּעוּפָה?	ma**tay** tza**rikh** leha**gia** lin**mal** hateu**fa**
Is there a bus to the airport?	יֵשׁ אוֹטוֹבּוּס לִנְמַל הַתְּעוּפָה?	yesh **o**tobus lin**mal** hateu**fa**

What's the flight number?	מַה מִסְפַּר הַטִּיסָה?	ma mis**par** hati**sa**
What time do we arrive?	מָתַי נוֹחֲתִים?	ma**tay** noḥa**tim**
I'd like to … my reservation.	בִּרְצוֹנִי … אֶת הַהַזְמָנָה.	birtzo**ni** … et hahazma**na**
cancel	לְבַטֵּל	leva**tel**
change	לְשַׁנּוֹת	lesha**not**
confirm	לְאַשֵּׁר	lea**sher**

בָּאִים
ARRIVAL

יוֹצְאִים
DEPARTURE

Train רַכֶּבֶת

Few people travel by train to and from Jerusalem as bus and *sherut* service (shared taxis) is so quick and inexpensive. Israel Railways provides a regular service between Tel Aviv and Herzliyya, Netanya, Hadera, Haifa, Akko (Acre) and Nahariyya, as well as a daily train between Tel Aviv and Jerusalem, following a particularly scenic route. Israeli trains are clean and comfortable, and, because the winter in Israel is so mild, they don't need to be heated.

The train is the cheapest means of transportation, and reductions are available for children, pensioners and groups. There are usually enough seats for everyone, except on the eves of holidays and during rush hours (early in the morning and in the evening). Reserved seats may be ordered in advance if you don't want to risk a tiring journey.

TELLING THE TIME, see page 153

All passenger services are provided with a buffet car or buffet service. Because distances are so short, only drinks, snacks and light meals are usually served. There is no railway service on Sabbaths and major holidays.

To the railway station לְתַחֲנַת הָרַכֶּבֶת

Where's the railway station?	אֵיפֹה תַּחֲנַת הָרַכֶּבֶת?	**ey**fo ta**ḥ**a**nat** hara**ke**vet
Taxi!	טָקְסִי/מוֹנִית	tak**si**/mo**nit**
Take me to the ...	סַע לְ...	sa le
main railway station	תַּחֲנַת הָרַכֶּבֶת הַמֶּרְכָּזִית	ta**ḥ**a**nat** hara**ke**vet hamerka**zit**
What's the fare?	כַּמָּה זֶה?	**ka**ma ze

כְּנִיסָה	ENTRANCE
יְצִיאָה	EXIT
לָרְצִיפִים	TO THE PLATFORMS
מוֹדִיעִין	INFORMATION

Where's the ...? אֵיפֹה ...?

Where is/are (the) ...?	אֵיפֹה ...?	**ey**fo
bar	הַבָּר	ha**bar**
booking office	אֶשְׁנָב הַכַּרְטִיסִים	esh**nav** hakarti**sim**
currency exchange office	הַחֲלָפַת מַטְבֵּעַ חוּץ	ha**ḥ**la**fat** mat**bea** **ḥ**utz
left luggage office (baggage check)	שְׁמִירַת הַחֲפָצִים	shmi**rat** **ḥ**afa**tzim**
lost property (lost and found) office	מַחְלֶקֶת הָאֲבֵדוֹת	ma**ḥle**ket haave**dot**
luggage lockers	תָּאֵי שְׁמִירַת הַחֲפָצִים	ta**ey** shmi**rat** ha**ḥ**afa**tzim**
newsstand	דּוּכַן הָעִתּוֹנִים	du**khan** haito**nim**
platform 7	רָצִיף 7	ra**tzif** **she**va
reservations office	אֶשְׁנָב הַכַּרְטִיסִים	esh**nav** hakarti**sim**
restaurant	הַמִּסְעָדָה	hamisa**da**
snack bar	הַמִּזְנוֹן	hamiz**non**
ticket office	אֶשְׁנָב הַכַּרְטִיסִים	esh**nav** hakarti**sim**
waiting room	חֲדַר הַהַמְתָּנָה	**ḥ**a**dar** hahamta**na**
Where are the toilets?	אֵיפֹה הַשֵּׁרוּתִים?	**ey**fo hasheru**tim**

Inquiries מוֹדִיעִין

When is the ... train to Jerusalem?	מָתַי הָרַכֶּבֶת ... לִירוּשָׁלַיִם?	ma**tay** hara**ke**vet ... lirusha**la**yim
first/last/next	הָרִאשׁוֹנָה/הָאַחֲרוֹנָה/הַבָּאָה	harisho**na**/haaḥa**ro**na/ ha**ba**a
What time does the train to Tel Aviv leave?	מָתַי יוֹצֵאת הָרַכֶּבֶת לְתֵל אָבִיב?	ma**tay** yo**tzet** hara**ke**vet le**tel** a**viv**
What's the fare to Haifa?	כַּמָּה עוֹלֶה כַּרְטִיס לְחֵיפָה?	**ka**ma o**le** kar**tis** lehey**fa**
Is it a through train?	זוֹ רַכֶּבֶת יְשִׁירָה?	zo ra**ke**vet yeshi**ra**
Is there a connection to ...?	יֵשׁ מִשָּׁם קֶשֶׁר לְ...?	yesh mi**sham** **ke**sher le
Do I have to change trains?	צָרִיךְ לְהַחֲלִיף רַכֶּבֶת?	tza**rikh** lehaḥa**lif** ra**ke**vet
Is the train running on time?	הָרַכֶּבֶת מַגִּיעָה בַּזְּמַן?	hara**ke**vet magi**a** baz**man**
What time does the train arrive in Hadera?	מָתַי מַגִּיעָה הָרַכֶּבֶת לַחֲדֵרָה?	ma**tay** magi**a** hara**ke**vet leḥa**de**ra
Is there a dining car on the train?	יֵשׁ מִזְנוֹן?	yesh miz**non**
Does the train stop in Beyt Shemesh?	הָרַכֶּבֶת עוֹצֶרֶת בְּבֵית שֶׁמֶשׁ?	hara**ke**vet o**tze**ret be**veyt** **she**mesh
Which platform does the train to Be'er Sheba leave from?	מֵאֵיזֶה רָצִיף יוֹצֵאת הָרַכֶּבֶת לִבְאֵר שֶׁבַע?	mee**yze** ra**tzif** yo**tzet** hara**ke**vet li**ver** **she**va
Which platform does the train from Haifa arrive at?	לְאֵיזֶה רָצִיף מַגִּיעָה הָרַכֶּבֶת מֵחֵיפָה?	lee**yze** ra**tzif** magia hara**ke**vet miḥey**fa**
I'd like a timetable.	אֶפְשָׁר לְקַבֵּל לוּחַ זְמַנִּים?	ef**shar** leka**bel** **lu**aḥ zma**nim**

TAXI, see page 21

צָרִיךְ לְהַחֲלִיף רַכֶּבֶת בְּ...	You have to change at …
רָצִיף 2 זֶה …	Platform 2 is …
שָׁם/לְמַעְלָה	over there/upstairs
שְׂמֹאלָה/יְמִינָה	on the left/on the right
הָרַכֶּבֶת לְ … הִיא …	There's a train to … at …
הָרַכֶּבֶת שֶׁלְךָ (שֶׁלָּךְ) תֵּצֵא מֵרָצִיף 1.	Your train will leave from platform 1.
הָרַכֶּבֶת תְּאַחֵר … דַּקּוֹת.	There will be a delay of … minutes.

Tickets כַּרְטִיסִים

I'd like a ticket to Haifa.	אֲבַקֵּשׁ כַּרְטִיס לְחֵיפָה.	ava**kesh** kar**tis** leḥey**fa**
single (one-way)	בְּכִוּוּן אֶחָד	bekhi**vun** e**ḥad**
return (round trip)	הָלוֹךְ וָשׁוֹב	ha**lokh** va**shov**
half price	כַּרְטִיסֵי הֲנָחָה	karti**sey** hana**ḥa**

Reservation מְקוֹמוֹת שְׁמוּרִים

I'd like to reserve a …	אֲבַקֵּשׁ לִשְׁמוֹר …	ava**kesh** lish**mor**
seat (by the window)	מוֹשָׁב (לְיַד הַחַלּוֹן)	mo**shav** (le**yad** haḥa**lon**)

All aboard נוֹסְעִים

Is this the right platform for the train to Haifa?	הָרַכֶּבֶת לְחֵיפָה יוֹצֵאת מֵהָרָצִיף הַזֶּה?	hara**ke**vet leḥey**fa** yo**tzet** miharatz**if** ha**ze**
Is this the right train to Jerusalem?	זוֹ הָרַכֶּבֶת לִירוּשָׁלַיִם?	zo hara**ke**vet lirusha**la**yim
Excuse me. Could I get past?	סְלִיחָה. אוּכַל לַעֲבוֹר?	sli**ḥa** u**khal** laa**vor**
Is this seat taken?	הַמּוֹשָׁב הַזֶּה תָּפוּס?	hamo**shav** ha**ze** ta**fus**

מְעַשְּׁנִים SMOKER	לֹא מְעַשְּׁנִים NONSMOKER

I think that's my seat.	סְלִיחָה זֶה הַמּוֹשָׁב שֶׁלִּי.	sli**ḥa** ze hamo**shav** she**li**
Would you let me know before we get to Hadera?	תּוּכַל (תּוּכְלִי) לוֹמַר לִי כְּשֶׁנַּגִּיעַ לַחֲדֵרָה?	tu**khal** (tukh**li**) lo**mar** li keshena**gi**a leḥa**de**ra
What station is this?	אֵיזוֹ תַּחֲנָה זוֹ?	**ey**zo taḥa**na** zo
How long does the train stop here?	כַּמָּה זְמַן עוֹצֶרֶת הָרַכֶּבֶת כָּאן?	**ka**ma zman ot**ze**ret hara**ke**vet kan
When do we arrive in Jerusalem?	מָתַי נַגִּיעַ לִירוּשָׁלַיִם?	ma**tay** na**gi**a lirusha**la**yim

Eating אוֹכְלִים

In view of the short distances covered, restaurant cars serve only light meals, drinks and snacks en route.

Where's the dining car?	אֵיפֹה הַמִּזְנוֹן?	**ey**fo hamiz**non**

Baggage מִזְוָדוֹת

Porters are not available at Israeli railway stations, but your taxi drivers may be willing to help with your baggage.

Can you help me with my luggage?	תּוּכַל לַעֲזוֹר לִי עִם הַמִּזְוָדוֹת?	tu**khal** la**azor** li im hamizva**dot**
Where are the luggage trolleys (carts)?	אֵיפֹה הָעֲגָלוֹת?	**ey**fo haaga**lot**
Where are the luggage lockers?	אֵיפֹה תָּאֵי שְׁמִירַת הַחֲפָצִים?	**ey**fo ta**ey** shmi**rat** haḥafa**tzim**
Where's the left luggage office (baggage check)?	אֵיפֹה שְׁמִירַת הַחֲפָצִים?	**ey**fo shmi**rat** haḥafa**tzim**
I'd like to leave my luggage, please.	אֲנִי רוֹצֶה (רוֹצָה) לְהַשְׁאִיר חֲפָצִים בְּבַקָּשָׁה.	a**ni** rot**ze** (rot**za**) leha**shir** ḥafa**tzim** bevaka**sha**

Underground (subway) רַכֶּבֶת תַּחְתִּית

Haifa is the only city with an underground railway: the Carmelit —כַּרְמְלִית—which goes up Mt Carmel and is a bit like an "underground" Swiss mountain railway. There is one line (no branches), with five stops.

Where's the nearest underground station?	אֵיפֹה תַּחֲנַת הַכַּרְמְלִית הַקְּרוֹבָה?	**ey**fo ta**ḥa**nat hakarme**lit** hakro**va**
Does this train go to ...?	הָרַכֶּבֶת הַזוֹ מַגִּיעָה לְ...?	hara**ke**vet ha**zo** magi**a** le
Is the next station ...?	הַאִם הַתַּחֲנָה הַבָּאָה הִיא ...?	ha**im** hataḥa**na** haba**a** hi

Coach (long-distance bus) אוֹטוֹבּוּס בֵּין-עִירוֹנִי

Buses are the most important means of transport in Israel. There are two sorts of bus lines: city buses and inter-urban buses. Inter-urban buses offer both fast and slow services.

The Egged Bus Cooperative operates nearly all inter-city bus lines, and provides urban service in most cities and towns as well. The greater Tel Aviv area is serviced by the Dan Cooperative and independent bus companies operate in Be'er Sheva and Nazareth. Fares are reasonable; you can obtain special monthly tickets for Egged's urban bus lines as well as "Israbus" passes, valid on all Egged's bus lines for periods of 7, 14, 21 and 30 days. Student discounts are also available.

If you intend to do a lot of travelling by bus, it might be a good idea to buy a timetable. These work on the 24-hour clock system and are on sale at ticket offices, information desks and in some bookshops.
Note: Children up to the age of five travel free.

When's the next coach to ...?	מָתַי הָאוֹטוֹבּוּס הַבָּא לְ...?	ma**tay** ha**o**tobus ha**ba** le
Does this coach stop at ...?	הָאוֹטוֹבּוּס עוֹצֵר בְּ...?	ha**o**tobus o**tzer** be
How long does the journey (trip) take?	כַּמָּה זְמַן נִמְשֶׁכֶת הַנְּסִיעָה?	**ka**ma zman nim**she**khet hanesi**a**

Note: Most of the phrases on the previous pages can be used or adapted for travelling on local transport.

Bus אוטובוס

It is not recommended to travel by bus in the cities during rush hours: in Tel Aviv especially, buses can get very crowded. One option (though more expensive) is to try a taxi or *sherut* (shared taxi). Don't forget that buses do not run on Saturdays (except in Haifa and its suburban area, Eilat and some tourist areas; enquire at the local Egged office).

I'd like a booklet of tickets.	אֲבַקֵּשׁ כַּרְטִיסִיָּה.	ava**kesh** kartisi**ya**
Which bus goes to the town centre?	אֵיזֶה אוֹטוֹבּוּס נוֹסֵעַ לְמֶרְכַּז הָעִיר?	**ey**ze **o**tobus no**sea** lemer**kaz** ha**ir**
Where can I get a bus to the opera?	אֵיפֹה תַּחֲנַת הָאוֹטוֹבּוּס לָאוֹפֶּרָה?	**ey**fo taḥa**nat** ha**o**tobus la**o**pera
Which bus do I take to Jaffa?	אֵיזֶה אוֹטוֹבּוּס נוֹסֵעַ לְיָפוֹ?	**ey**ze **o**tobus no**sea** le**ya**fo
Where's the bus stop?	אֵיפֹה תַּחֲנַת הָאוֹטוֹבּוּס?	**ey**fo taḥa**nat** ha**o**tobus
When is the ... bus to Akko (Acre)?	מָתַי הָאוֹטוֹבּוּס ... לְעַכּוֹ?	ma**tay** ha**o**tobus ... le**a**ko
first/last/next	הָרִאשׁוֹן/הָאַחֲרוֹן/הַבָּא	hari**shon**/haaḥa**ron**/ha**ba**
How much is the fare to ...?	כַּמָּה עוֹלֶה כַּרְטִיס לְ...?	**ka**ma o**le** kar**tis** le
Do I have to change buses?	צָרִיךְ לְהַחֲלִיף אוֹטוֹבּוּס?	tza**rikh** lehaḥa**lif** **o**tobus
How many bus stops are there to ...?	כַּמָּה תַּחֲנוֹת עַד ...?	**ka**ma taḥa**not** ad
Will you tell me when to get off?	תּוּכַל (תּוּכְלִי) לוֹמַר לִי אֵיפֹה אֲנִי צָרִיךְ לָרֶדֶת?	tu**khal** (tukh**li**) lo**mar** li **ey**fo a**ni** tza**rikh** la**re**det
I want to get off at the University.	אֲנִי רוֹצֶה (רוֹצָה) לָרֶדֶת בָּאוּנִיבֶרְסִיטָה.	a**ni** rot**ze** (rot**za**) la**re**det bauni**ver**sita

תַּחֲנַת אוֹטוֹבּוּס	BUS STOP
תַּחֲנַת בֵּינַיִם	REQUEST STOP

Boat service שִׁיט

It is possible to make boat trips from Eilat around the Gulf of Aquaba or from Tiberias across the Sea of Galilee. If you wish to venture further afloat, ferries regularly leave Haifa to Cyprus and Greece.

When does the next boat for ... leave?	מָתַי יוֹצֵאת הַסְּפִינָה הַבָּאָה ל...?	matay yotzet hasfina habaa le
Where's the embarkation point?	אֵיפֹה עוֹלִים לַסְּפִינָה?	eyfo olim lasfina
How long does the crossing take?	כַּמָּה זְמַן לוֹקַחַת הַהַפְלָגָה?	kama zman lokaḥat hahaflaga
Which port(s) do we stop at?	אֵיפֹה עוֹגְנִים?	eyfo ognim
I'd like to take a cruise/tour of the harbour.	אֶפְשָׁר לַעֲשׂוֹת שַׁיִט/טִיּוּל בַּנָּמֵל?	efshar laasot shayit/tiyol banamal
boat	סְפִינָה	sfina
cabin	תָּא	ta
single/double	לְיָחִיד/לְזוּג	leyaḥid/lezug
deck	סִפּוּן	sipun
ferry	מַעֲבּוֹרֶת	maaboret
hydrofoil	רַחֶפֶת	raḥefet
life belt/boat	חֲגוֹרַת/סִירַת הַצָּלָה	ḥagorat/sirat hatzala
port	נָמֵל	namal
river cruise	שַׁיִט בַּנָּהָר	shayit banahar
ship	אֳנִיָּה	oniya
steamer	סְפִינַת קִיטוֹר	sfinat kitor
reclining seat	כִּסֵּא נוֹחַ	kise noaḥ

Other means of transport אֶמְצָעֵי תַחְבּוּרָה אֲחֵרִים

Israelis are notably generous about picking up hitchhikers, though you may have a long time to wait for a lift. It is possible to hitch from bus stops, though soldiers hitching take priority over others. It's generally an enjoyable and safe way of travelling, but you should still be wary at all times.

helicopter	מָסוֹק	masok
moped	אוֹפַנַּיִם עִם מָנוֹעַ	ofanayim im manoa
motorbike/scooter	אוֹפָנוֹעַ/קַטְנוֹעַ	ofanoa/katnoa

Or perhaps you prefer:

to hitchhike	לָקַחַת טְרֶמְפּ	la**ka**ḥat tremp
to walk	לָלֶכֶת בָּרֶגֶל	la**le**khet ba**re**gel

Bicycle hire שְׂכִירַת אוֹפַנַּיִם

Bicycle hire is not common in Israel, nor is it possible in any of the major towns and cities. Some holiday villages and resorts may, however, provide this service.

I'd like to hire a ... bicycle.	אֲבַקֵּשׁ לִשְׂכּוֹר אוֹפַנַּיִם ...	ava**kesh** lis**kor** ofa**na**yim
5-gear	עִם חֲמִישָּׁה הִלּוּכִים	im ḥami**sha** hilu**khim**
mountain	לְשֶׁטַח הֲרָרִי	le**she**taḥ hara**ri**

Car מְכוֹנִית

Apart from the stretches of motorway (freeway) along the coast and between Tel Aviv and Jerusalem, roads in Israel are mostly simple two-way ones. They are well-maintained but not built for high-speed driving. There are no motorway tolls. After the first rains, the dirt and grease accumulated during the dry season form a slippery layer on streets, so exercise caution. You should drive a hired car only on surfaced roads—insurance coverage does not usually apply if you use backroads or tracks.

The wearing of seatbelts is compulsory for drivers, front-seat passengers and children travelling in the rear. Fuel is available as 92, 94 or 96 octane; diesel and some unleaded fuel are also available. You'll find no self-service stations in Israel; all pumps are manned.

Most visitors agree that the Israeli style of driving is spirited, bordering on the reckless, so watch out for everything. Local drivers are extremely quick off the mark at traffic lights and tend to lean on their horns. Brisk acceleration and good reflexes are essential.

Where's the nearest filling station?	אֵיפֹה תַּחֲנַת הַדֶּלֶק הַקְּרוֹבָה (לְשֵׁרוּת עַצְמִי)?	**ey**fo taḥa**nat** ha**de**lek hakro**va** (lesher**ut** atz**mi**)
Fill it up, please.	מָלֵא בְּבַקָּשָׁה.	ma**le** bevaka**sha**
Give me ... litres of petrol (gasoline).	שִׂים ... לִיטֶר בֶּנְזִין.	sim ... **li**ter ben**zin**
super (premium)/ regular/unleaded/ diesel	סוּפֶּר/רָגִיל/נְטוּל עוֹפֶרֶת/סוֹלֶר	**su**per/ra**gil**/ne**tul** o**fe**ret/ **so**ler
Please check the ...	בְּדוֹק בְּבַקָּשָׁה אֶת הַ...	be**dok** bevaka**sha** et ha
battery	מַצְבֵּר	matz**ber**
brake fluid	שֶׁמֶן בְּלָמִים	**she**men bla**mim**
oil/water	שֶׁמֶן/מַיִם	**she**men/**ma**yim
Would you check the tyre pressure?	בְּדוֹק בְּבַקָּשָׁה אֶת הַלַּחַץ בַּצְּמִיגִים.	bdok bevaka**sha** et hala**ḥ**atz batzmi**gim**
1.6 front, 1.8 rear.	אֶחָד נְקוּדָה שֵׁשׁ (1.6) מִלְּפָנִים אֶחָד נְקוּדָה שְׁמוֹנֶה (1.8) מֵאָחוֹר.	e**ḥ**ad neku**da** shesh milfa**nim** e**ḥad** neku**da** sh**mo**ne mea**ḥor**
Please check the spare tyre, too.	בְּדוֹק בְּבַקָּשָׁה גַּם אֶת הָרֶזֶרְבִי.	bdok bevaka**sha** gam et hare**zer**vi
Can you mend this puncture (fix this flat)?	אֶפְשָׁר לְתַקֵּן אֶת הַתֶּקֶר הַזֶּה?	ef**shar** leta**ken** et hate**ke**r haze
Would you change the ... please?	תּוּכַל (תּוּכְלִי) לְהַחֲלִיף אֶת הַ..., בְּבַקָּשָׁה?	tu**khal** (tukh**li**) lehaḥa**lif** et ha... bevaka**sha**
bulb	נוּרָה	**nu**ra
fan belt	חֲגוֹרַת הַמְּאַוְרֵר	ḥago**rat** hameav**rer**
spark(ing) plugs	מַצָּתִים	matza**tim**
tyre	צָמִיג	tza**mig**
wipers	מַגָּבִים	maga**vim**
Would you clean the windscreen (windshield)?	תּוּכַל (תּוּכְלִי) לְנַקּוֹת אֶת הַחַלּוֹן הַקִּדְמִי, בְּבַקָּשָׁה?	tu**khal** (tukh**li**) lena**kot** et haḥa**lon** hakid**mi** bevaka**sha**

CAR HIRE, see page 20

Asking the way—Street directions בַּקָּשַׁת עֶזְרָה—הוֹרָאוֹת דֶּרֶךְ

Can you tell me the way to …?	אֵיךְ מַגִּיעִים לְ...?	eykh magi**im** le
In which direction is …?	בְּאֵיזֶה כִּוּוּן ...?	be**ey**ze ki**vun**
How do I get to …?	אֵיךְ אַגִּיעַ לְ...?	eykh a**gi**a le
Are we on the right road for …?	זוֹ הַדֶּרֶךְ לְ...?	zo ha**de**rekh le
How far is the next village?	מַה הַמֶּרְחָק לַיִּשּׁוּב הַקָּרוֹב?	ma hamer**ḥak** layi**shuv** haka**rov**
How far is it to … from here?	מַה הַמֶּרְחָק לְ...?	ma hamer**ḥak** le
Is there a motorway (expressway)?	יֵשׁ דֶּרֶךְ מְהִירָה?	yesh **de**rekh mehi**ra**
How long does it take by car/on foot?	כַּמָּה זְמַן זֶה לוֹקֵחַ בִּמְכוֹנִית/בָּרֶגֶל?	**ka**ma zman ze lo**ke**aḥ bimkho**nit**/ba**re**gel
Can I drive to the centre of town?	אֶפְשָׁר לִנְהוֹג עַד מֶרְכַּז הָעִיר?	ef**shar** lin**hog** ad mer**kaz** ha**ir**
Is traffic allowed in the town centre?	מְכוֹנִיּוֹת מוּתָּרוֹת בְּמֶרְכַּז הָעִיר?	mekhoni**yot** muta**rot** bemer**kaz** ha**ir**
Can you tell me where … is?	תּוּכַל (תּוּכְלִי) לוֹמַר לִי אֵיפֹה ...?	tu**khal** (tukh**li**) lo**mar** li **ey**fo
How can I find this place/address?	אֵיךְ אוּכַל לִמְצוֹא אֶת הַמָּקוֹם הַזֶּה/הַכְּתֹבֶת הַזּוֹ?	eykh u**khal** lim**tzo** et hama**kom** ha**ze**/hak**to**vet ha**zo**
Where's this?	אֵיפֹה זֶה?	**ey**fo ze
Can you show me on the map where I am?	תּוּכַל (תּוּכְלִי) לְהַרְאוֹת לִי עַל הַמַּפָּה אֵיפֹה אֲנִי?	tu**khal** (tukh**li**) leha**rot** li al hama**pa** **ey**fo a**ni**
Where are the nearest public toilets?	אֵיפֹה יֵשׁ שֵׁרוּתִים צִבּוּרִיִּים בַּסְּבִיבָה?	**ey**fo yesh sheru**tim** tziburi**yim** basvi**va**

CAR HIRE, see page 20

זֶה הַכְּבִישׁ הַלֹּא נָכוֹן.	You're on the wrong road.
יָשָׁר קָדִימָה.	Go straight ahead.
זֶה בְּצַד שְׂמֹאל/יָמִין.	It's down there on the left/ right.
מוּל/מֵאֲחוֹרֵי...	opposite/behind ...
לְיַד/אַחֲרֵי ...	next to/after ...
צָפוֹן/דָּרוֹם	north/south
מִזְרָח/מַעֲרָב	east/west
סַע לַהִצְטַלְּבוּת הָרִאשׁוֹנָה/הַשְּׁנִיָּה.	Go to the first/second crossroads (intersection).
פְּנֵה (פְּנִי) שְׂמֹאלָה בָּרַמְזוֹר.	Turn left at the traffic lights.
פְּנֵה (פְּנִי) יָמִינָה בַּפִּנָּה הַבָּאָה.	Turn right at the next corner.
קַח (קְחִי) אֶת הַכְּבִישׁ הַ...	Take the ... road.
זֶה רְחוֹב חַד סִטְרִי.	It's a one-way street.
סַע (סְעִי) חֲזָרָה לְ...	You have to go back to ...
סַע (סְעִי) לְפִי הַשְּׁלוּט לִטְבֶרְיָה.	Follow signs for Tiberias.

Parking חֲנָיָה

Parking is indicated by the use of colour-coded kerbs: blue and white means that you must purchase a parking ticket, red and white means no parking, red and yellow means buses only, and a yellow line along the side of the road indicates a bus lane.

Where can I park?	אֵיפֹה אוּכַל לַחֲנוֹת?	**ey**fo u**khal** la**ḥ**a**not**
Is there a car park nearby?	יֵשׁ מִגְרַשׁ חֲנָיָה בַּסְּבִיבָה?	yesh mig**rash** **ḥ**ana**ya** basvi**va**
May I park here?	אוּכַל לַחֲנוֹת פֹּה?	u**khal** la**ḥ**a**not** po
How long can I park here?	כַּמָּה זְמַן אוּכַל לַחֲנוֹת פֹּה?	**ka**ma zman u**khal** la**ḥ**a**not** po
What's the charge per hour?	כַּמָּה זֶה לְשָׁעָה?	**ka**ma ze leshaa
Do you have some change for the parking meter?	יֵשׁ לְךָ (לָךְ) כֶּסֶף קָטָן לַמַּדְחָן?	yesh le**kha** (lakh) **ke**sef ka**tan** lamad**ḥ**an

CAR HIRE, see page 20

Breakdown—Road assistance קִלְקוּל בַּמְּכוֹנִית—עֶזְרָה בַּדֶּרֶךְ

The MMSI is an automobile club and can be called out in an emergency, but you will have to pay if you're not a subscriber.

Where's the nearest garage?	אֵיפֹה הַמּוּסָךְ הַקָּרוֹב?	**ey**fo hamu**sakh** haka**rov**
My car has broken down.	הַמְּכוֹנִית שֶׁלִּי הִתְקַלְקְלָה.	hamkho**nit** she**li** hitkalke**la**
Where can I make a phone call?	מֵאֵיפֹה אוּכַל לְטַלְפֵּן?	me**ey**fo u**khal** letal**pen**
I've had a breakdown at ...	הַמְּכוֹנִית שֶׁלִּי הִתְקַלְקְלָה בְּ...	hamkho**nit** she**li** hitkalke**la** be
Can you send a mechanic?	תּוּכְלוּ לִשְׁלוֹחַ מְכוֹנַאי?	tukh**lu** lish**lo**aḥ mekho**nay**
My car won't start.	הַמְּכוֹנִית שֶׁלִּי לֹא מַתְנִיעָה.	hamkho**nit** she**li** lo matnia
The battery is dead.	הַמַּצְבֵּר לֹא פּוֹעֵל.	hamatz**ber** lo po**el**
I've run out of petrol (gasoline).	נִגְמַר לִי הַבֶּנְזִין.	nig**mar** li haben**zin**
I have a flat tyre.	יֵשׁ לִי תֶּקֶר.	yesh li **te**ker
The engine is overheating.	הַמָּנוֹעַ מִתְחַמֵּם.	hama**no**a mitḥa**mem**
There's something wrong with the ...	מַשֶּׁהוּ לֹא בְּסֵדֶר עִם ...	**ma**shehu lo be**se**der im
brakes	הַבְּלָמִים	habla**mim**
carburettor	הַמְּאַיֵּד	hamea**yed**
exhaust pipe	צִנּוֹר הַמַּפְלֵט	tzi**nor** hama**flet**
radiator	הַמַּקְרֵן	hamak**ren**
wheel	הַגַּלְגַּל	hagal**gal**
Can you send a breakdown van (tow truck)?	תּוּכְלוּ לִשְׁלוֹחַ מַשָּׂאִית גְּרָר?	tukh**lu** lish**lo**aḥ masa**it** grar
How long will you be?	כַּמָּה זְמַן זֶה יִקַּח?	**ka**ma zman ze yi**kaḥ**
Can you give me an estimate?	אֶפְשָׁר לְקַבֵּל הַעֲרָכַת מְחִיר?	ef**shar** leka**bel** haara**khat** me**ḥir**

CAR HIRE, see page 20

Accident—Police תְּאוּנָה—מִשְׁטָרָה

Please call the police.	צַלְצֵל לַמִּשְׁטָרָה בְּבַקָּשָׁה.	tzal**tzel** lamishta**ra** bevaka**sha**
There's been an accident. It's about 2 km. from …	קָרְתָה תְּאוּנָה. זֶה בְּעֶרֶךְ שְׁנֵי קִילוֹמֶטֶר מִ...	kar**ta** teu**na**. ze beerekh shney kilo**me**ter mi
Where's there a telephone?	אֵיפֹה יֵשׁ טֶלֶפוֹן?	**ey**fo yesh **te**lefon
Call a doctor/an ambulance quickly.	צַלְצֵל מַהֵר לְרוֹפֵא/לְאַמְבּוּלַנְס.	tzal**tzel** ma**her** lero**fe**/ le**am**bulans
There are people injured.	יֵשׁ פְּצוּעִים.	yesh petzu**im**
Here's my driving licence.	הִנֵּה רִשְׁיוֹן הַנְּהִיגָה שֶׁלִּי.	hi**ne** rish**yon** hanehi**ga** she**li**
What's your name and address?	מָה הַשֵּׁם וְהַכְּתֹבֶת שֶׁלְּךָ (שֶׁלָּךְ)?	ma ha**shem** vehak**to**vet shel**kha** (she**lakh**)
What's your insurance company?	מִי חֶבְרַת הַבִּטּוּחַ שֶׁלְּךָ (שֶׁלָּךְ)?	mi ḥev**rat** habi**tuaḥ** shel**kha** (she**lakh**)

Road signs תַּמְרוּרִים

אֵין כְּנִיסָה (חַד סִטְרִי)	No entry (one-way street)
אֵין כְּנִיסָה לְרֶכֶב מְמוּנָע	No entry for vehicular traffic
מְהִירוּת מוּגְבֶּלֶת	Speed limit
שֶׁטַח בָּנוּי	Built-up area
עֲצוֹר	Stop
עֲקוּמָה	Curve
הִצְטַלְּבוּת לְפָנֶיךָ	Cross-roads ahead
צֹמֶת לְפָנֶיךָ	Junction ahead
זְהִירוּת	Take care
שֶׁלֶט עֲצוֹר לְפָנֶיךָ	Stop sign ahead
פְּנֵה יָמִינָה	Turn right
מַעֲבָר חֲצִיָּה	Pedestrian crossing
חֲנָיָה	Parking
אֵין חֲנָיָה	No parking
דֶּרֶךְ מְהִירָה	Motorway
אֵין פְּנִיָּה	No turning
אֵין עֲקִיפָה	No overtaking
גֶּשֶׁר צַר	Narrow bridge
כְּבִישׁ חַד סִטְרִי	One way
תֵּן זְכוּת קְדִימָה	Give way
מַעֲבָר רַכֶּבֶת לְפָנֶיךָ	Level crossing ahead

CAR HIRE, see page 20

Sightseeing

Numerous civilizations have risen and collapsed on the territory that is now the state of Israel. Jerusalem has always been a cradle of spiritual life, and the biblical past is present in every inch of its soil.

Israel has a very varied terrain—remarkable in such a small country. You can choose between snow-capped Mt Harmon up near the Lebanese border, the lush, wholesome areas around the Galilee and Sharon Valley, or the arid desert areas of the Dead Sea and the Negev.

Where's the tourist office?	איפה לשכת התיירות?	**ey**fo lish**kat** hataya**rut**
What are the main points of interest?	מה כדאי לראות?	ma ke**day** li**rot**
We're here for ...	אנחנו כאן ...	ana**ḥ**nu kan
only a few hours	רק לכמה שעות	rak leka**ma** sha**ot**
a day	ליום אחד	le**yom** e**ḥad**
a week	לשבוע אחד	lesha**vua** e**ḥad**
Can you recommend a sightseeing tour/an excursion?	תוכל (תוכלי) להמליץ על טיול מאורגן/טיול קצר?	tu**khal** (tukh**li**) leham**litz** al ti**yul** meur**gan**/ti**yul** katzar
Where do we leave from?	מאיפה יוצא הטיול?	me**ey**fo yo**tze** hati**yul**
Will the bus pick us up at the hotel?	האוטובוס יאסוף אותנו מהמלון?	ha**o**tobus yee**sof** o**ta**nu mehama**lon**
How much does the tour cost?	כמה עולה הטיול?	**ka**ma **ole** hati**yul**
What time does the tour start?	באיזו שעה מתחיל הטיול?	be**ey**zo sha**a** ma**tḥil** hati**yul**
Is lunch included?	זה כולל ארוחה?	ze ko**lel** aru**ḥa**
What time do we get back?	באיזו שעה מגיעים חזרה?	be**ey**zo sha**a** magi**im** ḥaza**ra**
Is there an English-speaking guide?	יש מדריך דובר אנגלית?	yesh mad**rikh** do**ver** ang**lit**
I'd like to hire a private guide for ...	הייתי רוצה (רוצה) לשכור מדריך פרטי ל...	ha**yi**ti ro**tze** (ro**tza**) lis**kor** mad**rikh** pra**ti** le
half a day	חצי יום	ḥa**tzi** yom
a day	יום אחד	yom e**ḥad**

Where is/Where are the ...?	?... אֵיפֹה	**ey**fo
abbey	הַמִּנְזָר	hamin**zar**
art gallery	גָּלֶרְיַת הָאָמָנוּת	ga**le**riyat haoma**nut**
artists' quarter	רֹובַע הָאָמָנִים	**ro**va hauma**nim**
botanical gardens	הַגַּנִּים הַבּוֹטָנִיִּים	haga**nim** habota**ni**im
building	הַבִּנְיָן	habin**yan**
business district	אֵזוֹר הָעֲסָקִים	e**zor** haasa**kim**
castle	הַטִּירָה	hati**ra**
catacombs	מְעָרוֹת הַקֶּבֶר	mea**rot** ha**ke**ver
cathedral	הַקָּתֶדְרָלָה	hakate**dra**la
cave	הַמְּעָרָה	hamea**ra**
cemetery	בֵּית הַקְּבָרוֹת	beyt hakva**rot**
city centre	מֶרְכַּז הָעִיר	mer**kaz** ha**ir**
chapel	הַקָּפֶּלָה	haka**pe**la
church	הַכְּנֵסִיָּה	haknesi**ya**
concert hall	אוּלָם הַקּוֹנְצֶרְטִים	u**lam** hakon**tzer**tim
convent	הַמִּנְזָר	hamin**zar**
court house	בֵּית הַמִּשְׁפָּט	beyt hamish**pat**
downtown area	מֶרְכַּז הָעִיר	mer**kaz** ha**ir**
embankment	הַחוֹף	haḥ**of**
exhibition	הַתַּעֲרוּכָה	hataaru**kha**
factory	בֵּית הַחֲרֹשֶׁת	beyt haḥa**ro**shet
fair	הַיָּרִיד	haya**rid**
flea market	שׁוּק הַפִּשְׁפְּשִׁים	shuk hapishpe**shim**
fortress	הַמִּבְצָר	hamiv**tzar**
fountain	הַמִּזְרָקָה	hamizra**ka**
gardens	הַגַּנִּים	haga**nim**
harbour	הַנָּמָל	hana**mal**
lake	הָאֲגַם	haa**gam**
library	הַסִּפְרִיָּה	hasifri**ya**
market	הַשּׁוּק	ha**shuk**
memorial	הָאַנְדַּרְטָה	haandar**ta**
monastery	הַמִּנְזָר	hamin**zar**
monument	הָאַנְדַּרְטָה	haandar**ta**
museum	הַמּוּזֵאוֹן	hamuze**on**
old town	הָעִיר הָעַתִּיקָה	ha**ir** haati**ka**
opera house	הָאוֹפֶּרָה	ha**o**pera
palace	הָאַרְמוֹן	haar**mon**
park	הַפָּארְק	ha**park**
parliament building	הַכְּנֶסֶת	hak**ne**set
planetarium	הַפְּלָנֶטַרְיוּם	haplane**ta**riyum
royal palace	אַרְמוֹן הַמֶּלֶךְ	ar**mon** ha**me**lekh
ruins	הַחֳרָבוֹת	haḥora**vot**
shopping area	אֵזוֹר הַקְּנִיּוֹת	e**zor** hakni**yot**
square	הַכִּכָּר	haki**kar**

stadium	הָאִצְטַדְיוֹן	haitztad**yon**
statue	הַפֶּסֶל	ha**pe**sel
stock exchange	בּוּרְסַת הַמְּנָיוֹת	bur**sat** hamna**yot**
synagogue	בֵּית כְּנֶסֶת	beyt **kne**set
theatre	הַתֵּאַטְרוֹן	hateat**ron**
tomb	הַקֶּבֶר	ha**ke**ver
tower	הַמִּגְדָּל	hamig**dal**
town hall	הָעִירִיָּה	hairi**ya**
university	הָאוּנִיבֶרְסִיטָה	hauni**ver**sita
zoo	גַּן הַחַיּוֹת	gan haḥa**yot**
theme park	גַּן הַשַּׁעֲשׁוּעִים	gan hashaashu**im**

Admission דְּמֵי כְּנִיסָה

Most tourist attractions provide reductions for pensioners, students and children, though it's always best to ask. Except in Arab areas and holiday resorts, attractions are closed on Saturdays.

Is ... open on Sundays?	הַאִם ... פָּתוּחַ בְּיוֹם רִאשׁוֹן?	ha**im** ... patuaḥ be**yom** ri**shon**
What are the opening hours?	מַה שְּׁעוֹת הַפְּתִיחָה?	ma she**ot** hapti**ḥa**
When does it close?	מָתַי סוֹגְרִים?	ma**tay** sog**rim**
How much is the entrance fee?	כַּמָּה זֶה עוֹלֶה?	**ka**ma ze o**le**
Is there any reduction for (the) ...?	יֵשׁ הֲנָחוֹת לְ...?	yesh hana**ḥot** le
children	יְלָדִים	yela**dim**
disabled	נְכִים	ne**khim**
groups	קְבוּצוֹת	kvu**tzot**
pensioners	גִּימְלָאִים	gimla**im**
students	תַּלְמִידִים	talmi**dim**
Do you have a guidebook (in English)?	יֵשׁ לָכֶם מַדְרִיךְ טִיּוּלִים (בְּאַנְגְּלִית)?	yesh la**khem** mad**rikh** tiyu**lim** (beang**lit**)
Can I buy a catalogue?	אוּכַל לִקְנוֹת קָטָלוֹג?	u**khal** lik**not** kata**log**
Is it all right to take pictures?	מוּתָּר לְצַלֵּם?	mu**tar** letza**lem**

הַכְּנִיסָה חָפְשִׁית	ADMISSION FREE
אָסוּר לְצַלֵּם	NO CAMERAS ALLOWED

Is there easy access for the disabled?	יֵשׁ גִּישָׁה קַלָּה לְנָכִים?	yesh gi**sha** ka**la** lene**khim**
Are there facilities/ activities for children?	יֵשׁ מִתְקָנִים/פְּעוּלוֹת לִילָדִים?	yesh mitka**nim**/peu**lot** lila**dim**

Who—What—When? מִי—מָה—מָתַי?

What's that building?	מַה הַבִּנְיָן הַהוּא?	ma habin**yan** ha**hu**
Who was the ...?	מִי הַ...?	mi ha
architect	אַדְרִיכָל	adri**khal**
artist	אָמָן	o**man**
painter	צַיָּר	tza**yar**
sculptor	פַּסָּל	pa**sal**
Who built it?	מִי בָּנָה אוֹתוֹ?	mi **ba**na oto
Who painted that picture?	מִי צִיֵּר אֶת הַתְּמוּנָה הַהִיא?	mi tzi**yer** et hatmu**na** ha**hi**
When did he live?	מָתַי הוּא חַי?	ma**tay** hu ḥay
When was it built?	מָתַי זֶה נִבְנָה?	ma**tay** ze niv**na**
Where's the house where ... lived?	אֵיפֹה הַבַּיִת בּוֹ גָּר ...?	**ey**fo ha**ba**yit bo gar
We're interested in ...	אֲנַחְנוּ מִתְעַנְיְנִים בְּ...	ana**ḥ**nu mitanye**nim** be
antiques	עַתִּיקוֹת	ati**kot**
archaeology	אַרְכֵאוֹלוֹגְיָה	arkheo**lo**giya
art	אָמָנוּת	oma**nut**
botany	בּוֹטָנִיקָה	bo**ta**nika
ceramics	קֶרָמִיקָה	ke**ra**mika
coins	מַטְבְּעוֹת	matbe**ot**
fine arts	אָמָנוּת יָפָה	oma**nut** ya**fa**
furniture	רָהִיטִים	rahi**tim**
geology	גֵאוֹלוֹגְיָה	geo**lo**giya
handicrafts	מְלֶאכֶת יָד	m**le**khet yad
history	הִסְטוֹרְיָה	his**to**riya
medicine	רְפוּאָה	refu**a**
music	מוּסִיקָה	**mu**sika
natural history	טֶבַע	**te**va
ornithology	צִפֳּרִים	tzipo**rim**
painting	צִיּוּר	tzi**yur**
pottery	קַדָּרוּת	kada**rut**
religion	דָּתוֹת	da**tot**
sculpture	פִּסּוּל	pi**sul**
zoology	זוֹאוֹלוֹגְיָה	zoo**lo**giya
Where's the ... department?	אֵיפֹה מַחְלֶקֶת הַ...?	**ey**fo maḥ**le**ket ha

It's ...	זֶה ...	ze
amazing	מַפְלִיא	maf**li**
awful	נוֹרָא	no**ra**
beautiful	נֶהְדָר	nehe**dar**
impressive	מַרְשִׁים	mar**shim**
interesting	מְעַנְיֵן	mean**yen**
magnificent	נִפְלָא	nif**la**
pretty	יָפֶה	ya**fe**
strange	מוּזָר	mu**zar**
superb	נִפְלָא	nif**la**
terrifying	מַפְחִיד	maf**ḥid**
tremendous	עָצוּם	a**tzum**
ugly	מְכוֹעָר	mekho**ar**

Churches—Religious services כְּנֵסִיּוֹת—תְּפִילּוֹת

In Israel, where Judaism, Islam and Christianity all have roots, you'll find places of worship of all three faiths. Remember that in a synagogue you cover your head, in a church men should *un*cover their heads, and in a mosque you must remove your shoes, and it would be wise to cover up arms and legs at all religious sites.

The *shabbat* (the Hebrew word for rest) starts at sundown on Friday and ends on Saturday evening. The Moslems' day of religious observance starts on Thursday at sunset and continues until sunset on Friday. Christians observe the day of rest all day on Sunday.

Is there a ... nearby?	יֵשׁ ... בַּסְּבִיבָה?	yesh ... bas**viva**
Catholic church	כְּנֵסִיָּה קָתוֹלִית	kne**siya** kato**lit**
Protestant church	כְּנֵסִיָּה פְּרוֹטֶסְטַנְטִית	kne**siya** protes**tan**tit
mosque	מִסְגָּד	mis**gad**
synagogue	בֵּית כְּנֶסֶת	beyt **kne**set
What time is ...?	מָתַי ...?	ma**tay**
mass/the service	הַמִּיסָה/הַתְּפִילָּה?	ha**mi**sa/hatfi**la**
Where can I find a ... who speaks English?	אֵיפֹה אוּכַל לִמְצֹא ... דּוֹבֵר אַנְגְּלִית?	**ey**fo u**khal** lim**tzo** ... do**ver** ang**lit**
priest/minister/rabbi	כֹּמֶר קָתוֹלִי/כֹּמֶר פְּרוֹטֶסְטַנְטִי/רַב	**ko**mer kat**o**lli/**ko**mer protes**tan**ti/rav
I'd like to visit the church.	הָיִיתִי רוֹצֶה (רוֹצָה) לְבַקֵּר בַּכְּנֵסִיָּה.	ha**yi**ti rot**ze** (rot**za**) leva**ker** bakne**siya**
I'd like to go to confession.	הָיִיתִי רוֹצֶה (רוֹצָה) לָלֶכֶת לְוִדּוּי.	ha**yi**ti rot**ze** (rot**za**) la**le**khet levi**duy**

In the countryside מחוץ לָעִיר

Is there a scenic route to ...?	יֵשׁ דֶּרֶךְ נוֹפִית לְ...?	yesh **de**rekh no**fit** le
How far is it to ...?	מַה הַמֶּרְחָק לְ...?	ma hamerḥ**ak** le
Can we walk there?	אֶפְשָׁר לָלֶכֶת לְשָׁם בָּרֶגֶל?	ef**shar** la**le**khet le**sham** baregel
How high is that mountain?	מַה גֹּבַהּ הָהָר הַהוּא?	ma **go**va ha**har** ha**hu**
What kind of ... is that?	אֵיזֶה מִין ... זֶה?	**ey**ze min ... ze
animal	חַיָּה	ḥa**ya**
bird	צִפּוֹר	tzi**por**
flower	פֶּרַח	**pe**raḥ
tree	עֵץ	etz

Landmarks אֲתָרִים

bridge	גֶּשֶׁר	**ge**sher
cliff	צוּק	tzuk
farm	מֶשֶׁק	**me**shek
field	שָׂדֶה	sa**de**
footpath	שְׁבִיל	shvil
forest	יַעַר	**ya**ar
garden	גַּן	gan
hill	גִּבְעָה	giv**a**
house	בַּיִת	**ba**yit
lake	אֲגַם	a**gam**
meadow	אָחוּ	a**ḥu**
mountain	הַר	har
(mountain) pass	מַעֲבָר (הָרִים)	maa**var** (ha**rim**)
path	שְׁבִיל	shvil
peak	פִּסְגָּה	pis**ga**
pond	בְּרֵיכָה אֲגַם קָטָן	bre**kha**, a**gam** ka**tan**
river	נָהָר	na**har**
road	כְּבִישׁ	kvish
sea	יָם	yam
spring	מַעְיָן	maa**yan**
valley	עֵמֶק	**e**mek
village	כְּפָר	kfar
vineyard	כֶּרֶם	**ke**rem
wall	חוֹמָה	ḥo**ma**
waterfall	מַפַּל מַיִם	ma**pal** **ma**yim
wood	חוּרְשָׁה	ḥur**sha**

ASKING THE WAY, see page 76

Relaxing

Cinema (movies)—Theatre קוֹלְנוֹעַ—תֵּאַטְרוֹן

Cinemas usually have three showings per day. A few have continuous programmes starting at 10 or 11 am, mostly showing action films.

All films are shown in their original version with Hebrew subtitles. Films which aren't in English also carry English subtitles, so you'll have no language problems. For evening showings, seats are numbered and it's advisable to make advance reservations.

The Israeli theatre enjoys a high reputation. Performances generally start at 8.30 pm, but you should check curtain time in a newspaper or on a billboard. The weekly country-wide guide "Hello Israel" details all the information you'll need, and it is worth reading Friday morning's *Jerusalem Post* for weekend listings.

What's on at the cinema tonight?	מַה מַצִּיגִים בַּקּוֹלְנוֹעַ הָעֶרֶב?	ma matzi**gim** bakol**noa** ha**e**rev
What's playing at the ... Theatre?	מַה מַצִּיגִים בְּתֵאַטְרוֹן ... הָעֶרֶב?	ma matzi**gim** beteat**ron** ... ha**e**rev
What sort of play is it?	אֵיזֶה מִין מַחֲזֶה זֶה?	**ey**ze min mahа**ze** ze
Who's it by?	מִי כָּתַב אוֹתוֹ?	mi ka**tav** **oto**
Can you recommend a ...?	תּוּכַל (תּוּכְלִי) לְהַמְלִיץ עַל ...?	tu**khal** (tukh**li**) leham**litz** al
good film	סֶרֶט טוֹב	**se**ret tov
comedy	קוֹמֶדְיָה	ko**med**ya
musical	מַחֲזֶמֶר	maḥa**ze**mer
Where's that new film directed by ... being shown?	אֵיפֹה מַצִּיגִים אֶת הַסֶּרֶט הֶחָדָשׁ שֶׁבּוּיַם עַל יְדֵי ...?	**ey**fo matzi**gim** et ha**se**ret haḥa**dash** shebu**yam** al ye**dey**
Who's in it?	מִי מְשַׂחֵק בּוֹ?	mi mesa**ḥek** bo

Who's playing the lead?	מִי בַּתַּפְקִיד הָרָאשִׁי?	mi batafkid harashi
Who's the director?	מִי הַבִּימַאי?	mi habimay
At which theatre is that new play by ... being performed?	אֵיפֹה מַצִּיגִים אֶת הַמַּחֲזֶה הֶחָדָשׁ שֶׁנִּכְתַּב עַל יְדֵי ...?	eyfo matzigim et hamahaze hahadash shenikhtav al yedey
What time does it begin?	בְּאֵיזוֹ שָׁעָה הוּא מַתְחִיל?	beeyzo shaa hu mathil
Are there any seats for tonight?	יֵשׁ כַּרְטִיסִים לְהָעֶרֶב?	yesh kartisim lehaerev
How much are the seats?	כַּמָּה עוֹלִים הַכַּרְטִיסִים?	kama olim hakartisim
I'd like to reserve 2 seats for the show on Friday evening.	אֲבַקֵּשׁ לְהַזְמִין שְׁנֵי כַּרְטִיסִים לַהַצָּגָה בְּיוֹם שִׁשִּׁי בָּעֶרֶב.	avakesh lehazmin shney kartisim lahatzaga beyom shishi baerev
Can I have a ticket for the matinée on Tuesday?	אוּכַל לְקַבֵּל כַּרְטִיס לַהַצָּגָה הַיּוֹמִית בְּיוֹם שְׁלִישִׁי?	ukhal lekabel kartis lahatzaga hayomit beyom shlishi
I'd like a seat in the stalls (orchestra).	אֲבַקֵּשׁ מָקוֹם בַּשּׁוּרוֹת הַקִּדְמִיּוֹת.	avakesh makom bashurot hakidmiyot
Not too far back.	לֹא יוֹתֵר מִדַּי רָחוֹק.	lo yoter miday rahok
Somewhere in the middle.	בְּעֵרֶךְ בָּאֶמְצַע.	beerekh baemtza
How much are the seats in the circle (mezzanine)?	כַּמָּה עוֹלִים הַכַּרְטִיסִים בַּיָּצִיעַ?	kama olim hakartisim bayatzia
May I have a programme, please?	אֶפְשָׁר לְקַבֵּל תָּכְנִיָּה בְּבַקָּשָׁה?	efshar lekabel tokhniya bevakasha
Where's the cloakroom?	אֵיפֹה הַמֶּלְתָּחָה?	eyfoameltaha

מִצְטַעֵר (מִצְטַעֶרֶת) הַכֹּל נִמְכָּר.	I'm sorry, we're sold out.
נִשְׁאֲרוּ רַק כַּמָּה כַּרְטִיסִים בַּיָּצִיעַ.	There are only a few seats left in the circle (mezzanine).
אֶפְשָׁר לִרְאוֹת אֶת הַכַּרְטִיס שֶׁלְּךָ (שֶׁלָּךְ)?	May I see your ticket?
זֶה הַמָּקוֹם שֶׁלְּךָ (שֶׁלָּךְ).	This is your seat.

DAYS OF THE WEEK, see page 151

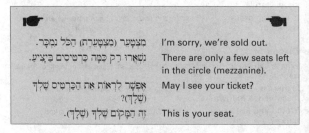

Opera—Ballet—Concert אוֹפֶּרָה—בָּלֶט—קוֹנְצֶרְט

Can you recommend a(n) ...?	...תּוּכַל) לְהַמְלִיץ עַל ...?)	tukhal (tukhli) lehamlitz al
ballet	בָּלֶט	balet
concert	קוֹנְצֶרְט	kontzert
opera	אוֹפֶּרָה	opera
operetta	אוֹפֶּרֶטָה	opereta

Where's the opera house/the concert hall?	אֵיפֹה בִּנְיַן הָאוֹפֶּרָה/אוּלַם הַקוֹנְצֶרְטִים?	eyfo binyan haopera/ulam hakontzertim
What's on at the opera tonight?	מָה מַצִּיגִים בָּאוֹפֶּרָה הָעֶרֶב?	ma matzigim baopera haerev
Who's singing/ dancing?	מִי שָׁר/רוֹקֵד?	mi shar/roked
Which orchestra is playing?	אֵיזוֹ תִּזְמֹרֶת מְנַגֶנֶת?	eyzo tizmoret menagenet
What are they playing?	מָה הֵם מְנַגְנִים?	ma hem menagnim
Who's the conductor/ soloist?	מִי הַמְנַצֵּחַ/הַסוֹלָן?	mi hamenatzeah/hasolan

Nightclubs מוֹעֲדוֹנֵי לַיְלָה

There are some reasonably priced places that provide good entertainment, so ask around. Find out the prices before you order—and allow for various surcharges.

Can you recommend a good nightclub?	אַתָּה (אַתְּ) מַכִּיר (מַכִּירָה) מוֹעֲדוֹן לַיְלָה טוֹב?	ata (at) makir (makira) moadon layla tov
Is there a floor show?	יֵשׁ הוֹפָעָה?	yesh hofaa
What time does the show start?	מָתַי מַתְחִילָה הַהוֹפָעָה?	matay mathila hahofaa
Is evening dress required?	הַאִם תִּלְבֹּשֶׁת עֶרֶב הֶכְרֵחִית?	haim tilboshet erev hekhrehit

Discos דִיסְקוֹטֵק

Where can we go dancing?	לְאָן אֶפְשָׁר לָלֶכֶת לִרְקוֹד?	lean efshar lalekhet lirkod
Is there a discotheque in town?	יֵשׁ דִיסְקוֹטֵק בָּעִיר?	yesh diskotek bair
Would you like to dance?	תִּרְצֶה (תִּרְצִי) לִרְקוֹד?	tirtze (tirtzi) lirkod

Sports סְפּוֹרְט

Football (soccer), basketball, tennis, fishing, hiking, water sports, golf and swimming are the most popular sports in Israel. In the winter there is also skiing on Mt Harmon.

Is there a football (soccer) match anywhere today?	יֵשׁ אֵיזוֹ תַּחֲרוּת כַּדּוּרֶגֶל הַיּוֹם	yesh **ey**zo ta**ḥa**rut kadu**re**gel hayom
Which teams are playing?	אֵילוּ קְבוּצוֹת מְשַׂחֲקוֹת?	**ey**lu kvu**tzot** mesa**ḥa**kot
Can you get me a ticket?	תּוּכַל (תּוּכְלִי) לְהַשִּׂיג לִי כַּרְטִיס?	tu**khal** (tukh**li**) leha**sig** li kar**tis**

basketball	כַּדּוּרְסַל	kadur**sal**
boxing	אִגְרוּף	ig**ruf**
car racing	מֵרוֹץ מְכוֹנִיּוֹת	me**rotz** mekhoni**yot**
cycling	רְכִיבָה בְּאוֹפַנַּיִם	rekhi**va** beofa**nayim**
football (soccer)	כַּדּוּרֶגֶל	kadu**re**gel
horse racing	מֵרוֹץ סוּסִים	me**rotz** su**sim**
(horse-back) riding	רְכִיבָה (עַל סוּס)	rekhi**va** (al sus)
mountaineering	טִפּוּס בֶּהָרִים	ti**pus** beha**rim**
skiing	סְקִי	ski
swimming	שְׂחִיָּה	sḥi**ya**
tennis	טֶנִיס	**te**nis
volleyball	כַּדּוּרְעָף	kadu**raf**

I'd like to see a boxing match.	הָיִיתִי רוֹצֶה (רוֹצָה) לִרְאוֹת תַּחֲרוּת אִגְרוּף.	ha**yi**ti rot**ze** (rot**za**) li**rot** ta**ḥa**rut ig**ruf**
What's the admission charge?	כַּמָּה דְּמֵי הַכְּנִיסָה?	**ka**ma dmey hakni**sa**
Where's the nearest golf course?	אֵיפֹה מַסְלוּל הַגּוֹלְף הַקָּרוֹב?	**ey**fo mas**lul** ha**golf** haka**rov**
Where are the tennis courts?	אֵיפֹה מִגְרְשֵׁי הַטֶּנִיס?	**ey**fo migre**shey** ha**te**nis
What's the charge per ...?	מַה הַמְּחִיר לְ...?	ma hame**ḥir** le
day/round/hour	יוֹם/מִשְׂחָק/שָׁעָה	yom/mis**ḥak**/sha**a**

Can I hire (rent) rackets?	אֶפְשָׁר לִשְׂכּוֹר מַחְבְּטִים?	ef**shar** lis**kor** maḥbe**tim**
Where's the race course (track)?	אֵיפֹה מַסְלוּל הַמְּרוֹצִים?	**ey**fo mas**lul** hameru**tzim**
Is there any good fishing/hunting around here?	יֵשׁ מָקוֹם טוֹב לָדוּג/לָצוּד בַּסְּבִיבָה?	yesh ma**kom** tov la**dug**/ la**tzud** basvi**va**
Do I need a permit?	צָרִיךְ רִשָּׁיוֹן?	tza**rikh** risha**yon**
Where can I get one?	אֵיפֹה אֶפְשָׁר לְהַשִּׂיג אוֹתוֹ?	**ey**fo ef**shar** leha**sig** o**to**
Can one swim in the lake/river?	אֶפְשָׁר לִשְׂחוֹת בָּאֲגַם/בַּנָּהָר?	ef**shar** lis**ḥot** baa**gam**/ bana**har**
Is there a swimming pool here?	יֵשׁ כָּאן בְּרֵיכַת שְׂחִיָּה?	yesh kan bre**khat** s**ḥi**ya
Is it open-air or indoor?	הִיא פְּתוּחָה אוֹ סְגוּרָה?	hi ptu**ḥa** o sgu**ra**
Is it heated?	הִיא מְחוּמֶּמֶת?	hi meḥu**me**met
What's the temperature of the water?	מַה טֶמְפֶּרָטוּרַת הַמַּיִם?	ma tempera**turat** ha**ma**yim
Is there a sandy beach?	יֵשׁ חוֹף עִם חוֹל?	yesh ḥof im ḥol

On the beach בַּחוֹף

Beaches are generally sandy, safe and clean. If you venture to Eilat and the Red Sea you'll find diving centres aplenty; for the less adventurous, snorkelling is a popular way of discovering the superb coral reef and underwater life. It is, however, illegal to take any coral away as a souvenir.

Is it safe to swim here?	זֶה בָּטוּחַ לִשְׂחוֹת כָּאן?	ze ba**tuaḥ** lis**ḥot** kan
Is there a lifeguard?	יֵשׁ מַצִּיל?	yesh ma**tzil**
Is it safe for children?	זֶה בָּטוּחַ לִילָדִים?	ze ba**tuaḥ** lila**dim**
The sea is very calm.	הַיָּם שָׁקֵט מְאוֹד.	ha**yam** sha**ket** meod
There are some big waves.	יֵשׁ גַּלִּים גְּדוֹלִים.	yesh ga**lim** gdo**lim**
Are there any dangerous currents?	יֵשׁ זְרָמִים מְסוּכָּנִים?	yesh zra**mim** mesuka**nim**

I want to hire (rent) a/an/some ...	בִּרְצוֹנִי לִשְׂכּוֹר ...	birtzo**ni** lis**kor**
bathing hut (cabana)	סוּכָּה	su**ka**
deck chair	כִּסֵּא נוֹחַ	**ki**se **no**aḥ
motorboat	סִירַת מָנוֹעַ	si**rat** ma**no**a
rowing-boat	סִירַת חֲתִירָה	si**rat** ḥati**ra**
sailing boat	סִירַת מִפְרָשׂ	si**rat** mif**ras**
skin-diving equipment	צִיּוּד צְלִילָה	tzi**yud** tzli**la**
sunshade (umbrella)	סוֹכֵךְ	so**khekh**
surfboard	גַּלְשָׁן	gal**shan**
water-skis	מִגְלָשִׁים לְסְקִי מַיִם	migla**shim** lis**ki** **ma**yim
windsurfer	גַּלְשַׁן רוּחַ	gal**shan** **ru**aḥ

חוֹף פְּרָטִי	PRIVATE BEACH
אָסוּר לִשְׂחוֹת	NO SWIMMING

Winter sports סְפּוֹרְט חֹרֶף

I'd like to ski.	אֲנִי רוֹצֶה (רוֹצָה) לַעֲשׂוֹת סְקִי.	a**ni** rot**ze** (rot**za**) laa**sot** ski
Are there any ski lifts?	יֵשׁ מַעֲלִיּוֹת סְקִי?	yesh maali**yot** ski
I want to hire ...	אֲבַקֵּשׁ לִשְׂכּוֹר ...	ava**kesh** lis**kor**
poles	מוֹטוֹת	mo**tot**
ski boots	נַעֲלֵי סְקִי	naa**ley** ski
skiing equipment	צִיּוּד סְקִי	tzi**yud** ski
skis	מִגְלְשֵׁי סְקִי	migle**shey** ski

Making friends

Introductions הַכָּרוֹת

Many Israeli families are happy to extend hospitality to tourists and engage visitors in lively conversation. Here are a few phrases to help break the ice.

May I introduce ...?	... תַּכִּיר (תַּכִּירִי) אֶת	**takir** (ta**kiri**) et
John, this is ...	... נוֹהֶן זֶה (זוֹ)	jon ze (zo)
My name is ...	... שְׁמִי	shmi
Pleased to meet you!	נָעִים לְהַכִּיר!	naim leha**kir**
What's your name?	מַה שִּׁמְךָ (שְׁמֵךְ)?	ma shim**kha** (shmekh)
How are you?	מַה שְׁלוֹמְךָ (שְׁלוֹמֵךְ)?	ma shlom**kha** (shlo**mekh**)
Fine, thanks. And you?	בְּסֵדֶר, תּוֹדָה. וְאַתָּה (וְאַתְּ)?	be**seder** toda. ve**ata** (veat)

Follow up מְשׁוֹחֲחִים

How long have you been here?	כַּמָּה זְמַן אַתָּה (אַתְּ) כָּאן?	**ka**ma zman ata (at) kan
We've been here a week.	אֲנַחְנוּ כָּאן כְּבָר שָׁבוּעַ.	a**nah**nu kan kvar shavua
Is this your first visit?	זֶה הַבִּקּוּר הָרִאשׁוֹן שֶׁלְּךָ (שֶׁלָּךְ)?	ze habi**kur** hari**shon** shel**kha** (she**lakh**)
No, we came here last year.	לֹא הָיִינוּ כָּאן בַּשָּׁנָה שֶׁעָבְרָה.	lo ha**yinu** kan basha**na** sheavra
Are you enjoying your stay?	אַתָּה נֶהֱנֶה (אַתְּ נֶהֱנֵית) כָּאן?	ata ne**hene** (at ne**henet**) kan
Yes, I like it very much.	כֵּן אֲנִי נֶהֱנֶה (נֶהֱנֵית) מְאֹד.	ken ani ne**hene** (ne**henet**) meod
I like the scenery a lot.	הַנּוֹף מְאֹד מוֹצֵא חֵן בְּעֵינַי.	ha**nof** meod motze hen bey**nay**
What do you think of the country/people?	מַה דַּעְתְּךָ (דַּעְתֵּךְ) עַל הָאָרֶץ/הָאֲנָשִׁים?	ma daat**kha** (daa**tekh**) al ha**aretz**/haana**shim**
Where do you come from?	מֵאֵיפֹה אַתָּה (אַתְּ)?	mee**yfo** ata (at)
I'm from ...	... אֲנִי מ	ani mi
What nationality are you?	מַה הָאֶזְרָחוּת שֶׁלְּךָ (שֶׁלָּךְ)?	ma haezra**hut** shel**kha** (she**lakh**)

I'm ...	אֲנִי ...	**ani**
American	אַמֶרִיקָאִי (אַמֶרִיקָאִית)	ameri**kai** (ameri**kait**)
British	בְּרִיטִי (בְּרִיטִית)	**bri**ti (**bri**tit)
Canadian	קָנָדִי (קָנָדִית)	ka**na**di (ka**na**dit)
English	אַנְגְלִי (אַנְגְלִיָה)	ang**li** (angli**ya**)
Irish	אִירִי (אִירִית)	**iri** (**irit**)
Where are you staying?	אֵיפֹה אַתָּה שׁוֹהֶה (אַתְּ שׁוֹהָה)?	**ey**fo **ata** sho**he** (at sho**ha**)
Are you on your own?	אַתָּה (אַתְּ) לְבָד?	**ata** (at) le**vad**
I'm with my ...	אֲנִי עִם ...	**ani** im
wife	אִשְׁתִּי	ish**ti**
husband	בַּעֲלִי	ba**ali**
family	הַמִּשְׁפָּחָה	hamishpa**ḥa**
children	הַיְלָדִים	hayla**dim**
parents	הַהוֹרִים	ha**horim**
boyfriend/girlfriend	הֶחָבֵר שֶׁלִּי/הַחֲבֵרָה שֶׁלִּי	haḥa**ver** she**li**/haḥave**ra** she**li**

father/mother	אָבִי/אִמִּי	a**vi**/i**mi**
son/daughter	בְּנִי/בִּתִּי	b**ni**/bi**ti**
brother/sister	אָחִי/אֲחוֹתִי	a**ḥi**/aḥo**ti**
uncle/aunt	דּוֹדִי/דּוֹדָתִי	do**di**/doda**ti**
nephew/niece	אַחְיָנִי/אַחְיָנִיתִי	aḥya**ni**/aḥyani**ti**
cousin	בֶּן (בַּת) דּוֹדִי	ben (bat) do**di**

Are you married/single?	אַתָּה נָשׂוּי (אַתְּ נְשׂוּאָה)/רַוָּק (רַוָּקָה)?	**ata** na**suy** (at nesua)/ra**vak** (rava**ka**)
Do you have children?	יֵשׁ לְךָ (לָךְ) יְלָדִים?	**yesh** le**kha** (lakh) yela**dim**
What do you do?	מַה אַתָּה עוֹשֶׂה (אַתְּ עוֹשָׂה)?	ma a**ta** o**se** (at o**sa**)
I'm a student.	אֲנִי סְטוּדֶנְט (סְטוּדֶנְטִית).	**ani** stu**dent** (stu**den**tit)
What are you studying?	מַה אַתָּה לוֹמֵד (אַתְּ לוֹמֶדֶת)?	ma a**ta** lo**med** (at lo**me**det)
I'm here on a business trip/on holiday.	אֲנִי כָּאן לַעֲסָקִים/בְּחֹפֶשׁ.	**ani** kan leasa**kim**/be**ḥo**fesh
Do you travel a lot?	אַתָּה נוֹסֵעַ (אַתְּ נוֹסַעַת) הַרְבֵּה?	**ata** no**sea** (at no**saat**) har**be**
Do you play cards/chess?	אַתָּה מְשַׂחֵק (אַתְּ מְשַׂחֶקֶת) קְלָפִים/שַׁחְמָט?	**ata** mesa**ḥek** (at mesa**ḥe**ket) kla**fim**/shaḥ**mat**

COUNTRIES, see page 146

The weather מֶזֶג הָאֲוִיר

What a lovely day!	אֵיזֶה יוֹם יָפֶה!	**ey**ze yom ya**fe**
What awful weather!	אֵיזֶה מֶזֶג אֲוִיר נוֹרָא!	**ey**ze mezeg avir no**ra**
Isn't it cold/hot today?	אֵיזֶה קֹר/חֹם הַיּוֹם!	eyze kor/ḥom ha**yom**
Is it usually as warm as this?	תָּמִיד כָּל כָּךְ חַם?	ta**mid** kol kakh ḥam
Do you think it's going to ... tomorrow?	אַתָּה חוֹשֵׁב (אַתְּ חוֹשֶׁבֶת) שֶׁיִּהְיֶה ... מָחָר?	a**ta** ḥo**shev** (at ḥo**she**vet) sheyih**ye** ... ma**ḥar**
be a nice day	מֶזֶג אֲוִיר יָפֶה	**me**zeg a**vir** ya**fe**
rain	גֶּשֶׁם	**ge**shem
snow	שֶׁלֶג	**she**leg
What's the weather forecast?	מַה הַתַּחֲזִית?	ma hataḥa**zit**

cloud	עָנָן	a**nan**
fog	עֲרָפֶל	ara**fel**
frost	כְּפוֹר	kfor
ice	קֶרַח	**ke**raḥ
lightning	בָּרָק	ba**rak**
moon	יָרֵחַ	ya**re**aḥ
rain	גֶּשֶׁם	**ge**shem
sky	שָׁמַיִם	sha**ma**yim
snow	שֶׁלֶג	**she**leg
star	כּוֹכָב	ko**khav**
sun	שֶׁמֶשׁ	**she**mesh
thunder	רַעַם	**ra**am
thunderstorm	סוּפַת רְעָמִים	su**fat** rea**mim**
wind	רוּחַ	**ru**aḥ

Invitations הַזְמָנוֹת

Would you like to have dinner with us on ...?	תִּרְצֶה (תִּרְצִי) לֶאֱכוֹל אִתָּנוּ אֲרוּחַת עֶרֶב בְּיוֹם ...?	tir**tze** (tir**tzi**) lee**khol** ita**nu** aru**ḥat** **e**rev be**yom**
May I invite you to lunch?	אוּכַל לְהַזְמִין אוֹתְךָ (אוֹתָךְ) לַאֲרוּחַת צָהֳרַיִם?	**u**khal lehaz**min** ot**kha** (o**takh**) learu**khat** tzoho**ra**yim

Can you come round for a drink this evening?	תּוּכַל (תּוּכְלִי) לָבוֹא אֵלַי לִשְׁתּוֹת מַשֶּׁהוּ הָעֶרֶב?	tu**khal** (tukh**li**) la**vo** e**lay** lish**tot** **ma**shehu hae**rev**
There's a party. Are you coming?	יֵשׁ מְסִיבָּה. תִּרְצֶה (תִּרְצִי) לָבוֹא?	yesh mesi**ba**. tir**tze** (tir**tzi**) la**vo**
That's very kind of you.	מְאֹד נֶחְמָד מִצִּדְּךָ (מִצִּדֵּךְ).	me**od** neh**mad** mitzid**kha** (mitzi**dekh**)
Great. I'd love to come.	יוֹפִי. אֶשְׂמַח לָבֹא.	**yofi**. es**maḥ** la**vo**
What time shall we come?	בְּאֵיזוֹ שָׁעָה נָבֹא?	be**ey**zo sha**a** na**vo**
May I bring a friend?	אוּכַל לְהָבִיא עוֹד מִישֶׁהוּ?	u**khal** leha**vi** od **mi**shehu
I'm afraid we have to leave now.	לְצַעֲרִי נִצְטָרֵךְ לָלֶכֶת עַכְשָׁו.	letzaa**ri** nitzta**rekh** la**le**khet akh**shav**
Next time you must come to visit us.	בַּפַּעַם הַבָּאָה תָּבֹא לְבַקֵּר אֶצְלֵנוּ.	ba**pa**am haba**a** ta**vo** leva**ker** etz**le**nu
Thanks for the evening. It was great.	תּוֹדָה, הָיָה עֶרֶב נֶהֱדָר.	to**da**. ha**ya** e**rev** nehe**dar**

Dating פְּגִישָׁה בִּשְׁנַיִם

Do you mind if I smoke?	אִכְפַּת לְךָ (לָךְ) אִם אֲעַשֵּׁן?	ikh**pat** le**kha** (lakh) im aa**shen**
Would you like a cigarette?	תִּרְצֶה (תִּרְצִי) סִיגַרְיָה?	tir**tze** (tir**tzi**) sigari**ya**
Do you have a light, please?	יֵשׁ לְךָ (לָךְ) אֵשׁ בְּבַקָּשָׁה?	yesh le**kha** (lakh) esh bevaka**sha**
Why are you laughing?	לָמָּה אַתָּה צוֹחֵק (אַתְּ צוֹחֶקֶת)?	**la**ma a**ta** tzo**ḥek** (at tzo**ḥe**ket)
Is my Hebrew that bad?	הָעִבְרִית שֶׁלִּי כָּל כָּךְ גְּרוּעָה?	haiv**rit** she**li** kol kakh gru**a**
Do you mind if I sit here?	אִכְפַּת לְךָ (לָךְ) אִם אֵשֵׁב כָּאן?	ikh**pat** le**kha** (lakh) im e**shev** kan
Can I get you a drink?	אוּכַל לְהָבִיא לְךָ (לָךְ) מַשֶּׁהוּ לִשְׁתּוֹת?	u**khal** leha**vi** le**kha** (lakh) **ma**shehu lish**tot**
Are you waiting for someone?	אַתָּה מְחַכֶּה (אַתְּ מְחַכָּה) לְמִישֶׁהוּ?	a**ta** me**ḥa**ke (at me**ḥa**ka) le**mi**shehu
Are you free this evening?	אַתָּה פָּנוּי (אַתְּ פְּנוּיָה) הָעֶרֶב?	a**ta** pa**nuy** (at pnu**ya**) hae**rev**

DAYS OF THE WEEK, see page 151

Would you like to go out with me tonight?	תִּרְצֶה (תִּרְצִי) לָצֵאת אִתִּי הָעֶרֶב?	**tirtze** (**tirtzi**) la**tzet** i**ti** ha**erev**
Would you like to go dancing?	תִּרְצֶה (תִּרְצִי) לָלֶכֶת לִרְקוֹד?	**tirtze** (**tirtzi**) la**le**khet lir**kod**
I know a good discotheque.	אֲנִי מַכִּיר (מַכִּירָה) דִּיסְקוֹטֶק טוֹב.	**ani** ma**kir** (maki**ra**) **dis**kotek tov
Shall we go to the cinema (movies)?	אוּלַי נֵלֵךְ לְקוֹלְנוֹעַ?	u**lay** ne**lekh** lekol**noa**
Would you like to go for a drive?	תִּרְצֶה (תִּרְצִי) לִנְסוֹעַ לְטִיּוּל בִּמְכוֹנִית?	**tirtze** (**tirtzi**) lin**soa** leti**yul** bimkho**nit**
Where shall we meet?	אֵיפֹה נִפָּגֵשׁ?	**ey**fo nipa**gesh**
I'll pick you up at your hotel.	אֶאֱסוֹף אוֹתְךָ (אוֹתָךְ) מֵהַמָּלוֹן שֶׁלְּךָ (שֶׁלָּךְ).	ee**sof** ot**kha** (o**takh**) mehama**lon** shel**kha** (she**lakh**)
I'll call for you at 8.	אָבוֹא בִּשְׁמוֹנֶה.	**avo** bishmo**ne**
May I take you home?	אוּכַל לָקַחַת אוֹתְךָ (אוֹתָךְ) הַבַּיְתָה?	u**khal** la**ka**ḥat ot**kha** (o**takh**) ha**bay**ta
Can I see you again tomorrow?	אוּכַל לִרְאוֹת אוֹתְךָ (אוֹתָךְ) שׁוּב מָחָר?	u**khal** li**rot** ot**kha** (o**takh**) shuv ma**ḥar**
I hope we'll meet again.	אֲנִי מְקַוֶּה (מְקַוָּה) שֶׁנִּפָּגֵשׁ שׁוּב.	**ani** meka**ve** (meka**va**) shenipa**gesh** shuv

... and you might answer:

I'd love to, thank you.	כֵּן בְּרָצוֹן.	ken bera**tzon**
Thank you, but I'm busy.	תּוֹדָה אֲבָל אֲנִי עָסוּק (עֲסוּקָה).	**toda** a**val** a**ni** a**suk** (asu**ka**)
No, I'm not interested, thank you.	לֹא אֲנִי לֹא מְעוּנְיָן (מְעוּנְיֶנֶת) תּוֹדָה.	lo **ani** lo meun**yan** (meun**ye**net) to**da**
Leave me alone, please!	עֲזוֹב (עִזְבִי) אוֹתִי בְּבַקָּשָׁה!	a**zov** (**izvi**) o**ti** bevaka**sha**
Thank you, it's been a wonderful evening.	תּוֹדָה הָיָה עֶרֶב נֶהְדָּר.	to**da** ha**ya** **e**rev neh**edar**
I've enjoyed myself.	נֶהֱנֵיתִי מְאוֹד.	nehe**ne**ti me**od**

Shopping Guide

This shopping guide is designed to help you find what you want with ease, accuracy and speed. It features:

1. A list of all major shops, stores and services (p. 98).
2. Some general expressions required when shopping to allow you to be specific and selective (p. 100).
3. Full details of the shops and services most likely to concern you. Here you'll find advice, alphabetical lists of items and conversion charts listed under the headings below.

LAUNDRY, see page 29/HAIDRESSER'S, see page 30

Shops, stores and services חֲנֻיּוֹת וְשֵׁרוּתִים

Shopping hours are usually from 8 am to 1 pm and 4 pm to 7 pm, but on the eve of the Jewish or Moslem Sabbaths shop-keepers may close around 2 pm. Some shops close on either Monday, Tuesday or Wednesday afternoons. Moslem shops close on Fridays, Jewish shops on Saturdays, and Christian-owned establishments on Sundays.

In large stores prices are fixed, but in the *souks* and many small shops it is customary to bargain. A value-added tax is levied on all goods and services and is included in the quoted price. Some shops have duty-free schemes.

Where's the nearest ...?	אֵיפֹה הַ... הַקָּרוֹב (הַקְּרוֹבָה)?	**ey**fo ha... haka**rov** (hakro**va**)
antique shop	חֲנוּת עַתִּיקוֹת	ḥa**nut** ati**kot**
art gallery	גָּלֶרְיָה לְאָמָּנוּת	gal**e**riya leoma**nut**
baker's	מַאֲפִיָּה	maafi**ya**
bank	בַּנְק	bank
barber's	מִסְפָּרָה	mispa**ra**
beauty salon	מְכוֹן יוֹפִי	me**khon yo**fi
bookshop	חֲנוּת סְפָרִים	ḥa**nut** sfa**rim**
butcher's	אִטְלִיז	it**liz**
camera shop	חֲנוּת צִלּוּם	ḥa**nut** tzi**lum**
chemist's	בֵּית מִרְקַחַת	beyt mir**ka**ḥat
dairy	חֲנוּת לְמוּצְרֵי חָלָב	ḥa**nut** lemutz**rey** ḥa**lav**
delicatessen	מַעֲדָנִיָּה	maadani**ya**
dentist	רוֹפֵא שִׁנַּיִם	ro**fe** shi**na**yim
department store	חֲנוּת כָּל-בּוֹ	ḥa**nut** kol bo
drugstore	בֵּית מִרְקַחַת	beyt mir**ka**ḥat
dry cleaner's	מִכְבָּסָה לְנִקּוּי יָבֵשׁ	mikhba**sa** leni**kuy** ya**vesh**
electrical goods shop	חֲנוּת לְדִבְרֵי חַשְׁמַל	ḥa**nut** ledi**vrey** ḥash**mal**
fishmonger's	חֲנוּת דָּגִים	ḥa**nut** da**gim**
florist's	חֲנוּת פְּרָחִים	ḥa**nut** pra**ḥim**
furrier's	חֲנוּת פַּרְווֹת	ḥa**nut** lepar**vot**
greengrocer's	יַרְקָן	yar**kan**
grocer's	חֲנוּת מַכֹּלֶת	ḥa**nut** ma**ko**let
hairdresser's (ladies/men)	מִסְפָּרָה (לְנָשִׁים/לִגְבָרִים)	mispa**ra** (lena**shim**/ liga**rim**)

hardware store	חֲנוּת לְחָמְרֵי בִּנְיָן	ḥa**nut** leḥom**rey** bin**yan**
health food shop	חֲנוּת טִבְעוֹנִית	ḥa**nut** tivo**nit**
hospital	בֵּית חוֹלִים	beyt ḥo**lim**
ironmonger's	חֲנוּת לְחָמְרֵי בִּנְיָן	ḥa**nut** leḥom**rey** bin**yan**
jeweller's	צוֹרֵף	tzo**ref**
launderette	מִכְבָּסָה לְשֵׁרוּת עַצְמִי	mikhba**sa** lesher**ut** atz**mi**
laundry	מִכְבָּסָה	mikhba**sa**
library	סִפְרִיָּה	sifri**ya**
market	שׁוּק	shuk
newsagent's	חֲנוּת עִתּוֹנִים	ḥa**nut** ito**nim**
newsstand	דּוּכַן עִתּוֹנִים	du**khan** ito**nim**
optician	אוֹפְּטִיקַאי	opti**kay**
pastry shop	חֲנוּת עוּגוֹת	ḥa**nut** u**got**
photographer	צַלָּם	tza**lam**
police station	תַּחֲנַת מִשְׁטָרָה	taḥa**nat** mishta**ra**
post office	דֹּאַר	**doar**
second-hand shop	חֲנוּת מְצִיאוֹת	ḥa**nut** metzi**ot**
shoemaker's (repairs)	סַנְדְּלָר	sand**lar**
shoe shop	חֲנוּת נַעֲלַיִם	ḥa**nut** naa**la**yim
shopping centre	מֶרְכַּז קְנִיּוֹת	mer**kaz** kni**yot**
souvenir shop	חֲנוּת מַזְכָּרוֹת	ḥa**nut** mazka**rot**
sporting goods shop	חֲנוּת לְדִבְרֵי סְפּוֹרְט	ḥa**nut** lediv**rey** sport
stationer's	חֲנוּת לְמַכְשִׁירֵי כְּתִיבָה	ḥa**nut** lemakhshi**rey** kti**va**
supermarket	סוּפֶּרְמַרְקֶט	super**market**
sweet shop	מִגְדָּנִיָּה	migdani**ya**
tailor's	חַיָּט	ḥa**yat**
tobacconist's	חֲנוּת טַבָּק	ḥa**nut** ta**bak**
toy shop	חֲנוּת צַעֲצוּעִים	ḥa**nut** tzaatzu**im**
travel agency	סוֹכְנוּת נְסִיעוֹת	sokh**nut** nesi**ot**
vegetable store	יַרְקָן	yar**kan**
veterinarian	רוֹפֵא חַיּוֹת	ro**fe** ḥa**yot**
watchmaker's	שָׁעָן	shean
wine merchant	חֲנוּת מַשְׁקָאוֹת	ḥa**nut** mashka**ot**

כְּנִיסָה	ENTRANCE
יְצִיאָה	EXIT
יְצִיאַת חֵרוּם	EMERGENCY EXIT

General expressions כְּלָלִי

Where? אֵיפֹה?

Where's there a good ...?	אֵיפֹה יֵשׁ ... טוֹב (טוֹבָה)?	**ey**fo yesh ... tov (**to**va)
Where can I find a ...?	אֵיפֹה אוּכַל לִמְצֹא ...?	**ey**fo u**khal** lim**tzo**
Where's the main shopping area?	אֵיפֹה אֵזוֹר הַקְּנִיּוֹת הָרָאשִׁי?	**ey**fo **ezor** hakni**yot** hara**shi**
Is it far from here?	זֶה רָחוֹק מִפֹּה?	ze ra**ḥok** mi**po**
How do I get there?	אֵיךְ מַגִּיעִים לְשָׁם?	eykh magi**im** le**sham**

מְכִירָה
SALE

Service שֵׁרוּת

Can you help me?	תּוּכַל (תּוּכְלִי) לַעֲזוֹר לִי?	tu**khal** (tukh**li**) laa**zor** li
I'm just looking.	אֲנִי רַק מִסְתַּכֵּל (מִסְתַּכֶּלֶת).	**ani** rak mista**kel** (mista**ke**let)
Do you sell ...?	אַתֶּם מוֹכְרִים ...?	**atem** mokh**rim**
I'd like to buy ...	אֲנִי רוֹצֶה (רוֹצָה) לִקְנוֹת ...?	**ani** rot**ze** (rot**za**) lik**not**
I'd like ...	אֲבַקֵּשׁ ...?	ava**kesh**
Can you show me some ...?	תּוּכַל (תּוּכְלִי) לְהַרְאוֹת לִי ...?	tu**khal** (tukh**li**) lehar**ot** li
Do you have any ...?	יֵשׁ לָכֶם ...?	yesh la**khem**
Where's the ... department?	אֵיפֹה מַחְלֶקֶת הַ...?	**ey**fo maḥ**le**ket ha
Where is the lift (elevator)/escalator?	אֵיפֹה הַמַּעֲלִית/הַמַּדְרֵגוֹת הַנָּעוֹת?	**ey**fo hamaa**lit**/hamadre**got** hana**ot**

That one הַהוּא

Can you show me ...?	תּוּכַל (תּוּכְלִי) לְהַרְאוֹת לִי ...?	tu**khal** (tukh**li**) lehar**ot** li
this/that	אֶת זֶה/אֶת הַהוּא	et ze/et ha**hu**
the one in the window/in the display case	אֶת זֶה שֶׁבַּחַלּוֹן/שֶׁבָּאָרוֹן	et ze shebeḥa**lon**/ shebaa**ron**

Defining the article תֵּאוּר הַסְּחוֹרָה

I'd like a ... one.	הָיִיתִי רוֹצֶה (רוֹצָה) ...	ha**yi**ti rot**ze** (rot**za**)
big	גָּדוֹל (גְּדוֹלָה)	ga**dol** (gdo**la**)
cheap	זוֹל (זוֹלָה)	zol (zo**la**)
dark	כֵּהֶה (כֵּהָה)	ke**he** (ke**ha**)
good	טוֹב (טוֹבָה)	tov (to**va**)
heavy	כָּבֵד (כְּבֵדָה)	ka**ved** (kve**da**)
large	גָּדוֹל (גְּדוֹלָה)	ga**dol** (gdo**la**)
light (weight)	קַל (קַלָּה)	kal (ka**la**)
light (colour)	בָּהִיר (בְּהִירָה)	ba**hir** (nehi**ra**)
oval	אֱלִיפְּטִי (אֱלִיפְּטִית)	elip**ti** (elip**tit**)
rectangular	מַלְבֵּנִי (מַלְבֵּנִית)	malbe**ni** (malbe**nit**)
round	עָגוֹל (עֲגוּלָה)	a**gol** (agu**la**)
small	קָטָן (קְטַנָּה)	ka**tan** (kta**na**)
square	מְרוּבָּע (מְרוּבַּעַת)	meru**ba** (meru**baat**)
sturdy	חָזָק (חֲזָקָה)	ḥa**zak** (ḥaza**ka**)
I don't want anything too expensive.	אֲנִי לֹא רוֹצֶה (רוֹצָה) מַשֶּׁהוּ יוֹתֵר מִדַּי יָקָר.	a**ni** lo rot**ze** (rot**za**) **ma**shehu yo**ter** mi**day** ya**kar**

Preference הַעֲדָפָה

Can you show me some others?	תּוּכַל (תּוּכְלִי) לְהַרְאוֹת לִי עוֹד כַּמָּה?	tu**khal** (tukh**li**) leha**rot** li od **ka**ma
Don't you have anything ...?	אֵין לָכֶם מַשֶּׁהוּ ...?	eyn la**khem** **ma**shehu
cheaper/better	יוֹתֵר זוֹל (זוֹלָה)/יוֹתֵר טוֹב (טוֹבָה)	yo**ter** zol (zo**la**)/yo**ter** tov (to**va**)
larger/smaller	יוֹתֵר גָּדוֹל (גְּדוֹלָה)/יוֹתֵר קָטָן (קְטַנָּה)	yo**ter** ga**dol** (gdo**la**)/yo**ter** ka**tan** (kta**na**)
How much	כַּמָּה	**ka**ma
How much is this?	כַּמָּה זֶה?	**ka**ma ze
How much are they?	כַּמָּה הֵם?	**ka**ma hem
I don't understand.	אֵינֶנִּי מֵבִין (מְבִינָה).	ey**ne**ni me**vin** (mevi**na**)
Please write it down.	כְּתֹב (כִּתְבִי) אֶת זֶה בִּשְׁבִילִי, בְּבַקָּשָׁה.	ktov et ze bishvi**li** bevaka**sha**
I don't want to spend more than ... shekels.	אֵינֶנִּי רוֹצֶה (רוֹצָה) לְהוֹצִיא יוֹתֵר מֵאֲשֶׁר ... שְׁקָלִים.	ey**ne**ni rot**ze** (rot**za**) leho**tzi** yo**ter** mea**sher** ... shka**lim**

Decision הַחְלָטָה

It's not quite what I want.	זֶה לֹא בְּדִיּוּק מַה שֶּׁאֲנִי רוֹצֶה (רוֹצָה).	ze lo bedi**yuk** ma shea**ni** ro**tze** (ro**tza**)
No, I don't like it.	לֹא, זֶה לֹא מוֹצֵא חֵן בְּעֵינַי.	lo ze lo mo**tze** ḥen beey**nay**
I'll take it.	בְּסֵדֶר, אֶקַּח אוֹתוֹ.	be**se**der e**kaḥ** o**to**

Ordering הַזְמָנוֹת

Can you order it for me?	תּוּכַל (תּוּכְלִי) לְהַזְמִין אֶת זֶה בִּשְׁבִילִי?	tu**khal** (tukh**li**) lehaz**min** et ze bishvi**li**
How long will it take?	כַּמָּה זְמַן זֶה יִקַּח?	**ka**ma zman ze yi**kaḥ**

Delivery מִשְׁלוֹחַ

I'll take it with me.	אֶקַּח אֶת זֶה אִתִּי.	e**kaḥ** et ze i**ti**
Deliver it to the ... Hotel.	שִׁלְחוּ אֶת זֶה לְמָלוֹן ...	shil**ḥu** et ze lema**lon**
Please send it to this address.	שִׁלְחוּ אֶת זֶה לַכְּתֹבֶת הַזֹּו בְּבַקָּשָׁה.	shil**ḥu** et ze lak**to**vet ha**zo** bevaka**sha**
Will I have any difficulty with the customs?	תִּהְיֶינָה לִי בְּעָיוֹת עִם הַמֶּכֶס?	tih**ye**na li bea**yot** im ha**me**khes

Paying תַּשְׁלוּם

How much is it?	כַּמָּה זֶה?	**ka**ma ze
Can I pay by traveller's cheque?	אֶפְשָׁר לְשַׁלֵּם בְּהַמְחָאוֹת נוֹסְעִים?	ef**shar** lesha**lem** behamḥa**ot** no**sim**
Do you accept dollars/pounds?	אַתֶּם מְקַבְּלִים דּוֹלָרִים/לִירוֹת שְׁטֶרְלִינְג?	a**tem** mekab**lim** do**la**rim/ **li**rot **ster**ling
Do you accept credit cards?	אַתֶּם מְקַבְּלִים כַּרְטִיסֵי אַשְׁרַאי?	a**tem** mekabvlim karti**sey** ash**ray**
Do I have to pay the VAT (sales tax)?	אֲנִי צָרִיךְ (צְרִיכָה) לְשַׁלֵּם מַעַ"מ?	**ani** tza**rikh** (tzri**kha**) lesha**lem** ma**am**
I think there's a mistake in the bill.	אֲנִי חוֹשֵׁב (חוֹשֶׁבֶת) שֶׁיֵּשׁ טָעוּת בַּחֶשְׁבּוֹן.	she**yesh** ta**ut** baḥesh**bon** a**ni** ḥo**shev** (ḥo**she**vet)

Anything else? עוֹד מַשֶׁהוּ?

No, thanks, that's all.	לֹא תּוֹדָה, זֶה הַכֹּל.	lo to**da** ze ha**kol**
Yes, I'd like …	כֵּן אֲבַקֵּשׁ …	ken ava**kesh**
Can you show me …?	תּוּכַל (תּוּכְלִי) לְהַרְאוֹת לִי …?	tu**khal** (tukh**li**) leha**rot** li
May I have a bag, please?	אוּכַל לְקַבֵּל שַׂקִּית בְּבַקָּשָׁה?	u**khal** leka**bel** sa**kit** bevaka**sha**
Could you wrap it up for me, please?	תּוּכַל (תּוּכְלִי) לַעֲטוֹף אֶת זֶה בִּשְׁבִילִי, בְּבַקָּשָׁה?	tu**khal** (tukh**li**) laa**tof** et ze bishvi**li** bevaka**sha**
May I have a receipt?	תּוּכַל (תּוּכְלִי) לָתֵת לִי קַבָּלָה?	tu**khal** (tukh**li**) la**tet** li kaba**la**

Dissatisfied? תְּלוּנוֹת?

Can you exchange this, please?	תּוּכַל (תּוּכְלִי) לְהַחֲלִיף אֶת זֶה בְּבַקָּשָׁה?	tu**khal** (tukh**li**) lehaḥa**lif** et ze bevaka**sha**
I want to return this.	אֲנִי רוֹצֶה (רוֹצָה) לְהַחֲזִיר אֶת זֶה.	a**ni** rot**ze** (rot**za**) lehaḥa**zir** et ze
I'd like a refund. Here's the receipt.	אֲבַקֵּשׁ הֶחְזֵר. הִנֵּה הַקַּבָּלָה.	ava**kesh** heḥ**zer**. hi**ne** hakaba**la**

אוּכַל לַעֲזוֹר לְךָ (לָךְ)?	Can I help you?
מַה תִּרְצֶה (תִּרְצִי)?	What would you like?
אֵיזֶה … תִּרְצֶה (תִּרְצִי)?	What … would you like?
צֶבַע/צוּרָה/אֵיכוּת	colour/shape/quality
צַר לִי, אֵין לָנוּ כָּזֶה.	I'm sorry, we don't have any.
זֶה אָזַל.	We're out of stock.
לְהַזְמִין אֶת זֶה בִּשְׁבִילְךָ (בִּשְׁבִילֵךְ)?	Shall we order it for you?
תִּקַּח אִתְּךָ (תִּקְחִי אִתָּךְ) אוֹ שֶׁנִּשְׁלַח אֶת זֶה?	Will you take it with you or shall we send it?
עוֹד מַשֶּׁהוּ?	Anything else?
… שְׁקָלִים בְּבַקָּשָׁה.	That's … shekels, please.
הַקֻּפָּה שָׁם.	The cash desk is over there.

Bookshop—Stationer's חֲנוּת סְפָרִים—חֲנוּת לְמַכְשִׁירֵי כְּתִיבָה

In Israel, bookshops and stationers may be combined or separate. Newspapers and magazines may be sold in bookshops, newsagents, in kiosks or at the stationer's, but you're more likely to find foreign newspapers at newsagents rather than kiosks. The English-language daily is called the *Jerusalem Post*.

Where's the nearest ...?	אֵיפֹה הַ... הַקָּרוֹב (הַקְּרוֹבָה)?	**ey**fo ha... haka**rov** (hakro**va**)
bookshop	חֲנוּת סְפָרִים	ḥa**nut** sfa**rim**
stationer's	חֲנוּת לְמַכְשִׁירֵי כְּתִיבָה	ḥa**nut** lemakhshi**rey** kti**va**
newsstand	דּוּכַן עִתּוֹנִים	du**khan** ito**nim**
Where can I buy an English-language newspaper?	אֵיפֹה אוּכַל לִקְנוֹת עִתּוֹן בְּאַנְגְּלִית?	**ey**fo u**khal** lik**not** i**ton** beang**lit**
Where's the guide-book section?	אֵיפֹה מַדְרִיכֵי הַטִּיּוּלִים?	**ey**fo madri**khey** hatiyu**lim**
Where do you keep the English books?	אֵיפֹה יֵשׁ לָכֶם סְפָרִים בְּאַנְגְּלִית?	**ey**fo yesh la**khem** sfa**rim** beang**lit**
Have you any of ...'s books in English?	יֵשׁ לָכֶם סְפָרִים שֶׁל ... בְּאַנְגְּלִית?	yesh la**khem** sfa**rim** shel ... beang**lit**
Do you have second-hand books?	יֵשׁ לָכֶם סְפָרִים מְשׁוּמָּשִׁים?	yesh la**khem** sfa**rim** meshuma**shim**
I want to buy a/an/some ...	אֲנִי רוֹצֶה (רוֹצָה) לִקְנוֹת ...	a**ni** rot**ze** (rot**za**) lik**not**
address book	פִּנְקַס כְּתוֹבוֹת	pin**kas** kto**vot**
adhesive tape	נְיָר דֶּבֶק	ne**yar** **de**vek
ball-point pen	עֵט כַּדּוּרִי	et kadu**ri**
book	סֵפֶר	**se**fer
calendar	לוּחַ שָׁנָה	**lu**aḥ sha**na**
carbon paper	נְיָר פֶּחָם	ne**yar** pe**ḥam**
crayons	עֶפְרוֹנוֹת צִבְעוֹנִיִּים	efro**not** tzi**yur**
dictionary	מִלּוֹן	mi**lon**
Hebrew-English	עִבְרִי–אַנְגְּלִי	iv**ri**-ang**li**
pocket	... כִּיס	kis
drawing paper	נְיָר צִיּוּר	ne**yar** tzi**yur**
drawing pins	נְעָצִים	nea**tzim**
envelopes	מַעֲטָפוֹת	maata**fot**
eraser	מַחַק	ma**ḥak**

exercise book	מַחְבֶּרֶת	maḥ**be**ret
felt-tip pen	עֵט לוֹרְד	et lord
fountain pen	עֵט נוֹבֵעַ	et novea
glue	דֶּבֶק	**de**vek
grammar book	סֵפֶר דִּקְדּוּק	**se**fer dik**duk**
guidebook	מַדְרִיךְ טִיּוּלִים	mad**rikh** tiyu**lim**
ink	דְּיוֹ	dyo
black/red/blue	שָׁחוֹר/אָדוֹם/כָּחוֹל	sha**ḥor**/a**dom**/ka**ḥol**
(adhesive) labels	תָּוִיוֹת (מִדְבָּקוֹת)	tavi**yot** (midba**kot**)
magazine	מָגָזִין	maga**zin**
map	מַפָּה	ma**pa**
street map	מַפַּת רְחוֹבוֹת	ma**pat** reḥo**vot**
road map of ...	מַפַּת דְּרָכִים שֶׁל ...	ma**pat** dra**khim** shel
mechanical pencil	עִפָּרוֹן מֵכָנִי	ipa**ron** me**kha**ni
newspaper	עִתּוֹן	i**ton**
American/English	אָמֵרִיקָאִי/אַנְגְּלִי	ameri**kai**/angli
notebook	פִּנְקָס	pin**kas**
note paper	נְיָר כְּתִיבָה	ne**yar** kti**va**
paintbox	קֻפְסַת צְבָעִים	kuf**sat** tzva**im**
paper	נְיָר	ne**yar**
paperback	סֵפֶר כִּיס	**se**fer kis
paperclips	מְהַדְּקִים	mehad**kim**
paper napkins	מַפִּיּוֹת נְיָר	mapi**yot** ne**yar**
paste	דֶּבֶק	**de**vek
pen	עֵט	et
pencil	עִפָּרוֹן	ipa**ron**
pencil sharpener	מְחַדֵּד	meḥa**ded**
playing cards	קְלָפִים	kla**fim**
pocket calculator	מַחְשֵׁב כִּיס	maḥ**shev** kis
postcard	גְּלוּיָה	glu**ya**
propelling pencil	עִפָּרוֹן מֵכָנִי	ipa**ron** me**kha**ni
refill (for a pen)	מִלּוּי (לָעֵט)	mi**luy** (le**et**)
rubber	מַחַק	**ma**ḥak
ruler	סַרְגֵּל	sar**gel**
staples	סִכּוֹת לְשַׁדְכָן	si**kot** leshad**khan**
string	חוּט מְשִׁיחָה	ḥut meshi**ḥa**
thumbtacks	נְעָצִים	nea**tzim**
travel guide	מַדְרִיךְ טִיּוּלִים	mad**rikh** tiyu**lim**
typewriter ribbon	סֶרֶט לִמְכוֹנַת כְּתִיבָה	**se**ret limkho**nat** kti**va**
typing paper	נְיָר לִמְכוֹנַת כְּתִיבָה	ne**yar** limkho**nat** kti**va**
writing pad	בְּלוֹק לִכְתִיבָה	blok likhti**va**

Camping and sports equipment צִיּוּד מַחֲנָאוּת וּסְפּוֹרְט

I'd like a/an/some ...	אֲבַקֵּשׁ ...	ava**kesh**
I'd like to hire a(n)/ some ...	בִּרְצוֹנִי לִשְׂכּוֹר ...	birtzo**ni** lis**kor**
air bed (mattress)	מִזְרוֹן אֲוִיר	miz**ron** a**vir**
backpack	תַּרְמִיל גַּב	tar**mil** gav
butane gas	גַּז בִּשּׁוּל	gaz bi**shul**
campbed	מִטַּת שָׂדֶה	mi**tat sade**
(folding) chair	כִּסֵּא (מִתְקַפֵּל)	**kise** (mitka**pel**)
charcoal	פֶּחָמִים	peḥa**mim**
compass	מַצְפֵּן	matz**pen**
cool box	אַרְגַּז קַלְקָר	ar**gaz kal**kar
deck chair	כִּסֵּא נוֹחַ	**kise noaḥ**
fire lighters	מַצָּתִים	matza**tim**
fishing tackle	צִיּוּד דַּיִג	tzi**yud da**yig
flashlight	פַּנַּס יָד	pa**nas** yad
groundsheet	יְרִיעַת בִּדּוּד	yeri**at** bi**dud**
hammock	עַרְסָל	ar**sal**
ice pack	רְטִיַּת קֶרַח	reti**yat ke**raḥ
insect spray (killer)	תַּכְשִׁיר דּוֹחֶה חֲרָקִים	takh**shir** do**ḥe** ḥara**kim**
kerosene	נֵפְט	neft
lamp	מְנוֹרָה	meno**ra**
lantern	פַּנָּס	pa**nas**
mallet	פַּטִּישׁ	pa**tish**
matches	גַּפְרוּרִים	gafru**rim**
(foam rubber) mattress	מִזְרוֹן (גּוּמָאֲוִיר)	miz**ron** (guma**vir**)
mosquito net	כִּלָּה	ki**la**
paraffin	נֵפְט	neft
picnic basket	אַרְגַּז לְפִּיקְנִיק	ar**gaz** le**pik**nik
pump	מַשְׁאֵבָה	mashe**va**
rope	חֶבֶל	**ḥe**vel
rucksack	תַּרְמִיל גַּב	tar**mil** gav
screwdriver	מַבְרֵג	mav**reg**
skiing equipment	צִיּוּד סְקִי	tzi**yud** ski
skin-diving equipment	צִיּוּד צְלִילָה	tzi**yud** tzli**la**
sleeping bag	שַׂק שֵׁינָה	sak she**na**
(folding) table	שֻׁלְחָן (מִתְקַפֵּל)	shul**ḥan** (mitka**pel**)
tent	אֹהֶל	**o**hel
tent pegs	יְתֵדוֹת	yete**dot**
tent pole	מוֹט לְאֹהֶל	mot le**o**hel
torch	פַּנַּס יָד	pa**nas** yad
windsurfer	גַּלְשַׁן רוּחַ	gal**shan ruaḥ**
water flask	מֵימִיָּה	meymi**ya**

CAMPING, see page 32

Chemist's (drugstore) בֵּית מִרְקַחַת

Israeli chemists normally don't stock the great range of goods that you'll find in England or the U.S. In the window you'll see a notice telling you where the nearest all-night chemist is. Note that drugstores sell toiletries and not medication.

For ease of reference, this section is divided into two parts:

1. Pharmaceutical—medicine, first-aid, etc.
2. Toiletry—toilet articles, cosmetics.

General כְּלָלִי

Where's the nearest (all-night) chemist's?	אֵיפֹה בֵּית הַמִּרְקַחַת הַקָּרוֹב (הַפָּתוּחַ בַּלַּיְלָה)?	**ey**fo beyt hamir**ka**ḥat haka**rov** (hapa**tuaḥ** ba**lay**la)
What time does the chemist's open/close?	מָתַי בֵּית הַמִּרְקַחַת נִפְתָּח/נִסְגָּר?	ma**tay** beyt hamir**ka**ḥat nif**taḥ**/nis**gar**

1—Pharmaceutical תְּרוּפוֹת

I'd like something for ...	אֲבַקֵּשׁ מַשֶּׁהוּ לְ...	ava**kesh ma**shehu le
a cold/a cough	הִצְטַנְּנוּת/שִׁעוּל	hitztane**nut**/**shiul**
hay fever	קַדַּחַת הַשַּׁחַת	ka**da**ḥat ha**sha**ḥat
insect bites	עֲקִיצוֹת חֲרָקִים	aki**tzot** ḥara**kim**
sunburn	כְּוִיּוֹת שֶׁמֶשׁ	kvi**yot she**mesh
travel/altitude sickness	מַחֲלַת נְסִיעָה/גְּבָהִים	maḥa**lat** nesia/gva**him**
an upset stomach	קִלְקוּל קֵיבָה	kilvkul ke**va**
Can you prepare this prescription for me?	תוּכְלוּ לְהָכִין לִי אֶת הַמִּרְשָׁם הַזֶּה?	tukh**lu** leha**khin** li et hamir**sham** ha**ze**
Can I get it without a prescription?	אֶפְשָׁר לְקַבֵּל אֶת זֶה בְּלִי מִרְשָׁם?	ef**shar** leka**bel** et ze bli mir**sham**
Shall I wait?	לְחַכּוֹת?	leḥa**kot**
Can I have a/an/some ...?	אֲבַקֵּשׁ ...	ava**kesh**
adhesive plaster	פְּלַסְטֶר	**plas**ter
analgesic	תְּרוּפָה נֶגֶד כְּאֵבִים	tru**fa ne**ged kee**vim**
antiseptic cream	מִשְׁחָה אַנְטִיסֶפְּטִית	mish**ḥa** anti**sep**tit

aspirin	אַסְפִּירִין	aspi**rin**
bandage	תַּחְבֹּשֶׁת	taḥ**bo**shet
elastic bandage	תַּחְבֹּשֶׁת אֶלַסְטִית	taḥboshet elastit
Band-Aids	פְּלַסְטֶר	**plas**ter
condoms	אֶמְצָעֵי מְנִיעָה	emtza**ey** menia
contraceptives	אֶמְצָעֵי מְנִיעָה	emtza**ey** menia
corn plasters	פְּלַסְטֶרִים לְיַבָּלוֹת	**plas**terim leyaba**lot**
cotton wool (absorbent cotton)	צֶמֶר גֶּפֶן	**tze**mer **ge**fen
cough drops	טַבְלִיּוֹת נֶגֶד שִׁעוּל	tavli**yot ne**ged shi**ul**
disinfectant	חֹמֶר חִטּוּי	**ḥo**mer hi**tuy**
ear drops	טִפּוֹת אָזְנַיִם	ti**pot** oz**na**yim
eye drops	טִפּוֹת עֵינַיִם	ti**pot** ey**na**yim
first-aid kit	עֶרְכַּת עֶזְרָה רִאשׁוֹנָה	er**kat** ez**ra** risho**na**
gauze	גָּזָה	**ga**za
insect repellent/spray	תַּכְשִׁיר דּוֹחֶה חֲרָקִים	takh**shir** do**ḥe** ḥara**kim**
iodine	יוֹד	yod
laxative	חֹמֶר מְשַׁלְשֵׁל	**ḥo**mer meshal**shel**
mouthwash	תַּשְׁטִיף פֶּה	tash**tif** pe
nose drops	טִפּוֹת אַף	ti**pot** af
sanitary towels (napkins)	תַּחְבּוֹשׁוֹת הִגְיֵנִיּוֹת	taḥbo**shot** higi**ye**niyot
sleeping pills	גְּלוּלוֹת שֵׁינָה	glu**lot** she**na**
suppositories	נֵרוֹת	ne**rot**
... tablets	טַבְלִיּוֹת ...	tavli**yot**
tampons	טָמְפּוֹנִים	tam**po**nim
thermometer	מַדְחוֹם	mad**ḥom**
throat lozenges	טַבְלִיּוֹת לִכְאֵב גָּרוֹן	tavli**yot** likh**ev** ga**ron**
tranquillizers	גְּלוּלוֹת הַרְגָּעָה	glu**lot** harga**a**
vitamin pills	גְּלוּלוֹת וִיטָמִינִים	glu**lot** vita**mi**nim

רַעַל	POISON
לְשִׁמּוּשׁ חִצוֹנִי בִּלְבָד	FOR EXTERNAL USE ONLY

2—Toiletry תַּמְרוּקִים

I'd like a/an/some ...	אֲבַקֵּשׁ ...	ava**kesh**
after-shave lotion	מֵי גִּלּוּחַ	mey gi**luaḥ**
astringent	עוֹצֵר דִּמּוּם	o**tzer** di**mum**
bath salts	מִלְחֵי אַמְבַּטְיָה	mil**ḥey** am**bat**ya
blusher (rouge)	אֹדֶם	**o**dem
bubble bath	סַבּוֹן מַקְצִיף	sa**bon** mak**tzif**

cream	קְרֶם	krem
cleansing cream	קְרֶם נִקּוּי	krem ni**kuy**
foundation cream	קְרֶם בָּסִיס	krem ba**sis**
moisturizing cream	קְרֶם לַחוּת	krem la**ḥut**
night cream	קְרֶם לַיְלָה	krem **lay**la
cuticle remover	מִסְפְּרֵי צִפָּרְנַיִם	misper**ey** tzipor**na**yim
deodorant	דֵאוֹדוֹרַנְט	deodo**rant**
emery board	נְיַר לֶטֶשׁ	ne**yar le**tesh
eyebrow pencil	עִפָּרוֹן לְגַבּוֹת	ipa**ron** lega**bot**
eyeliner	עִפָּרוֹן לְעַפְעַפַּיִם	ipa**ron** leafa**pim**
eye shadow	צֶבַע לְעַפְעַפַּיִם	**tze**va leafa**pim**
face powder	פּוּדְרָה לְפָנִים	**pud**ra lepa**nim**
foot cream	מִשְׁחָה לְרַגְלַיִם	mish**ḥa** lerag**la**yim
hand cream	מִשְׁחָה לְיָדַיִם	mish**ḥa** leya**da**yim
lipsalve	מִשְׁחָה לִשְׂפָתַיִם	mish**ḥa** lisfa**ta**yim
lipstick	שִׂפְתּוֹן	sif**ton**
make-up remover pads	סְפוֹגִיּוֹת לְהוֹרָדַת אִפּוּר	sfogi**yot** lehora**dat ipur**
mascara	מַסְקָרָה	mas**ka**ra
nail brush	מִבְרֶשֶׁת לְצִפָּרְנַיִם	miv**re**shet letzipor**na**yim
nail clippers	גּוֹזֵז צִפָּרְנַיִם	go**zez** tzipor**na**yim
nail file	פְּצִירָה לְצִפָּרְנַיִם	ptzi**ra** letzipor**na**yim
nail polish	לַכָּה לְצִפָּרְנַיִם	**la**ka letzipor**na**yim
nail polish remover	תַּכְשִׁיר לְהוֹרָדַת לַכָּה	takh**shir** lehora**dat la**ka
nail scissors	מִסְפָּרַיִם לְצִפָּרְנַיִם	mispa**ra**yim letzipor**na**yim
perfume	בֹּשֶׂם	**bo**sem
powder	פּוּדְרָה	**pud**ra
powder puff	פּוּדְרִיָּה	pudri**ya**
razor	תַּעַר	**ta**ar
razor blades	סַכִּינֵי גִּלּוּחַ	saki**ney** gilu**aḥ**
rouge	אֹדֶם	**o**dem
safety pins	סִכּוֹת בִּטָּחוֹן	si**kot** bita**ḥon**
shaving brush	מִבְרֶשֶׁת גִּלּוּחַ	miv**re**shet gilu**aḥ**
shaving cream	מִשְׁחַת גִּלּוּחַ	mish**ḥat** gilu**aḥ**
soap	סַבּוֹן	sa**bon**
sponge	סְפוֹג	sfog
sun-tan cream	מִשְׁחַת שִׁזּוּף	mish**ḥat** shi**zuf**
sun-tan oil	שֶׁמֶן שִׁזּוּף	**she**men shi**zuf**
talcum powder	טַלְק	talk
tissues	מִטְפְּחוֹת נְיָר	mitpe**ḥot** ne**yar**
toilet paper	נְיַר טוֹאָלֶט	ne**yar** toa**let**
toilet water	מֵי פָּנִים	mey pa**nim**
toothbrush	מִבְרֶשֶׁת שִׁנַּיִם	miv**re**shet shi**na**yim
toothpaste	מִשְׁחַת שִׁנַּיִם	mish**ḥat** shi**na**yim
towel	מַגֶּבֶת	ma**ge**vet
tweezers	מֶלְקָחִית	melka**ḥit**

For your hair לִשְׂעָרֵךְ

bobby pins	סִכּוֹת רֹאשׁ	si**kot** rosh
colour shampoo	שַׁמְפּוּ צוֹבֵעַ	sham**pu** tzo**vea**
comb	מַסְרֵק	mas**rek**
curlers	גַּלְגַּלִּים	galga**lim**
dry shampoo	שַׁמְפּוּ יָבֵשׁ	sham**pu** ya**vesh**
dye	צֶבַע	**tze**va
hairbrush	מִבְרֶשֶׁת שֵׂעָר	miv**re**shet se**ar**
hair gel	גֶ'ל שֵׂעָר	jel se**ar**
hairgrips	מִצְבָּטִים לְשֵׂעָר	mitzba**tim** lese**ar**
hair lotion	קְרֶם לְשֵׂעָר	krem lese**ar**
hairpins	סִכּוֹת רֹאשׁ	si**kot** rosh
hair slide	סִכַּת שֵׂעָר	si**kat** se**ar**
hair spray	תַּרְסִיס לְשֵׂעָר	tar**sis** lese**ar**
setting lotion	מְיַצֵּב	meya**tzev**
shampoo	שַׁמְפּוּ	sham**pu**
for dry/greasy (oily) hair	לְשֵׂעָר יָבֵשׁ/שָׁמֵן	lese**ar** ya**vesh**/sha**men**
tint	צֶבַע	**tze**va
wig	פֵּאָה נָכְרִית	pe**a** nokh**rit**

For the baby לְתִינוֹק

baby food	מָזוֹן לְתִינוֹק	ma**zon** leti**nok**
dummy (pacifier)	מוֹצֵץ	mo**tzetz**
feeding bottle	בַּקְבּוּק לְתִינוֹק	bak**buk** leti**nok**
nappies (diapers)	חִתּוּלִים	ḥitu**lim**

Clothing בְּגָדִים

If you want to buy something specific, prepare yourself in advance. Look at the list of clothing on page 115. Get some idea of the colour, material and size you want. They're all listed on the next few pages.

General כְּלָלִי

I'd like ...	... אֲבַקֵּשׁ	avakesh
I'd like ... for a 10-year-old boy/girl.	אֲבַקֵּשׁ ... לְיֶלֶד/לְיַלְדָּה בֶּן (בַּת) עֶשֶׂר.	avakesh ... leyeled/leyalda ben (bat) eser
I'd like something like this.	אֲנִי רוֹצֶה (רוֹצָה) מַשֶּׁהוּ כָּזֶה.	ani rotze (rotza) mashehu kaze
I like the one in the window.	זֶה שֶׁבַּחַלּוֹן מוֹצֵא חֵן בְּעֵינַי.	ze shebahalon motze ḥen beeynay
How much is that per metre?	כַּמָּה זֶה לְמֶטֶר?	kama ze lemeter

1 centimetre (cm) = 0.39 in.	1 inch = 2.54 cm
1 metre (m) = 39.37 in.	1 foot = 30.5 cm
10 metres = 32.81 ft.	1 yard = 0.91 m.

Colour צֶבַע

I'd like something in ...	...אֲבַקֵּשׁ מַשֶּׁהוּ בְּ	avakesh mashehu be
I'd like a darker/lighter shade.	אֲנִי רוֹצֶה (רוֹצָה) גָּוֶן יוֹתֵר כֵּהֶה/בָּהִיר.	ani rotze (rotza) gavan yoter kehe/bahir
I'd like something to match this.	אֲבַקֵּשׁ מַשֶּׁהוּ דּוֹמֶה לְזֶה.	avakesh mashehu dome leze
I don't like the colour.	הַצֶּבַע אֵינוֹ מוֹצֵא חֵן בְּעֵינַי.	hatzeva eyno motze ḥen beeynay

beige	בֶּז'	bej
black	שָׁחוֹר	sha**ḥor**
blue	כָּחוֹל	ka**ḥol**
brown	חוּם	ḥum
fawn	חוּם–צְהַבְהַב	ḥum-tzehav**hav**
golden	זָהֹב	za**hov**
green	יָרוֹק	ya**rok**
grey	אָפוֹר	a**for**
mauve	סָגוֹל־אַרְגָּמָן	sa**gol**-arga**man**
orange	כָּתוֹם	ka**tom**
pink	וָרוֹד	va**rod**
purple	אַרְגָּמָן	arga**man**
red	אָדוֹם	a**dom**
scarlet	שָׁנִי	sha**ni**
silver	כֶּסֶף	**ke**sef
turquoise	טוּרְקִיז	tur**kiz**
white	לָבָן	la**van**
yellow	צָהוֹב	tza**hov**
light ...	... בָּהִיר	ba**hir**
dark ...	... כֵּהֶה	ke**he**

אָחִיד (a**ḥid**) — פַּסִּים (pa**sim**) — נְקוּדוֹת (neku**dot**) — מִשְׁבָּצוֹת (mishba**tzot**) — דּוּגְמָה (dug**ma**)

Fabric בַּד

Do you have anything in ...?	יֵשׁ לָכֶם מַשֶּׁהוּ בְּ...?	yesh la**khem ma**shehu be
Is that ...?	זֶה ...?	ze
handmade	עֲבוֹדַת יָד	avo**dat** yad
imported	מְיוּבָּא	meyu**va**
made here	תּוֹצֶרֶת הָאָרֶץ	to**tze**ret haa**retz**
I'd like something thinner.	אֲבַקֵּשׁ מַשֶּׁהוּ דַּק יוֹתֵר.	ava**kesh ma**shehu dak **yo**ter
Do you have anything of better quality?	יֵשׁ מַשֶּׁהוּ בְּאֵיכוּת יוֹתֵר טוֹבָה?	yesh **ma**shehu bee**khut** yoter **tova**
What's it made of?	מִמָּה זֶה עָשׂוּי?	mi**ma** ze a**suy**

cambric	בָּטִיסְט	ba**tist**
camel-hair	צֶמֶר גָּמָל	**tze**mer ga**mal**
chiffon	שִׁיפוֹן	shi**fon**
corduroy	קוֹרְדֶרוֹי	**kor**deroy
cotton	כּוּתְנָה	kut**na**
crepe	קְרֶפּ	krep
denim	דֶּנִים	**de**nim
felt	לֶבֶד	**le**ved
flannel	פְלָנֶל	fla**nel**
gabardine	גַּבַּרְדִּין	gabar**din**
lace	תַּחֲרָה	taḥa**ra**
leather	עוֹר	or
linen	פִּשְׁתָּן	pish**tan**
poplin	כּוּתְנַת פּוֹפְּלִין	kut**nat poplin**
satin	סָטִין	sa**tin**
silk	מֶשִׁי	**me**shi
suede	זַמְשׁ	zamsh
towelling	בַּד מַגֶּבֶת	bad ma**ge**vet
velvet	קְטִיפָה	kti**fa**
velveteen	חִקּוּי קְטִיפָה	ḥi**kuy** kti**fa**
wool	צֶמֶר	**tze**mer
worsted	צֶמֶר סָרוּק	**tze**mer sa**ruk**

Is it ...?	הַאִם זֶה ...?	ha**im** ze
pure cotton/wool	כּוּתְנָה נְקִיָּה/צֶמֶר נָקִי	kut**na** neki**ya**/**tze**mer na**ki**
synthetic	סִנְתֶטִי	sin**te**ti
colourfast	צֶבַע עָמִיד	**tze**va a**mid**
crease (wrinkle) resistant	בִּלְתִּי מִתְקַמֶּט	**bil**ti mitka**met**
Is it hand washable/ machine washable?	זֶה כָּבִיס בַּיָּד/כָּבִיס בִּמְכוֹנָה?	ze ka**vis** ba**yad**/ka**vis** bimkho**na**
Will it shrink?	זֶה יִתְכַּוֵּץ?	ze yitka**vetz**

Size מִדָּה

I take size 38.	אֲנִי מִדָּה שְׁלֹשִׁים וּשְׁמוֹנֶה.	a**ni** mi**da** shlo**shim** ush**mo**ne
Could you measure me?	תּוּכַל (תּוּכְלִי) לִמְדּוֹד אוֹתִי?	tu**khal** (tukh**li**) lim**dod** o**ti**
I don't know the Israeli sizes.	אֵינֶנִּי מַכִּיר (מַכִּירָה) אֶת הַמִּדּוֹת בְּיִשְׂרָאֵל.	ey**ne**ni ma**kir** (maki**ra**) et hami**dot** beyisra**el**

Women נָשִׁים

Dresses/Suits						
American	8	10	12	14	16	18
British	10	12	14	16	18	20
Israeli	36	38	40	42	44	46

Stockings						
American	8½	9	9½	10	10½	
British						
Israeli	0	1	2	3	4	5

Shoes				
American	6	7	8	9
British	4½	5½	6½	7½
Israeli	37	38	40	41

Men גְּבָרִים

Suits/overcoats						
American / British	36	38	40	42	44	46
Israeli	46	48	50	52	54	56

Shirts				
American / British	15	16	17	18
Israeli	38	40	42	44

Shoes									
American / British	5	6	7	8	8½	9	9½	10	11
Israeli	38	39	40	41	42	43	44	44	45

small (S) קָטָן ka**tan**
medium (M) בֵּינוֹנִי beyno**ni**
large (L) גָּדוֹל ga**dol**
extra large (XL) גֹּדֶל אֶקְסְטְרָא **go**del **eks**tra
larger/smaller יוֹתֵר גָּדוֹל/יוֹתֵר קָטָן yo**ter** ga**dol**/yo**ter** ka**tan**

A good fit? זֶה מַתְאִים?

Can I try it on? אֶפְשָׁר לִמְדּוֹד אֶת זֶה? ef**shar** lim**dod** et ze
Where's the fitting room? אֵיפֹה חֲדַר הַהַלְבָּשָׁה? **ey**fo ḥa**dar** hahalba**sha**
Is there a mirror? יֵשׁ רְאִי? yesh rei
It fits very well. זֶה מַתְאִים לִי מְאֹד. ze ma**tim** li me**od**
It doesn't fit. זֶה לֹא מַתְאִים לִי. ze lo ma**tim** li
It's too ... זֶה יוֹתֵר מִדַּי ... ze yo**ter** mi**day**
short/long קָצָר/אָרוֹךְ ka**tzar**/a**rokh**
tight/loose הָדוּק/חָפְשִׁי ha**duk**/ḥof**shi**
How long will it take to alter? כַּמָּה זְמַן יִקַּח לְשַׁנּוֹת אֶת זֶה? **ka**ma zman yi**kaḥ** lesha**not** et ze

NUMBERS, see page 147

Clothes and accessories בְּגָדִים וְאַבִיזָרִים

I would like a/an/ some ...	... אֲבַקֵּשׁ	ava**kesh**
anorak	מְעִיל רוּחַ	me**il ruaḥ**
bathing cap	כּוֹבַע יָם	**ko**va yam
bathing suit	בֶּגֶד יָם	**be**ged yam
bathrobe	חֲלוּק רַחֲצָה	ḥa**luk** raḥatza
blouse	כֻּתֹּנֶת	ku**to**net
bow tie	עֲנִיבַת פַּרְפַּר	ani**vat** par**par**
bra	חֲזִיָּה	ḥazi**ya**
braces	כְּתֵפִיּוֹת	ktefi**yot**
cap	כּוֹבַע מִצְחִיָּה	**ko**va mitzḥi**ya**
cardigan	אֲפוּדַת צֶמֶר	afu**dat tze**mer
coat	מְעִיל	me**il**
dress	שִׂמְלָה	sim**la**
with long sleeves	עִם שַׁרְוּוּלִים אֲרוּכִּים	im sharvu**lim** aru**kim**
with short sleeves	עִם שַׁרְוּוּלִים קְצָרִים	im sharvu**lim** ktza**rim**
sleeveless	בְּלִי שַׁרְוּוּלִים	bli sharvu**lim**
dressing gown	חָלוּק	ḥa**luk**
evening dress (woman's)	שִׂמְלַת עֶרֶב	sim**lat e**rev
girdle	מָחוֹךְ	ma**ḥokh**
gloves	כְּפָפוֹת	kfa**fot**
handbag	תִּיק יָד	tik yad
handkerchief	מִמְחָטָה	mimḥa**ta**
hat	כּוֹבַע	**ko**va
jacket	זָקֶט	**ja**ket
jeans	גִ׳ינְס	jins
jersey	חֻלְצַת טְרִיקוֹ	ḥul**tzat** tri**ko**
jumper (Br.)	סוּדָר	su**dar**
kneesocks	גַּרְבַּיִם אֲרוּכּוֹת	gar**ba**yim aru**kot**
nightdress	כֻּתֹּנֶת לַיְלָה	kutonet **lay**la
overalls	סַרְבָּל	sar**bal**
pair of ...	... זוּג	zug
panties	תַּחְתּוֹנִים	taḥto**nim**
pants (Am.)	מִכְנָסַיִם	mikhna**sa**yim
panty girdle	מְחוֹךְ גַּרְבּוֹנִים	me**ḥokh** garbo**nim**
panty hose	גַּרְבּוֹנִים	garbo**nim**
parka	פַּרְקָה , מְעִיל רוּחַ מְרוּפָּד	**par**ka, me**il ruaḥ** meru**pad**
pullover	סוּדָר	su**dar**
polo (turtle)-neck	פּוֹלוֹ	**po**lo
round-neck	עִם צַוָּאר עָגֹל	im tza**var** a**gol**
V-neck	עִם צַוָּארוֹן וִי	im tza**va**ron vi
with long sleeves	עִם שַׁרְוּוּלִים אֲרוּכִּים	im sharvu**lim** aru**kim**
with short sleeves	עִם שַׁרְוּוּלִים קְצָרִים	im sharvu**lim** ktza**rim**
without sleeves	בְּלִי שַׁרְוּוּלִים	bli sharvu**lim**

pyjamas	פִּיגָ'מָה	pi**ja**ma
raincoat	מְעִיל גֶּשֶׁם	me**il** **ge**shem
scarf	צָעִיף	tza**if**
shirt	חוּלְצָה	ḥul**tza**
shorts	מִכְנָסַיִם קְצָרִים	mikhna**sa**yim ktza**rim**
skirt	חֲצָאִית	ḥatza**it**
slip	שִׂמְלָה תַּחְתּוֹנִית	sim**la** taḥto**nit**
socks	גַּרְבַּיִם	gar**ba**yim
stockings	גַּרְבֵּי נָשִׁים	gar**bey** na**shim**
suit (man's)	חֲלִיפָה	ḥa**li**fa
suit (woman's)	חֲלִיפַת נָשִׁים	ḥali**fat** na**shim**
suspenders (Am.)	כְּתֵפִיּוֹת	ktefi**yot**
sweater	סוּדָר	su**dar**
sweatshirt	חוּלְצַת מֵיזָע	ḥul**tzat** mey**za**
swimming trunks	בֶּגֶד יָם	**be**ged yam
swimsuit	בֶּגֶד יָם	**be**ged yam
T-shirt	חוּלְצַת טִי	ḥul**tzat** ti
tie	עֲנִיבָה	a**ni**va
tights	גַּרְבּוֹנִים	garbo**nim**
tracksuit	אִמּוּנִית , טְרֵינִינְג	imu**nit**, **trey**ning
trousers	מִכְנָסַיִם	mikhna**sa**yim
umbrella	מִטְרִיָּה	mitri**ya**
underpants	תַּחְתּוֹנִים	taḥto**nim**
undershirt	גּוּפִיָּה	gufi**ya**
vest (Am.)	וֶסְט	vest
vest (Br.)	גּוּפִיָּה	gufi**ya**
waistcoat	וֶסְט	vest

belt	חֲגוֹרָה	ḥa**go**ra
buckle	אַבְזָם	av**zam**
button	כַּפְתּוֹר	kaf**tor**
collar	צַוָּארוֹן	tzava**ron**
pocket	כִּיס	kis
press stud (snap fastener)	לַחְצָנִית	laḥtza**nit**
zip (zipper)	רוֹכְסָן	rokh**san**

Shoes נַעֲלַיִים

I'd like a pair of ...	... אֲבַקֵשׁ זוּג	ava**kesh** zug
boots	נַעֲלַיִים גְבוֹהוֹת	naa**la**yim gvo**hot**
moccasins	מוֹקָסִינִים	moka**si**nim
plimsolls (sneakers)	נַעֲלֵי סְפּוֹרְט	naa**ley** sport
sandals	סַנְדָלִים	sanda**lim**
shoes	נַעֲלַיִים	naa**la**yim
flat	שְׁטוּחוֹת	shtu**ḥot**
with (high) heels	עִם עֲקֵבִים (גְבוֹהִים)	im ake**vim** (gvo**him**)
with leather soles	עִם סוּלְיוֹת עוֹר	im suli**yot** or
with rubber soles	עִם סוּלְיוֹת גוּמִי	im suli**yot** **gu**mi
slippers	נַעֲלֵי בַּיִת	naa**ley** **ba**yit
These are too ...	... אֵלֶה יוֹתֵר מִדַי	**e**le yo**ter** mi**day**
narrow/wide	צָרוֹת/רְחָבוֹת	tza**rot**/reḥa**vot**
big/small	גְדוֹלוֹת/קְטַנוֹת	gdo**lot**/kta**not**
Do you have a larger/ smaller size?	יֵשׁ לָכֶם מִדָה יוֹתֵר גְדוֹלָה/קְטַנָה?	yesh la**khem** mi**da** yo**ter** gdo**la**/kta**na**
Do you have the same in black?	יֵשׁ לָכֶם כָּזֶה בְּשָׁחוֹר?	yesh la**khem** ka**ze** besha**hoior**
cloth	בַּד	bad
leather	עוֹר	or
rubber	גוּמִי	**gu**mi
suede	זַמְשׁ	zamsh
Is it real leather?	זֶה עוֹר אֲמִיתִי?	ze or ami**ti**
I need some shoe polish/shoelaces.	אֲנִי זָקוּק (זְקוּקָה) לְמִשְׁחַת נַעֲלַיִים/לִשְׂרוֹכִים.	a**ni** za**kuk** (zeku**ka**) lemish**ḥat** naa**la**yim/ lisro**khim**

Shoes worn out? Here's the key to getting them fixed again:

Can you repair these shoes?	תּוּכְלוּ לְתַקֵן אֶת הַנַעֲלַיִים הָאֵלֶה?	tukh**lu** leta**ken** et hanaa**la**yim ha**e**le
Can you stitch this?	תּוּכְלוּ לִתְפּוֹר אֶת זֶה?	tukh**lu** lit**por** et ze
I want new soles and heels.	אֲנִי רוֹצֶה (רוֹצָה) סוּלְיוֹת וַעֲקֵבִים חֲדָשִׁים.	a**ni** ro**tze** (rot**za**) suli**yot** veake**vim** ḥada**shim**
When will they be ready?	מָתַי הֵם יִהְיוּ מוּכָנִים?	ma**tay** hem yihi**yu** mukha**nim**

COLOURS, see page 113

Electrical appliances מִכְשִׁירֵי חַשְׁמַל

The voltage in Israel is 220 volts AC—50 cycles. An adaptor plug will be necessary.

What's the voltage?	מָה הַמֶּתַח?	ma ha**me**taḥ
Do you have a battery for this?	אֶפְשָׁר לְקַבֵּל סוֹלְלָה?	ef**shar** leka**bel** sole**la**
This is broken. Can you repair it?	זֶה שָׁבוּר. תּוּכְלוּ לְתַקֵּן אוֹתוֹ?	ze sha**vur**. tukh**lu** leta**ken** o**to**
Can you show me how it works?	תּוּכַל (תּוּכְלִי) לְהַרְאוֹת לִי אֵיךְ זֶה פּוֹעֵל?	tu**khal** (tukh**li**) leha**rot** li eykh ze po**el**
I'd like (to hire) a video cassette.	אֲבַקֵּשׁ (לִשְׂכּוֹר) קַסֶּטַת וִידֵאוֹ.	ava**kesh** (lis**kor**) ka**se**tat **vi**deo
I'd like a/an/some ...	אֲבַקֵּשׁ ...	ava**kesh**
adaptor	מַתְאֵם	ma**tem**
amplifier	מַגְבֵּר	mag**ber**
bulb	נוּרָה	nu**ra**
CD player	פָּטֵפוֹן לְתַקְלִיטוֹנֵי סִידִי (אוֹפְּטִיִּים)	**pa**tefon letaklito**ney** si di (**op**tiyim)
clock-radio	שְׁעוֹן־רַדְיוֹ	sha**on**-**rad**yo
electric toothbrush	מִבְרֶשֶׁת שִׁנַּיִם חַשְׁמַלִּית	miv**re**shet shi**na**yim ḥashma**lit**
extension lead (cord)	כֶּבֶל הַאֲרָכָה	**ke**vel haara**kha**
hair dryer	מְיַבֵּשׁ שֵׂעָר	meya**besh** se**ar**
headphones	אָזְנִיּוֹת	ozni**yot**
(travelling) iron	מַגְהֵץ (לִנְסִיעוֹת)	mag**hetz** (linsi**ot**)
lamp	מְנוֹרָה	meno**ra**
plug	תֶּקַע	**te**ka
portable ...	... נַיָּד	na**yad**
radio	רַדְיוֹ	**rad**yo
car radio	רַדְיוֹ לִמְכוֹנִית	**rad**yo limkho**nit**
(cassette) recorder	רְשַׁמְקוֹל (קַסֶּטוֹת)	resham**kol** (ka**se**tot)
record player	פָּטֵפוֹן	**pa**tefon
shaver	מְכוֹנַת גִּלּוּחַ	mekho**nat** gilu**aḥ**
speakers	רַמְקוֹלִים	ramko**lim**
(colour) television	טֶלֶוִיזְיָה (צֶבַע)	tele**viz**ya (**tze**va)
transformer	שַׁנַּאי	sha**nay**
video-recorder	מְכוֹנַת הַקְלָטָה וִידֵאוֹ	mekho**nat** hakla**ta** **vi**deo

Grocer's חֲנוּת מַכֹּלֶת

All towns and cities have well-stocked supermarkets which sell a broad range of home-produced and imported goods, although at inflated prices. The following list of basic food and drink items will be useful if you want a picnic or light snack.

I'd like some bread, please.	אֲבַקֵּשׁ לֶחֶם.	ava**kesh** le**ḥ**em
What sort of cheese do you have?	אֵילוּ גְּבִינוֹת יֵשׁ לָכֶם?	**elu** gvi**not** yesh la**khem**
A piece of …	פְּרוּסַת …	pru**sat**
that one	הַהוּא	ha**hu**
the one on the shelf	זֶה שֶׁעַל הַמַּדָּף	ze she**al** hama**daf**
I'll have one of those, please.	אֶחָד מֵאֵלֶּה , בְּבַקָּשָׁה.	e**ḥad** meele bevaka**sha**
May I help myself?	אוּכַל לָקַחַת בְּעַצְמִי?	u**khal** laka**ḥ**at beatz**mi**
I'd like …	אֲבַקֵּשׁ …	ava**kesh**
a kilo of apples	קִילוֹ תַּפּוּחִים	**ki**lo tapu**ḥim**
half a kilo of tomatoes	חֲצִי קִילוֹ עַגְבָנִיּוֹת	ḥa**tzi** **ki**lo agvani**yot**
100 grams of butter	מֵאָה גְּרַם חֶמְאָה	me**a** gram **ḥ**ema
a litre of milk	לִיטֶר חָלָב	**li**ter ḥa**lav**
half a dozen eggs	שֵׁשׁ בֵּיצִים	shesh bey**tzim**
a packet of tea	חֲבִילַת תֵּה	ḥavi**lat** te
a jar of jam	צִנְצֶנֶת רִיבָּה	tzin**tze**net **ri**ba
a tin (can) of peaches	פַּחִית אֲפַרְסְקִים	pa**ḥit** afarse**kim**
a tube of mustard	שְׁפוֹפֶרֶת חַרְדָּל	shfo**fe**ret ḥar**dal**
a box of chocolates	קוּפְסַת שׁוֹקוֹלָד	kuf**sat** **sho**kolad

1 kilogram or kilo (kg.) =	1000 grams (g.)
100 g. = 3.5 oz.	½ kg. = 1.1 lb.
200 g. = 7.0 oz.	1 kg. = 2.2 lb.
1 oz. = 28.35 g.	
1 lb. = 453.60 g.	

1 litre (l.) = 0.88 imp. quarts = 1.06 U.S. quarts	
1 imp. quart = 1.14 l.	1 U.S. quart = 0.95 l.
1 imp. gallon = 4.55 l.	1 U.S. gallon = 3.8 l.

FOOD, see also page 63

Household articles מוּצָרִים לַבַּיִת

aluminium foil	נְיָר אֲלוּמִינְיוּם	neyar aluminiyum
bottle opener	פּוֹתְחָן בַּקְבּוּקִים	potḥan bakbukim
bucket	דְּלִי	dli
can/tin opener	פּוֹתְחָן קוּפְסָאוֹת	potḥan kufsaot
candles	נֵרוֹת	nerot
clothes pegs (pins)	אַטְבֵי כְּבִיסָה	itvey kvisa
dish detergent	תַּכְשִׁיר נִקּוּי לְכֵלִים	takhshir nikuy lekhelim
food box	צֵידָנִית	tzeydanit
frying pan	מַחֲבַת	maḥavat
matches	גַּפְרוּרִים	gafrurim
paper napkins	מַפִּיוֹת נְיָר	mapiyot neyar
paper towel	מַגֶּבֶת נְיָר	magevet neyar
plastic bags	שַׂקִּיוֹת פְּלַסְטִיק	sakiyot plastik
saucepan	סִיר בִּשּׁוּל	sir bishul
tea towel	מַגֶּבֶת מִטְבָּח	magevet mitbaḥ
vacuum flask	תֶּרְמוֹס	termos
washing powder	אַבְקַת כְּבִיסָה	avkat kvisa
washing-up liquid	תַּכְשִׁיר נִקּוּי לְכֵלִים	takhshir nikuy lekhelim

... and some useful items

hammer	פַּטִּישׁ	patish
nails	מַסְמְרִים	masmerim
penknife	אוֹלָר	olar
pliers	פְּלָיֶר	player
scissors	מִסְפָּרַיִם	misparayim
screws	בְּרָגִים	bragim
screwdriver	מַבְרֵג	mavreg
spanner	מַפְתֵּחַ בְּרָגִים (שְׁוֵדִי)	mafteaḥ bragim (shvedi)
tools	כֵּלִים	kelim

Crockery כְּלֵי חֶרֶס

cups	סְפָלִים	sfalim
mugs	סְפָלִים גְּדוֹלִים	sfalim gdolim
plates	צַלָּחוֹת	tzalaḥot
saucers	תַּחְתִּיוֹת	taḥtiyot
tumblers	כּוֹסוֹת גְּדוֹלוֹת	kosot gdolot

Cutlery (flatware) סַכּוּ"ם

forks/knives	מַזְלֵגוֹת/סַכִּינִים	mazlegot/sakinim
spoons	כַּפּוֹת	kapot
teaspoons	כַּפִּיוֹת	kapiyot
(made of) plastic	מִפְּלַסְטִיק	miplastik

Jeweller's—Watchmaker's שָׁעָן—צוֹרֵף

Could I see that, please?	אֶפְשָׁר לִרְאוֹת אֶת זֶה בְּבַקָּשָׁה?	ef**shar** li**rot** et ze bevaka**sha**
Do you have anything in gold?	יֵשׁ לָכֶם מַשֶּׁהוּ מִזָּהָב?	yesh la**khem** **ma**shehu miza**hav**
How many carats is this?	כַּמָּה קָרָט זֶה?	**ka**ma ka**rat** ze
Is this real silver?	זֶה כֶּסֶף אֲמִתִּי?	ze **ke**sef ami**ti**
Can you repair this watch?	תּוּכַל (תּוּכְלִי) לְתַקֵּן אֶת הַשָּׁעוֹן הַזֶּה?	**tukhal** (tukh**li**) leta**ken** et hasha**on** ha**ze**
I'd like a/an/some ...	אֲבַקֵּשׁ ...	ava**kesh**
alarm clock	שְׁעוֹן מְעוֹרֵר	sha**on** meo**rer**
bangle	צָמִיד	tza**mid**
battery	סוֹלְלָה	sole**la**
bracelet	צָמִיד	tza**mid**
chain bracelet	צָמִיד שַׁרְשֶׁרֶת	tza**mid** **sharshe**ret
charm bracelet	צָמִיד עִם קָמֵעַ	tza**mid** im ka**me**a
brooch	סִכַּת נוֹי	si**kat** noy
chain	שַׁרְשֶׁרֶת	shar**she**ret
charm	קָמֵעַ	ka**me**a
cigarette case	נַרְתִּיק לְסִיגַרְיוֹת	nar**tik** lesigari**yot**
cigarette lighter	מַצִּית	ma**tzit**
clip	סִכָּה לַעֲנִיבָה	si**ka** leani**va**
clock	שְׁעוֹן קִיר	she**on** kir
cross	צְלָב	tzlav
cuckoo clock	שְׁעוֹן קוּקִיָּה	she**on** kuki**ya**
cuff links	כַּפְתּוֹרֵי חֲפָתִים	kafto**rey** ḥofa**tim**
cutlery	סַכּוּם	sa**kum**
earrings	עֲגִילִים	agi**lim**
gem	אֶבֶן יְקָרָה	**e**ven yeka**ra**
jewel box	קֻפְסַת תַּכְשִׁיטִים	kuf**sat** takhshi**tim**
mechanical pencil	עִפָּרוֹן מֵכָנִי	ipa**ron** me**kha**ni
music box	קֻפְסָה מְנַגֶּנֶת	kuf**sa** mena**ge**net
necklace	מַחֲרֹזֶת	maḥa**ro**zet
pendant	תִּלְיוֹן	til**yon**
pin	סִכָּה	si**ka**
pocket watch	שְׁעוֹן כִּיס	she**on** kis
powder compact	פּוּדְרִיָּה	pudri**ya**
propelling pencil	עִפָּרוֹן מֵכָנִי	ipa**ron** me**kha**ni

ring	טַבַּעַת	ta**baat**
engagement ring	טַבַּעַת אֵרוּסִים	ta**baat** eru**sim**
signet ring	טַבַּעַת חוֹתָם	ta**baat** ḥo**tam**
wedding ring	טַבַּעַת נִשּׂוּאִים	ta**baat** nisu**im**
rosary	מַחֲרֹזֶת תְּפִלָּה	maḥa**ro**zet tfi**la**
silverware	דִּבְרֵי כֶּסֶף	div**rey** **ke**sef
tie clip/pin	סִכָּה לַעֲנִיבָה	si**ka** leani**va**
watch	שָׁעוֹן	sha**on**
automatic	אוֹטוֹמָטִי	oto**ma**ti
digital	דִּיגִיטָלִי	digi**ta**li
quartz	קְוַרְץ	kvartz
with a second hand	עִם מְחוֹג שְׁנִיּוֹת	im me**ḥog** shni**yot**
waterproof	נֶגֶד מַיִם	**ne**ged **ma**yim
watchstrap	רְצוּעָה לְשָׁעוֹן	retzu**a** lesha**on**
wristwatch	שְׁעוֹן יָד	she**on** yad

amber	עִנְבָּר	in**bar**
amethyst	אַחְלָמָה	aḥla**ma**
chromium	כְּרוֹם	krom
copper	נְחֹשֶׁת	ne**ḥo**shet
coral	אַלְמֹג	al**mog**
crystal	בְּדֹלַח	b**do**laḥ
cut glass	זְכוּכִית מְלֻטֶּשֶׁת	zkhu**khit** melu**te**shet
diamond	יַהֲלֹמִים	yahalo**mim**
emerald	בָּרֶקֶת	ba**re**ket
enamel	אֱמַאיְל	**emayl**
gold	זָהָב	**zahav**
gold plate	מְצֻפֶּה זָהָב	metzu**pe** za**hav**
ivory	שֶׁנְהָב	shen**hav**
jade	יַרְקָן	yar**kan**
onyx	שֹׁהַם	**sho**ham
pearl	פְּנִינָה	**pnina**
pewter	בְּדִיל-עוֹפֶרֶת	bdil-o**fe**ret
platinum	פְּלָטִינָה	pla**ti**na
ruby	אֹדֶם	**o**dem
sapphire	סַפִּיר	sa**pir**
silver	כֶּסֶף	**ke**sef
silver plate	מְצֻפֶּה כֶּסֶף	metzu**pe** **ke**sef
stainless steel	פְּלָדַת אַלְחֶלֶד	pil**dat** al**ḥe**led
topaz	טוֹפָּז	to**paz**

Optician אוֹפְּטִיקַאי

I've broken my glasses.	הַמִּשְׁקָפַיִם שֶׁלִּי נִשְׁבְּרוּ.	hamishka**fa**yim sheli nishbe**ru**
Can you repair them for me?	תּוּכְלוּ לְתַקֵּן אוֹתָם?	tukh**lu** leta**ken** o**tam**
When will they be ready?	מָתַי הֵם יִהְיוּ מוּכָנִים?	ma**tay** hem yihi**yu** mukha**nim**
Can you change the lenses?	תּוּכְלוּ לְהַחֲלִיף אֶת הָעֲדָשׁוֹת?	tukh**lu** lehaḥa**lif** et haada**shot**
I'd like tinted lenses.	אֲבַקֵּשׁ עֲדָשׁוֹת כֵּהוֹת.	ava**kesh** ada**shot** ke**hot**
The frame is broken.	הַמִּסְגֶּרֶת שְׁבוּרָה.	hamis**ge**ret shvu**ra**
I'd like a spectacle case.	אֲבַקֵּשׁ נַרְתִּיק לְמִשְׁקָפַיִם.	ava**kesh** nar**tik** lemishka**fa**yim
I'd like to have my eyesight checked.	אֲבַקֵּשׁ לִבְדּוֹק אֶת הָרְאִיָּה שֶׁלִּי.	ava**kesh** liv**dok** et harei**ya** she**li**
I'm short-sighted/ long-sighted.	אֲנִי קְצַר (קִצְרַת) רְאוּת/מַרְחִיק (מַרְחִיקַת) רְאוּת.	**ani** ktzar (kitz**rat**) re**ut**/ mar**ḥik** (marḥi**kat**) re**ut**
I'd like some contact lenses.	אֲבַקֵּשׁ עַדְשׁוֹת מַגָּע.	ava**kesh** ad**shot** ma**ga**
I've lost one of my contact lenses.	אִבַּדְתִּי עַדְשַׁת מַגָּע.	i**ba**deti ad**shat** ma**ga**
Could you give me another one?	תּוּכְלוּ לָתֵת לִי אַחֶרֶת?	tukh**lu** la**tet** li a**ḥe**ret
I have hard/soft lenses.	יֵשׁ לִי עֲדָשׁוֹת קָשׁוֹת/רַכּוֹת.	yesh li ada**shot** ka**shot**/ ra**kot**
Do you have any contact-lens fluid?	יֵשׁ לָכֶם נוֹזֵל לְעַדְשׁוֹת מַגָּע?	yesh la**khem** no**zel** lead**shot** ma**ga**
I'd like to buy a pair of sunglasses.	אֲבַקֵּשׁ לִקְנוֹת מִשְׁקְפֵי שֶׁמֶשׁ.	ava**kesh** lik**not** mishke**fey** **she**mesh
May I look in a mirror?	אֶפְשָׁר לְהִסְתַּכֵּל בָּרְאִי?	ef**shar** lehista**kel** barei
I'd like to buy a pair of binoculars.	אֲבַקֵּשׁ לִקְנוֹת מִשְׁקֶפֶת.	ava**kesh** lik**not** mish**ke**fet

Photography צִלּוּם

You'll be able to buy film and batteries in drugstores, sweet kiosks and supermarkets as well as film-processing shops.

I'd like a(n) … camera.	אֲבַקֵּשׁ מַצְלֵמָה ...	ava**kesh** matzle**ma**
automatic	אוטוֹמָטִית	oto**ma**tit
inexpensive	לֹא יְקָרָה	lo yekara
simple	פְּשׁוּטָה	pshu**ta**
Can you show me some …, please?	תּוּכַל (תּוּכְלִי) לְהַרְאוֹת לִי ..., בְּבַקָּשָׁה?	tu**khal** (tukh**li**) leha**rot** li … bevaka**sha**
cine (movie) cameras	מַצְלֵמַת קוֹלְנוֹעַ	matzle**mat** kol**no**a
video cameras	מַצְלֵמַת וִידֵאוֹ	matzle**mat vi**deo
I'd like to have some passport photos taken.	אֲבַקֵּשׁ לַעֲשׂוֹת תְּמוּנוֹת דַּרְכּוֹן.	ava**kesh** laa**sot** tmu**not** dar**kon**

Film סֶרֶט

I'd like a film for this camera.	אֲבַקֵּשׁ סֶרֶט לַמַּצְלֵמָה הַזּוֹ.	ava**kesh se**ret lamatzle**ma** hazo
black and white	שָׁחוֹר-לָבָן	sha**ḥor**-la**van**
colour	צֶבַע	**tze**va
colour negative	נֶגָטִיב צֶבַע	**ne**gativ **tze**va
colour slide	שְׁקוּפִיּוֹת צֶבַע	shkufi**yot tze**va
cartridge	קָסֶטָה	ka**se**ta
disc film	דִּיסְק	disk
roll film	סֶרֶט מְגוּלְגָל	**se**ret megul**gal**
video cassette	קַסֶּטַת וִידֵאוֹ	ka**se**tat **vi**deo
24/36 exposures	עֶשְׂרִים וְאַרְבַּע/שְׁלֹשִׁים וָשֵׁשׁ תְּמוּנוֹת	es**rim** vearba/shlo**shim** ve**shesh** tmu**not**
this size	בַּגֹּדֶל הַזֶּה	ba**go**del haze
this ASA/DIN number	מִסְפַּר אַסָא/דִּין הַזֶּה	mis**par** asa/din haze
artificial light type	לְאוֹר מְלָאכוּתִי	le**or** mlakhuti
daylight type	לְאוֹר יוֹם	le**or** yom
fast (high-speed)	מָהִיר	ma**hir**
fine grain	גַּרְעִין דַּק	gar**in** dak

Processing פִּתּוּחַ

How much do you charge for processing?	כַּמָּה עוֹלֶה פִּתּוּחַ?	**ka**ma **ole** pituaḥ

I'd like ... prints of each negative.	אבקש ... תמונות מכל נגטיב.	ava**kesh** ... tmu**not** mi**kol** **ne**gativ
with a matt finish	גמור מט	gi**mur** mat
with a glossy finish	גמור מבריק	gi**mur** mav**rik**
Will you enlarge this, please?	אפשר להגדיל את זה, בבקשה?	ef**shar** lehag**dil** et ze bevaka**sha**
When will the photos be ready?	מתי תהיינה התמונות מוכנות?	ma**tay** tihi**ye**na hatmu**not** mukha**not**

Accessories and repairs אביזרים ותקונים

I'd like a/an/some ...	אבקש ...	ava**kesh**
battery	סוללה	sole**la**
cable release	מחשף גמיש	maḥ**isef** ga**mish**
camera case	נרתיק למצלמה	nar**tik** lematzle**ma**
(electronic) flash	מבזק (אלקטרוני)	mav**zek** (elek**tro**ni)
filter	מסנן	mas**nen**
for black and white	לשחור-לבן	lesha**ḥor**-la**van**
for colour	לצבע	le**tze**va
lens	עדשה	ada**sha**
telephoto lens	טלפוטו	tele**fo**to
wide-angle lens	רחבת זוית	reḥa**vat** za**vit**
lens cap	מכסה עדשה	mikh**se** ada**sha**
Can you repair this camera?	תוכלו לתקן את המצלמה הזו?	tukh**lu** leta**ken** et hamatzle**ma** ha**zo**
The film is jammed.	הסרט נתקע.	ha**se**ret nit**ka**
There's something wrong with the ...	משהו לא בסדר עם ...	**ma**shehu lo be**se**der im
exposure counter	סופר החשיפות	so**fer** haḥasi**fot**
film winder	קדום הסרט	ki**dum** ha**se**ret
flash attachment	החבור למבזק	haḥi**bur** lemav**zek**
lens	העדשה	haada**sha**
light meter	המדאור	hama**dor**
rangefinder	מד המרחק	mad hamer**ḥak**
shutter	התריס	hat**ris**

Tobacconist's חֲנוּת טַבָּק

Cigarettes are generally referred to by their brand name. Locally manufactured brands are quite cheap, while imported cigarettes are subject to tax and therefore more expensive. Cigarettes can be bought from sweet kiosks and shops, some bars and restaurants and from supermarkets.

A packet of cigarettes, please.	חֲפִיסַת סִיגָרִיּוֹת, בְּבַקָּשָׁה.	ḥa**fi**sat sigari**yot** bevaka**sha**
Do you have any American/English cigarettes?	יֵשׁ לָכֶם סִיגָרִיּוֹת אֲמֶרִיקָאִיּוֹת/אַנְגְּלִיּוֹת?	yesh la**khem** sigari**yot** ameri**kai**yot/angli**yot**
I'd like a carton.	אֲבַקֵּשׁ קַרְטוֹן אֶחָד.	ava**kesh** kar**ton** e**ḥad**
Give me a/some ..., please.	תֵּן (תְּנִי) לִי ... בְּבַקָּשָׁה.	ten (tni) li ... bevaka**sha**
candy	סוּכָּרִיּוֹת	sukari**yot**
chewing gum	מַסְטִיק	**mas**tik
chewing tobacco	טַבָּק לְעִיסָה	ta**bak** lei**sa**
chocolate	שׁוֹקוֹלָד	**sho**kolad
cigarette case	נַרְתִּיק לְסִיגָרִיּוֹת	nar**tik** lesigari**yot**
cigarette holder	פּוּמִית	pu**mit**
cigarettes	סִיגָרִיּוֹת	sigari**yot**
filter-tipped/without filter	עִם פִילְטֶר/בְּלִי פִילְטֶר	im **fil**ter/bli **fil**ter
light/dark tobacco	טַבָּק בָּהִיר/כֵּהֶה	ta**bak** ba**hir**/**ke**he
mild/strong	עֲדִינוֹת/חֲזָקוֹת	adi**not**/ḥaza**kot**
menthol	מֶנְטוֹל	men**tol**
king-size	אֲרוּכּוֹת	aru**kot**
cigars	סִיגָרִים	si**ga**rim
lighter	מַצִּית	ma**tzit**
lighter fluid/gas	נוֹזֵל/גַּז לְמַצִּית	**no**zel/gaz lema**tzit**
matches	גַּפְרוּרִים	gafru**rim**
pipe	מִקְטֶרֶת	mik**te**ret
pipe cleaners	כְּלֵי נִקּוּי לְמִקְטֶרֶת	kley ni**kuy** lemik**te**ret
pipe tobacco	טַבָּק לְמִקְטֶרֶת	ta**bak** lemik**te**ret
pipe tool	מַכְשִׁיר נִקּוּי לְמִקְטֶרֶת	makh**shir** ni**kuy** lemik**te**ret
postcard	גְּלוּיָה	glu**ya**
snuff	טַבָּק הֲרָחָה	ta**bak** hara**ḥa**
stamps	בּוּלִים	bu**lim**
sweets	מַמְתַּקִּים	mamta**kim**
wick	פְּתִילָה	pti**la**

Miscellaneous שׁוֹנוֹת

Souvenirs מַזְכָּרוֹת

In Israel you'll find modern shopping malls and supermarkets with fixed prices rubbing shoulders with traditional bazaars, or *souks*, where haggling is the time-honoured way of doing business. The old section of Jerusalem, with its narrow streets and merchant's stores, is an ideal place for a shopping expedition. Browse around, especially in the *souks*, and you'll find all sorts of exquisitely hand-crafted items fashioned from olive wood, mother-of-pearl, leather and straw, religious artefacts, ceramics, beautiful jewellery, hand-blown glass and exotic oriental clothing.

מַתָּנוֹת מֵעֵץ זַיִת	mata**not** me**etz za**yit	olivewood
כְּלֵי נְחֹשֶׁת	kley ne**ḥo**shet	copper and brass
כְּלֵי כֶּסֶף	kley kesef	silverware
קֶרָמִיקָה	ke**ra**mika	ceramics
תַּשְׁמִישֵׁי קְדוּשָּׁה	tashmi**shey** kdu**sha**	religious articles
עַתִּיקוֹת	ati**kot**	antiques
שְׁטִיחִים	shti**him**	carpets
רִקְמָה	rik**ma**	embroidery
יַהֲלוֹמִים	yahalo**mim**	diamonds
סְפָרִים	sfa**rim**	books

Records—Cassettes תַּקְלִיטִים—קַסֶּטוֹת

Music native to Israel tends to be in the folk tradition, but you'll also hear quite a variety of music around, including home-grown and Western pop.

I'd like a ...	... אֲבַקֵּשׁ	ava**kesh**
cassette	קַסֶּטָה	ka**se**ta
video cassette	קַסֶּטַת וִידֵאוֹ	ka**se**tat **vi**deo
compact disc	תַּקְלִיטוֹן סִי-דִי (אוֹפְּטִי)	takli**ton** si di (**op**ti)

L.P.(33 rpm)	אֲרִיךְ נֶגֶן (שְׁלֹשִׁים וְשָׁלֹשׁ)	**arikh ne**gen (shlo**shim** vesha**losh**)
E.P.(45 rpm)	אַרְבָּעִים וְחָמֵשׁ	arba**im** veḥa**mesh**
single	תַּקְלִיטוֹן	takli**ton**

Do you have any records by ...?	יֵשׁ לָכֶם תַּקְלִיטִים שֶׁל ...?	yesh la**khem** takli**tim** shel
Can I listen to this record?	אוּכַל לְהַקְשִׁיב לְתַקְלִיט זֶה?	u**khal** lehak**shiv** leta**klit** ze
chamber music	מוּסִיקָה קָמֶרִית	**mu**sika **ka**merit
classical music	מוּסִיקָה קְלָסִית	**mu**sika **kla**sit
folk music	שִׁירֵי עַם	shi**rey** am
folk song	שִׁיר עַם	shir am
instrumental music	מוּסִיקָה אִינְסְטְרוּמֶנְטָלִית	**mu**sika instrumen**ta**lit
jazz	גֶ'ז	jaz
light music	מוּסִיקָה קַלָּה	**mu**sika ka**la**
orchestral music	מוּסִיקָה תִּזְמָרְתִּית	**mu**sika tizmor**tit**
pop music	מוּסִיקַת פּוֹפ	**mu**sikat pop

Toys צַעֲצוּעִים

I'd like a toy/game...	אֲנִי מְחַפֵּשׂ (מְחַפֶּשֶׂת) צַעֲצוּעַ/מִשְׂחָק ...	**ani** meḥa**pes** (meḥa**pe**set) tzaatzua/mis**ḥak**
for a boy	לְיֶלֶד	le**ye**led
for a 5-year-old girl	לְיַלְדָּה בַּת חָמֵשׁ	leyal**da** bat ḥa**mesh**
(beach) ball	כַּדּוּר (יָם)	ka**dur** (yam)
bucket and spade (pail and shovel)	אֵת וּדְלִי	et ud**li**
building blocks (bricks)	קוּבִּיּוֹת מִשְׂחָק	kubi**yot** mis**ḥak**
card game	מִשְׂחַק קְלָפִים	mis**ḥak** kla**fim**
chess set	מַעֲרֶכֶת שַׁחְמָט	maa**re**khet shaḥ**mat**
doll	בּוּבָּה	bu**ba**
electronic game	מִשְׂחָק אֶלֶקְטְרוֹנִי	mis**ḥak** elek**tro**ni
roller skates	סְקֶטִים	**ske**tim
snorkel	שְׁנוֹרְקֶל	**shnor**kel
toy car	מְכוֹנִית צַעֲצוּעַ	mekho**nit** tzaa**tzu**a
teddy bear	דּוּבּוֹן	du**bon**
colouring book	סֵפֶר לִצְבִיעָה	**se**fer litzvia

Your money: banks—currency

At larger banks there's certain to be someone who speaks English. In most tourist centres you'll find small currency exchanges (banks), especially during high season. Always take your passport with you when changing money, and be prepared for a wait.

Business hours vary according to the season, but banks are normally open Sunday to Thursday from 8.30 am to 12.30 pm, from 4 pm to 6 pm on Sundays, Tuesdays and Thursdays and from 8.30 am to noon on Fridays and on the eve of major Jewish holidays. The currency exchange desks at Ben Gurion airport are always open.

In many tourist resorts hard currency may be exchanged on the black market—you should be wary of the rate offered.

The Israeli unit of currency is the *new shekel* (abbreviated NIS), divided into 100 *agorot*.
Coins: 5, 10 agorot, ½, 1 and 5 new shekels.
Notes: 10, 20, 50, 100 and 200 new shekels.

Where's the nearest bank?	אֵיפֹה הַבַּנְק הַקָּרוֹב?	**ey**fo ha**bank** haka**rov**
Where's the nearest currency exchange office?	אֵיפֹה אֶפְשָׁר לְהַחֲלִיף מַטְבֵּעַ חוּץ בַּסְּבִיבָה?	**ey**fo ef**shar** lehaḥa**lif** mat**be**a ḥutz basvi**va**

At the bank בַּבַּנְק

I want to change some dollars/pounds.	בִּרְצוֹנִי לְהַחֲלִיף דּוֹלָרִים/לִירוֹת שְׁטֶרְלִינג.	birtzo**ni** lehaḥa**lif** do**la**rim/ li**rot** **ster**ling
I want to cash a traveller's cheque.	בִּרְצוֹנִי לִפְדּוֹת הַמְחָאַת נוֹסְעִים.	birtzo**ni** lif**dot** hamḥaat no**sim**
What's the exchange rate?	מַה הַשַּׁעַר?	ma ha**shaar**
How much commission do you charge?	מַה הָעֲמָלָה שֶׁלָּכֶם?	ma haama**la** shela**khem**
Can you cash a personal cheque?	אֶפְשָׁר לִפְדּוֹת הַמְחָאָה אִישִׁית?	ef**shar** lif**dot** hamḥaa i**shit**
Can you telex my bank in London?	אֶפְשָׁר לִשְׁלוֹחַ טֶלֶקְס לַבַּנְק שֶׁלִּי בְּלוֹנְדוֹן?	ef**shar** lish**loaḥ** **te**leks la**bank** she**li** be**lon**don
I have a/an/some ...	יֵשׁ לִי ...	yesh li
credit card	כַּרְטִיס אַשְׁרַאי	kar**tis** ash**ray**
Eurocheques	יוּרוֹצֶ'ק	**yu**rotshek
letter of credit	כְּתָב אַשְׁרַאי	ktav ash**ray**
I'm expecting some money from New York. Has it arrived?	אֲנִי מְצַפֶּה (מְצַפָּה) לְכֶסֶף מִנְיוּ יוֹרְק. הַאִם הִגִּיעַ?	a**ni** metza**pe** (metza**pa**) le**khe**sef min**yu** york. ha**im** hi**gia**
Please give me ... notes (bills) and some small change.	תֵּן (תְּנִי) לִי בְּבַקָּשָׁה ... שְׁטָרוֹת וּקְצָת כֶּסֶף קָטָן.	ten (tni) li bevaka**sha** ... shta**rot** uk**tzat** **ke**sef ka**tan**
Give me ... large notes and the rest in small notes.	תֵּן (תְּנִי) לִי ... שְׁטָרוֹת גְּדוֹלִים וְהַשְּׁאָר בִּשְׁטָרוֹת קְטַנִּים.	ten (tni) li ... shta**rot** gdo**lim** vehash**ar** bishta**rot** kta**nim**

Deposits—Withdrawals הַפְקָדָה—מְשִׁיכָה

I want to ...	בִּרְצוֹנִי ...	birtzo**ni**
open an account	לִפְתּוֹחַ חֶשְׁבּוֹן	lif**toaḥ** ḥesh**bon**
withdraw ... shekels	לִמְשׁוֹךְ ... שְׁקָלִים	lim**shokh** ... shka**lim**
Where should I sign?	אֵיפֹה לַחְתּוֹם?	**ey**fo laḥa**tom**
I'd like to pay this into my account.	בִּרְצוֹנִי לְהַפְקִיד זֹאת בְּחֶשְׁבּוֹנִי.	birtzo**ni** lehaf**kid** zot beḥeshbo**ni**

NUMBERS, see page 147

Business terms מונְחֵי עֲסָקִים

My name is ...	שְׁמִי...	shmi
Here's my card.	הִנֵּה כַּרְטִיס הַבִּקּוּר שֶׁלִּי.	hi**ne** kar**tis** habi**kur** sheli
I have an appointment with ...	יֵשׁ לִי פְּגִישָׁה עִם...	yesh li pgi**sha** im
Can you give me an estimate of the cost?	תּוּכַל (תּוּכְלִי) לָתֵת לִי הַעֲרָכַת מְחִיר?	tu**khal** (tukh**li**) la**tet** li haara**khat** me**ḥir**
What's the rate of inflation?	מָה שַׁעַר הָאִינְפְלַצְיָה?	ma **sha**ar hainf**la**tzia
Can you provide me with an interpreter/a personal computer/a secretary?	אֶפְשָׁר לְסַדֵּר לִי תּוּרְגְמָן/מַחְשֵׁב אִישִׁי/ מַזְכִּירָה?	ef**shar** lesa**der** li turg**man**/ maḥ**shev** i**shi**/mazki**ra**
Where can I make photocopies?	אֵיפֹה אוּכַל לַעֲשׂוֹת הַעְתָּקִים?	**ey**fo u**khal** laa**sot** heete**kim**

amount	סְכוּם	skhum
balance	מַאֲזָן	maa**zan**
capital	הוֹן	hon
cheque	הַמְחָאָה	hamḥa**a**
contract	חוֹזֶה	ḥo**ze**
discount	הֲנָחָה	hana**ḥa**
expenses	הוֹצָאוֹת	hotza**ot**
interest	רִבִּית	ri**bit**
investment	הַשְׁקָעָה	hashka**a**
invoice	חֶשְׁבּוֹן	ḥesh**bon**
loss	הֶפְסֵד	hef**sed**
mortgage	מַשְׁכַּנְתָּא	mash**kan**ta
payment	תַּשְׁלוּם	tash**lum**
percentage	אָחוּז	a**ḥuz**
profit	רֶוַח	**re**vaḥ
purchase	קְנִיָּה	kni**ya**
sale	מְכִירָה	mekhi**ra**
share	מְנָיָה	mna**ya**
transfer	הַעֲבָרָה	haava**ra**
value	עֶרֶךְ	**e**rekh

At the post office

In Israel, the post office is indicated by a white deer on a blue background. Mailboxes are red. The opening hours are 8.30 am to 12.30 pm and 3.30 pm to 6.30 pm Sundays to Thursdays, and 8 am to 12 noon on Fridays and days before Jewish holy days.

Where's the nearest post office?	אֵיפֹה הַדֹּאַר הַקָּרוֹב?	**ey**fo ha**do**ar haka**rov**
What time does the post office open/close?	מָתַי הַדֹּאַר נִפְתָּח/נִסְגָּר?	ma**tay** ha**do**ar nif**taḥ**/nis**gar**
A stamp for this letter/postcard, please.	בּוּל בִּשְׁבִיל הַמִּכְתָּב/ הַגְּלוּיָה בְּבַקָּשָׁה.	bul bish**vil** hamikh**tav**/ haglu**ya** bevaka**sha**
A ...-agorot stamp, please.	בּוּל שֶׁל ... אֲגוֹרוֹת, בְּבַקָּשָׁה.	bul shel ... ago**rot** bevaka**sha**
What's the postage for a letter to London?	כַּמָּה עוֹלֶה מִכְתָּב לְלוֹנְדוֹן?	**ka**ma **ole** mikh**tav** le**lon**don
What's the postage for a postcard to Los Angeles?	כַּמָּה עוֹלָה גְּלוּיָה לְלוֹס אַנְגֶ'לֶס?	**ka**ma **ola** glu**ya** le**los** **an**jeles
Where's the letter box (mailbox)?	אֵיפֹה תֵּבַת הַדֹּאַר?	**ey**fo **tevat** ha**doar**
I want to send this parcel.	בִּרְצוֹנִי לִשְׁלוֹחַ אֶת הַחֲבִילָה הַזֹּאת.	birtzo**ni** lish**lo**aḥ et haḥavi**la** **hazot**
I'd like to send this (by) ...	בִּרְצוֹנִי לִשְׁלוֹחַ אֶת זֶה...	birtzo**ni** lish**loa**ḥ et ze
airmail	בְּדֹאַר אֲוִיר	be**doar** **avir**
express (special delivery)	אֶקְסְפְּרֶס	eks**pres**
registered mail	רָשׁוּם	ra**shum**

At which counter can I cash an international money order?	בְּאֵיזֶה אֶשְׁנָב אוּכַל לִפְדּוֹת הַמְחָאַת דֹּאַר בֵּינְלְאוּמִית?	beeyze esh**nav** u**khal** lif**dot** ham**ḥaat do**ar beynleu**mit**
Where's the poste restante (general delivery)?	אֵיפֹה הַדֹּאַר הַשָּׁמוּר?	**ey**fo ha**do**ar hasha**mur**
Is there any post (mail) for me? My name is ...	יֵשׁ דֹּאַר בִּשְׁבִילִי? שְׁמִי...	yesh **do**ar bishvi**li**? shmi

בּוּלִים	STAMPS
חֲבִילוֹת	PARCELS
הַמְחָאוֹת דֹּאַר	MONEY ORDERS

Telegrams—Telex—Fax מִבְרָקִים—טֶלֶקְס—פַקְס

Ordinary telex facilities are available to guests in most luxury hotels in Jerusalem and Tel Aviv and in main post offices. Fax services are available at most 4- and 5-star hotels.

I'd like to send a telegram/telex.	בִּרְצוֹנִי לִשְׁלוֹחַ מִבְרָק/טֶלֶקְס.	birtzo**ni** lish**lo**aḥ miv**rak**/ **te**leks
May I have a form, please?	אוּכַל לְקַבֵּל טוֹפֶס , בְּבַקָּשָׁה?	u**khal** leka**bel to**fes bevaka**sha**
How much is it per word?	כַּמָּה זֶה לְמִלָּה?	**ka**ma ze lemi**la**
How long will a cable to Boston take?	כַּמָּה זְמַן יִקַּח מִבְרָק לְבּוֹסְטוֹן?	**ka**ma zman yi**kaḥ** miv**rak** le**bos**ton
How much will this fax cost?	כַּמָּה יַעֲלֶה הַפַּקְס הַזֶּה?	**ka**ma yaa**le** ha**faks** ha**ze**

Telephoning שִׂיחוֹת טֶלֶפוֹן

Most public telephones operate with tokens (*asimonim*) or 20-unit telephone cards, on sale at post offices, kiosks, etc. There are also public phones in bars and cafés where a token isn't needed. These are indicated by the Israeli Postal Service emblem (a white deer on a blue background).

Where's the telephone?	אֵיפֹה הַטֶלֶפוֹן?	**ey**fo ha**te**lefon
I'd like a telephone token.	אֲסִימוֹן , בְּבַקָשָׁה.	asi**mon** bevaka**sha**
Where's the nearest telephone booth?	אֵיפֹה תָּא הַטֶלֶפוֹן הַקָרוֹב?	**ey**fo ta ha**te**lefon haka**rov**
May I use your phone?	אֶפְשָׁר לְהִשְׁתַּמֵשׁ בְּטֶלֶפוֹן שֶׁלְךָ (שֶׁלָךְ)?	ef**shar** lehishta**mesh** ba**te**lefon shel**kha** (she**lakh**)
Do you have a telephone directory for Tel Aviv?	יֵשׁ לְךָ (לָךְ) מַדְרִיךְ טֶלֶפוֹן שֶׁל תֵּל-אָבִיב?	yesh le**kha** (lakh) mad**rikh** **te**lefon shel tel a**viv**
I'd like to call ... in England.	בִּרְצוֹנִי לְצַלְצֵל לְ... בְּאַנְגְלִיָה.	birtzo**ni** letzal**tzel** le... be**ang**liya
What's the dialling (area) code for ... ?	מַה קוֹד הַחִיוּג לְ...?	ma kod haḥi**yug** le
How do I get the international operator?	אֵיךְ מַשִׂיגִים אֶת הַמֶרְכָּזִיָה הַבֵּינְלְאוּמִית?	eykh masi**gim** et hamerkazi**ya** habeynleu**mit**

Operator מֶרְכָּזִיָה

I'd like Eilat 23 45 67.	אֲבַקֵשׁ אֵילַת 234 567.	ava**kesh** ey**lat** **shta**yim sha**losh** **arba** ḥa**mesh** shesh **she**va
Can you help me get this number?	תּוּכַל (תּוּכְלִי) לַעֲזוֹר לִי לְהַשִׂיג אֶת הַמִסְפָּר הַזֶה?	**tu**khal (tukh**li**) laa**zor** li leha**sig** et hamis**par** **haze**
I'd like to place a personal (person-to-person) call.	בִּרְצוֹנִי לְהַזְמִין שִׂיחָה אִישִׁית.	birtzo**ni** lehaz**min** si**ḥa** **ishit**
I'd like to reverse the charges (call collect).	בִּרְצוֹנִי לְחַיֵיג בְּגוּבַיְנָא.	birtzo**ni** leḥa**yeg** begu**vay**na

NUMBERS, see page 147

Speaking מְשׂוֹחֲחִים

Hello. This is …	הַלוֹ. כָּאן …	ha**lo**. kan
I'd like to speak to …	אֲבַקֵשׁ אֶת…	ava**kesh** et
Extension …	שְׁלוּחָה …	shlu**ḥa**
Speak louder/more slowly, please.	אֶפְשָׁר לְדַבֵּר בְּקוֹל רָם יוֹתֵר/יוֹתֵר לְאַט , בְּבַקָּשָׁה?	ef**shar** leda**ber** be**kol** ram yo**ter**/yo**ter** le**at** bevaka**sha**

Bad luck בְּעָיוֹת

Would you try again later, please?	תּוּכַל (תּוּכְלִי) לְנַסּוֹת שׁוּב יוֹתֵר מְאוּחָר, בְּבַקָּשָׁה?	tu**khal** (tukh**li**) lena**sot** shuv yo**ter** meu**ḥar** bevaka**sha**
Operator, you gave me the wrong number.	מֶרְכָּזִיָּה , נָתַתְּ לִי מִסְפָּר לֹא נָכוֹן.	merkazi**ya** na**tat** li mis**par** lo na**khon**
Operator, we were cut off.	מֶרְכָּזִיָּה , נוּתַקְנוּ.	merkazi**ya** nu**tak**nu

Telephone alphabet אָלֶפְבֵּית טֶלֶפוֹנִי

A	עֲפוּלָה	a**fu**la	N	נַעַן	**na**an
B	בִּנְיָמִינָה	binya**mi**na	O	עֹגֶן	**o**gen
C	כַּרְמֶל	kar**mel**	P	פַּרְדֵּס	par**des**
D	דַּלְיָה	**dal**ya	Q	קְוִין	kvin
E	אֶרֶץ	**e**retz	R	רִאשׁוֹן	ri**shon**
F	פְרַנְס	frans	S	סֵפֶר	**se**fer
G	גְּדֵרָה	gede**ra**	T	טְבֶרְיָה	t**ver**ya
H	חֵיפָה	ḥey**fa**	U	אוּרִים	u**rim**
I	יִשְׂרָאֵל	yisra**el**	V	וֶרֶד	**ve**red
J	יָפָה	**ja**fa	W	וִינְגֵייט	**vin**geyt
K	כַּרְכּוּר	kar**kur**	X	אֶקְסְפְּרֶס	eks**pres**
L	לוֹד	lod	Y	יַבְנִיאֵל	**yav**niel
M	מוֹלֶדֶת	mo**le**det	Z	זִכְרוֹן	zikh**ron**

Not there לֹא נִמְצָא

When will he/she be back?	מָתַי יַחֲזוֹר/תַּחֲזוֹר?	ma**tay** yaḥazor/taḥazor
Will you tell him/her I called? My name is …	תּוּכַל (תּוּכְלִי) לוֹמַר לוֹ/לָהּ שֶׁצִּלְצַלְתִּי? שְׁמִי …	tu**khal** (tukh**li**) lo**mar** lo/la shetzil**tzal**ti? shmi
Would you ask him/her to call me? My number is …	תּוּכַל (תּוּכְלִי) לְבַקֵּשׁ שֶׁיְּצַלְצֵל/שֶׁתְּצַלְצֵל אֵלַי? מִסְפָּרִי …	tu**khal** (tukh**li**) leva**kesh** sheyetzal**tzel**/shetetzal**tzel** e**lay**? mispa**ri**
Would you take a message, please	תּוּכַל (תּוּכְלִי) לִרְשׁוֹם הוֹדָעָה בְּבַקָּשָׁה?	tu**khal** (tukh**li**) lir**shom** hoda**a** bevaka**sha**

Charges מְחִירִים

What was the cost of that call?	כַּמָּה עָלְתָה הַשִּׂיחָה הַהִיא?	**ka**ma al**ta** hasi**ḥa** ha**hi**
I want to pay for the call.	בִּרְצוֹנִי לְשַׁלֵּם עֲבוּר הַשִּׂיחָה.	birtzo**ni** lesha**lem** a**vur** hasi**ḥa**

יֵשׁ שִׂיחַת טֶלֶפוֹן בִּשְׁבִילְךָ (בִּשְׁבִילֵךְ).	There's a telephone call for you.
אֵיזֶה מִסְפָּר חִיַּגְתָּ (חִיַּגְתְּ)?	What number are you calling?
הַקַּו תָּפוּס.	The line's engaged.
אֵין תְּשׁוּבָה.	There's no answer.
חִיַּגְתָּ (חִיַּגְתְּ) מִסְפָּר לֹא נָכוֹן.	You've got the wrong number.
הַטֶּלֶפוֹן מְקוּלְקָל.	The phone is out of order.
רַק רֶגַע.	Just a moment.
חַכֵּה, בְּבַקָּשָׁה.	Hold on, please.
הוּא/הִיא לֹא פֹּה כָּרֶגַע.	He's/She's out at the moment.

Doctor

Medical assistance is obtainable at all times. Most doctors generally speak English and other foreign languages. You are strongly recommended to take out your own private health insurance; E111 forms are not valid in Israel.

General כְּלָלִי

Can you get me a doctor?	תּוּכַל (תּוּכְלִי) לְהַשִּׂיג לִי רוֹפֵא?	**tukhal** (tukh**li**) leha**sig** li ro**fe**
Is there a doctor here?	יֵשׁ כָּאן רוֹפֵא?	yesh kan ro**fe**
I need a doctor, quickly.	אֲנִי זָקוּק (זְקוּקָה) לְרוֹפֵא מָהֵר.	**ani** za**kuk** (zeku**ka**) lero**fe** ma**her**
Where can I find a doctor who speaks English?	אֵיפֹה אוּכַל לִמְצֹא רוֹפֵא דּוֹבֵר אַנְגְּלִית?	**ey**fo u**khal** lim**tzo** ro**fe** do**ver** ang**lit**
Where's the surgery (doctor's office)?	אֵיפֹה הַמִּרְפָּאָה?	**ey**fo hamirpaa
What are the surgery (office) hours?	מַה שְׁעוֹת הַקַּבָּלָה?	ma sheo**t** hakabala
Could the doctor come to see me here?	הָרוֹפֵא יוּכַל לָבוֹא אֵלַי?	haro**fe** yu**khal** la**vo** el**ay**
What time can the doctor come?	מָתַי יוּכַל הָרוֹפֵא לָבוֹא?	ma**tay** yu**khal** haro**fe** la**vo**
Can you recommend a/an ...?	תּוּכַל (תּוּכְלִי) לְהַמְלִיץ עַל ...?	tu**khal** (tukh**li**) leham**litz** al
general practitioner	רוֹפֵא כְּלָלִי	ro**fe** kla**li**
children's doctor	רוֹפֵא יְלָדִים	ro**fe** yela**dim**
eye specialist	רוֹפֵא עֵינַיִם	ro**fe** ey**na**yim
gynaecologist	רוֹפֵא נָשִׁים	ro**fe** na**shim**
Can I have an appointment ...?	אֶפְשָׁר לְקַבֵּל תּוֹר ...?	ef**shar** leka**bel** tor
tomorrow	לְמָחָר	lema**ḥar**
as soon as possible	בְּהֶקְדֵּם הָאֶפְשָׁרִי	behek**dem** haef**shari**

CHEMIST'S, see page 108

Parts of the body חלקי הגוף

appendix	תוספתן	tosef**tan**
arm	זרוע	**zro**a
back	גב	gav
bladder	שלפוחית שתן	shalpu**ḥit** ha**she**ten
bone	עצם	**e**tzem
bowel	מעיים	me**a**yim
breast	שד	shad
chest	חזה	ḥa**ze**
ear	אוזן	**o**zen
eye(s)	עין (עיניים)	**a**yin (ey**na**yim)
face	פנים	pa**nim**
finger	אצבע	**etz**ba
foot	כף רגל	kaf **re**gel
genitals	אברי המין	ev**rey** ha**min**
gland	בלוטה	balu**ta**
hand	יד	yad
head	ראש	rosh
heart	לב	lev
jaw	לסת	**le**set
joint	מפרק	mi**frak**
kidney	כליה	kil**ya**
knee	ברך	**be**rekh
leg	רגל	**re**gel
ligament	מיתר	mey**tar**
lip	שפה	sa**fa**
liver	כבד	ka**ved**
lung	ריאה	**rea**
mouth	פה	pe
muscle	שריר	shrir
neck	צוואר	tza**var**
nerve	עצב	**atzav**
nervous system	מערכת העצבים	maa**re**khet haatza**bim**
nose	אף	af
rib	צלע	**tze**la
shoulder	כתף	ka**tef**
skin	עור	or
spine	עמוד השדרה	**amud** ha**shidra**
stomach	קיבה	key**va**
tendon	גיד	gid
thigh	ירך	ya**rekh**
throat	גרון	ga**ron**
thumb	בוהן	**bo**hen
toe	אצבע הרגל	**etz**ba ha**re**gel
tongue	לשון	la**shon**
tonsils	שקדים	shke**dim**
vein	וריד	va**rid**

Accident—Injury תְּאוּנָה—פְּצִיעָה

There's been an accident.	קָרְתָה תְּאוּנָה.	kar**ta** teu**na**
My child has had a fall.	הַיֶּלֶד שֶׁלִּי נָפַל.	ha**ye**led she**li** na**fal**
He/She has hurt his/her head.	הוּא/הִיא נִפְגַּע/נִפְגְּעָה בָּרֹאשׁ.	hu/hi nif**ga**/nifge**a** ba**rosh**
He's/She's unconscious.	הוּא/הִיא חֲסַר/חַסְרַת הַכָּרָה.	hu/hi ḥa**sar**/ḥas**rat** haka**ra**
He's/She's bleeding (heavily).	הוּא/הִיא מְדַמֵּם/מְדַמֶּמֶת (קָשֶׁה).	hu/hi meda**mem**/ meda**me**met (ka**she**)
He's/She's (seriously) injured.	הוּא/הִיא נִפְצַע/נִפְצְעָה (קָשֶׁה).	hu/hi nif**tza**/niftze**a** (ka**she**)
His/Her arm is broken.	הַזְּרוֹעַ שֶׁלּוֹ/שֶׁלָּהּ שְׁבוּרָה.	haz**roa** she**lo**/she**la** shvu**ra**
His/Her ankle is swollen.	הַקַּרְסֹל שֶׁלּוֹ/שֶׁלָּהּ נָפוּחַ.	hakar**sol** she**lo**/she**la** nafu**aḥ**
I've been stung.	נֶעֱקַצְתִּי.	nee**katzti**
I've got something in my eye.	יֵשׁ לִי מַשֶּׁהוּ בָּעַיִן.	yesh li **ma**shehu ba**a**yin
I've got a/an ...	יֵשׁ לִי ...	yesh li
blister	בּוּעָה	bu**a**
bruise	חַבּוּרָה	ḥabu**ra**
burn	כְּוִיָּה	kvi**ya**
cut	חֲתָךְ	ḥa**takh**
graze	שִׁפְשׁוּף	shif**shuf**
insect bite	עֲקִיצַת חָרָק	aki**tzat** ḥa**rak**
lump	תְּפִיחָה	tfi**ḥa**
rash	פְּרִיחָה	pri**ḥa**
sting	עֲקִיצָה	aki**tza**
swelling	נְפִיחוּת	nefi**ḥut**
wound	פֶּצַע	**pe**tza
Could you have a look at it?	תּוּכַל (תּוּכְלִי) לְהִסְתַּכֵּל בְּזֶה?	tu**khal** (tukh**li**) lehista**kel** be**ze**
I can't move my ...	אֵינֶנִּי יָכוֹל (יְכוֹלָה) לְהָזִיז אֶת הַ... שֶׁלִּי.	eyn**e**ni ya**khol** (yekho**la**) leha**ziz** et ha... she**li**
It hurts.	זֶה כּוֹאֵב.	ze ko**ev**

אֵיפֹה זֶה כּוֹאֵב?	Where does it hurt?
אֵיזֶה מִין כְּאֵב זֶה?	What kind of pain is it?
קֵהֶה/חַד/דּוֹפֵק	dull/sharp/throbbing
כָּל הַזְּמַן/מִפַּעַם לְפַעַם	constant/on and off
זֶה ...	It's ...
שָׁבוּר/נָקוּעַ	broken/sprained
נָקוּעַ/קָרוּעַ	dislocated/torn
אַתָּה (אַתְּ) זָקוּק (זְקוּקָה) לְצִלּוּם רֶנְטְגֶן.	I'd like you to have an X-ray.
נִצְטָרֵךְ לָשִׂים אֵת זֶה בְּגֶבֶס.	We'll have to put it in plaster.
יֵשׁ זִהוּם.	It's infected.
קִבַּלְתָּ (קִבַּלְתְּ) חִסּוּן נֶגֶד טֶטָנוּס?	Have you been vaccinated against tetanus?
אֶתֵּן לְךָ (לָךְ) מַשֶּׁהוּ נֶגֶד כְּאֵבִים.	I'll give you a painkiller.

Illness מַחֲלָה

I'm not feeling well.	אֵינֶנִּי מַרְגִּישׁ (מַרְגִּישָׁה) טוֹב.	ey**ne**ni mar**gish** (margi**sha**) tov
I'm ill.	אֲנִי חוֹלֶה (חוֹלָה).	**ani** ḥ**ole** (ḥ**ola**)
I feel ...	אֲנִי מַרְגִּישׁ (מַרְגִּישָׁה) ...	**ani** mar**gish** (margi**sha**)
dizzy	סְחַרְחוֹרֶת	seḥar**ḥo**ret
nauseous	בְּחִילָה	beḥi**la**
shivery	צְמַרְמֹרֶת	tzemar**mo**ret
I have a temperature (fever).	יֵשׁ לִי חֹם.	yesh li ḥ**om**
My temperature is 38 degrees.	יֵשׁ לִי שְׁלֹשִׁים וּשְׁמוֹנֶה מַעֲלוֹת.	yesh li shlo**shim** ush**mone** maa**lot**
I've been vomiting.	יֵשׁ לִי הֲקָאוֹת.	yesh li haka**ot**
I'm constipated/I've got diarrhoea.	יֵשׁ לִי עֲצִירוּת/יֵשׁ לִי שִׁלְשׁוּל.	yesh li atzi**rut**/yesh li shil**shul**
My ... hurt(s).	הַ... שֶׁלִּי כּוֹאֵב.	ha... she**li** ko**ev**
I've got (a/an) ...	יֵשׁ לִי ...	yesh li
asthma	אַסְתְּמָה	**ast**ma
backache	כְּאֵבֵי גַּב	kee**vey** gav
cold	הִצְטַנְּנוּת	hitztane**nut**
cough	שִׁעוּל	shi**ul**

cramps	התכווצויות	hitkavtzu**yot**
earache	כאב אוזניים	ke**ev** oz**na**yim
hay fever	קדחת השחת	ka**da**ḥat ha**sha**ḥat
headache	כאב ראש	ke**ev** rosh
indigestion	קלקול קיבה	kil**kul** ke**va**
nosebleed	דמום מהאף	di**mum** meha**af**
palpitations	רעידות לב	rei**dot** lev
rheumatism	שגרון	shiga**ron**
sore throat	כאב גרון	ke**ev** ga**ron**
stiff neck	ערף נוקשה	**o**ref nuk**she**
stomach ache	כאב קיבה	ke**ev** ke**va**
sunstroke	מכת שמש	ma**kat she**mesh
I have difficulties breathing.	קשה לי לנשום.	ka**she** li lin**shom**
I have chest pains.	יש לי כאבים בחזה.	yesh li ke**evim** ba**ḥaze**
I had a heart attack ... years ago.	היה לי התקף לב לפני ... שנים.	ha**ya** li het**kef** lev lif**ney** ... sha**nim**
My blood pressure is too high/too low.	לחץ הדם שלי גבוה מדי/נמוך מדי.	**la**ḥatz ha**dam** she**li** ga**vo**ha mi**day**/na**mukh** mi**day**
I'm allergic to ...	אני אלרגי (אלרגית) ל...	**ani** aler**gi** (**al**er**git**) le
I'm diabetic.	אני חולה (חולת) סכרת.	**ani** ḥ**ole** (ḥo**lat**) sa**ke**ret

Women's section לנשים

I have period pains.	יש לי כאבי מחזור.	yesh li ke**evey** ma**ḥazor**
I have a vaginal infection.	יש לי זהום נרתיק.	yesh li da**le**ket nar**tik**
I'm on the pill.	אני לוקחת גלולות למניעת הריון.	**ani** loka**ḥ**at glu**lot** limni**at** hera**yon**
I haven't had a period for 2 months.	אין לי מחזור כבר חדשיים.	eyn li maḥ**azor** kvar ḥod**sha**yim
I'm (3 months) pregnant.	אני (שלשה חדשים) בהריון.	**ani** (shlo**sha** ḥoda**shim**) behera**yon**

כַּמָּה זְמַן אַתָּה מַרְגִּישׁ (אַתְּ מַרְגִּישָׁה) כָּכָה?	How long have you been feeling like this?
זוֹ הַפַּעַם הָרִאשׁוֹנָה שֶׁיֵּשׁ לְךָ (לָךְ) דָּבָר כָּזֶה?	Is this the first time you've had this?
אֶמְדּוֹד לְךָ (לָךְ) חֹם/לַחַץ דָּם.	I'll take your temperature/ blood pressure.
לְהַפְשִׁיל אֶת הַשַּׁרְווּל בְּבַקָּשָׁה.	Roll up your sleeve, please.
בְּבַקָּשָׁה לְהִתְפַּשֵּׁט (עַד הַמֹּתֶן).	Please undress (down to the waist).
בְּבַקָּשָׁה לִשְׁכַּב כָּאן.	Please lie down over here.
פְּתַח (פִּתְחִי) אֶת הַפֶּה.	Open your mouth.
לִנְשׁוֹם עָמוֹק.	Breathe deeply.
לְהִשְׁתַּעֵל בְּבַקָּשָׁה.	Cough, please.
אֵיפֹה זֶה כּוֹאֵב?	Where does it hurt?
יֵשׁ לְךָ (לָךְ) ...	You've got (a/an) ...
דַּלֶּקֶת תּוֹסֶפְתָּן	appendicitis
דַּלֶּקֶת שַׁלְפּוּחִית הַשֶּׁתֶן	cystitis
דַּלֶּקֶת קֵיבָה	gastritis
שַׁפַּעַת	flu
דַּלֶּקֶת ...	inflammation of ...
הַרְעָלַת קֵיבָה	food poisoning
צַהֶבֶת	jaundice
מַחֲלַת מִין	venereal disease
דַּלֶּקֶת רֵאוֹת	pneumonia
חַצֶּבֶת	measles
זֶה (לֹא) מִדַּבֵּק.	It's (not) contagious.
זוֹ אַלֶּרְגְיָה.	It's an allergy.
אֶתֵּן לְךָ (לָךְ) זְרִיקָה.	I'll give you an injection.
אֲנִי זָקוּק (זְקוּקָה) לְדוּגְמַת דָּם/צוֹאָה/שֶׁתֶן.	I want a specimen of your blood/stools/urine.
תִּצְטָרֵךְ (תִּצְטָרְכִי) לְהִשָּׁאֵר בַּמִּטָּה ... יָמִים.	You must stay in bed for ... days.
אֲנִי שׁוֹלֵחַ (שׁוֹלַחַת) אוֹתְךָ (אוֹתָךְ) לְמוּמְחֶה.	I want you to see a specialist.
אַתָּה צָרִיךְ (אַתְּ צְרִיכָה) לָלֶכֶת לְבֵית-חוֹלִים לִבְדִיקָה כְּלָלִית.	I want you to go to the hospital for a general check-up.

Prescription—Treatment מִרְשָׁם—טִפּוּל

This is my usual medicine.	זוֹ הַתְּרוּפָה הָרְגִילָה שֶׁלִּי.	zo hatru**fa** haregi**la** she**li**
Can you give me a prescription for this?	תּוּכַל (תּוּכְלִי) לָתֵת לִי מִרְשָׁם לָזֶה?	**tukhal** (**tukhli**) la**tet** li mir**sham** **leze**
Can you prescribe a/an/some ...?	תּוּכַל (תּוּכְלִי) לִרְשׁוֹם לִי ...?	**tukhal** (**tukhli**) lir**shom** **li**
antidepressant	תְּרוּפָה נֶגֶד דִּכָּאוֹן	tru**fa** **ne**ged dika**on**
sleeping pills	כַּדּוּרֵי שֵׁינָה	kadu**rey** she**na**
tranquillizer	כַּדּוּרֵי הַרְגָּעָה	kadu**rey** harga**a**
I'm allergic to certain antibiotics/penicillin.	אֲנִי אַלֶרְגִּי (אַלֶרְגִּית) לְאַנְטִיבְּיוֹטִיקָה מְסוּיֶּמֶת/פֶּנִיצִילִין.	**a**ni aler**gi** (aler**git**) leantibi**yo**tika mesu**ye**met/ penitzi**lin**
I don't want anything too strong.	אֵינֶנִּי רוֹצֶה (רוֹצָה) שׁוּם דָּבָר יוֹתֵר מִדַּי חָזָק.	ey**ne**ni rot**ze** (rot**za**) shum da**var** yo**ter** mi**day** ḥa**zak**
How many times a day should I take it?	כַּמָּה פְּעָמִים בְּיוֹם לָקַחַת אֶת זֶה?	**ka**ma pea**mim** be**yom** laka**ḥat** et ze
Must I swallow them whole?	צָרִיךְ לִבְלוֹעַ אוֹתָם כְּמוֹ שֶׁהֵם?	tza**rikh** liv**lo**a o**tam** kmo she**hem**

אֵיזֶה טִפּוּל אַתָּה מְקַבֵּל (אַתְּ מְקַבֶּלֶת)?	What treatment are you having?
אֵיזוֹ תְּרוּפָה אַתָּה לוֹקֵחַ (אַתְּ לוֹקַחַת)?	What medicine are you taking?
בִּזְרִיקָה אוֹ בַּפֶּה?	By injection or orally?
קַח (קְחִי) ... כַּפִּיּוֹת מֵהַתְּרוּפָה הַזּוֹ ...	Take ... teaspoons of this medicine ...
קַח (קְחִי) כַּדּוּר אֶחָד עִם כּוֹס מַיִם ...	Take one pill with a glass of water...
כָּל ... שָׁעוֹת	every ... hours
... פְּעָמִים בְּיוֹם	... times a day
לִפְנֵי/אַחֲרֵי כָּל אֲרוּחָה	before/after each meal
בַּבֹּקֶר/בָּעֶרֶב	in the morning/at night
אִם יֵשׁ כְּאֵבִים	if there is any pain
בְּמֶשֶׁךְ ... יָמִים	for ... days

Fee תַּשְׁלוּם

How much do I owe you?	כַּמָּה צָרִיךְ לְשַׁלֵּם?	**ka**ma tza**rikh** lesha**lem**
May I have a receipt for my health insurance?	אֶפְשָׁר לְקַבֵּל קַבָּלָה לְבִטּוּחַ שֶׁלִּי?	ef**shar** leka**bel** kaba**la** labi**tu**aḥ she**li**
Can I have a medical certificate?	אוּכַל לְקַבֵּל תְּעוּדָה רְפוּאִית?	u**khal** leka**bel** teu**da** refu**it**
Would you fill in this health insurance form, please?	תּוּכַל (תּוּכְלִי) לְמַלֵּא אֶת טֹפֶס הַבִּטּוּחַ הַזֶּה, בְּבַקָּשָׁה?	tu**khal** (tukh**li**) lema**le** et **to**fes habi**tu**aḥ ha**ze** bevaka**sha**

Hospital בֵּית חוֹלִים

Please notify my family.	הוֹדִיעוּ לְמִשְׁפַּחְתִּי, בְּבַקָּשָׁה.	ho**di**u lemishpaḥ**ti** bevaka**sha**
What are the visiting hours?	מַה שְׁעוֹת הַבִּקּוּר?	ma she**ot** habi**kur**
When can I get up?	מָתַי אוּכַל לָקוּם?	ma**tay** u**khal** la**kum**
When will the doctor come?	מָתַי יָבֹא הָרוֹפֵא?	ma**tay** ya**vo** haro**fe**
I'm in pain.	יֵשׁ לִי כְּאֵבִים.	yesh li kee**vim**
I can't eat/sleep.	אֵינֶנִּי יָכוֹל (יְכוֹלָה) לֶאֱכוֹל/לִישׁוֹן.	ey**ne**ni ya**khol** (yekho**la**) lee**khol**/li**shon**
Where is the bell?	אֵיפֹה הַפַּעֲמוֹן?	**ey**fo hapaa**mon**

nurse	אָחוֹת	a**ḥot**
patient	חוֹלֶה	**ḥo**le
anaesthetic	מְאַלְחֵשׁ	meal**ḥesh**
blood transfusion	עֵרוּי דָּם	i**ruy** dam
injection	זְרִיקָה	zri**ka**
operation	נִתּוּחַ	ni**tu**aḥ
bed	מִטָּה	mi**ta**
bedpan	סִיר-מִטָּה	sir-mi**ta**
thermometer	מַדְחוֹם	mad**ḥom**

Dentist רוֹפֵא שִׁנַּיִם

If you have to go to the dentist, read your insurance documents first as most policies cover emergency dental treatment (for the immediate relief of pain).

Can you recommend a good dentist?	תּוּכַל (תּוּכְלִי) לְהַמְלִיץ עַל רוֹפֵא שִׁנַּיִם טוֹב?	tukhal (tukhli) lehamlitz al rofe shinayim tov
Can I make an (urgent) appointment to see Dr ...?	אוּכַל לְבַקֵּשׁ תּוֹר (דָּחוּף) לִרְאוֹת אֶת דּוֹקְטוֹר ...?	ukhal levakesh tor (dahuf) lirot et doktor
Couldn't you make it earlier?	אוּלַי אֶפְשָׁר לִפְנֵי כֵן?	ulay efshar lifney khen
I have a broken tooth.	יֵשׁ לִי שֵׁן שְׁבוּרָה.	yesh li shen shvura
I have toothache.	יֵשׁ לִי כְּאֵב שִׁנַּיִם.	yesh li keev shinayim
I have an abscess.	יֵשׁ לִי מוּרְסָה.	yesh li mursa
This tooth hurts.	הַשֵּׁן הַזּוֹ כּוֹאֶבֶת.	hashen hazo koevet
at the top	לְמַעְלָה	lemala
at the bottom	לְמַטָּה	lemata
at the front	לְפָנִים	lefanim
at the back	מֵאָחוֹר	meahor
Can you fix it temporarily?	תּוּכַל (תּוּכְלִי) לְסַדֵּר אֶת זֶה בְּאֹפֶן זְמַנִּי?	tukhal (tukhli) lesader et ze beofen zmani
I don't want it pulled out.	אֵינֶנִּי רוֹצֶה (רוֹצָה) לַעֲקֹר אוֹתָהּ.	eyneni rotze (rotza) laakor ota
Could you give me an anaesthetic?	אֶפְשָׁר לְקַבֵּל אִלְחוּשׁ?	efshar lekabel ilhush
I've lost a filling.	נָפְלָה לִי סְתִימָה.	nafla li stima
My gums ...	הַחֲנִיכַיִם שֶׁלִּי ...	hahanikhayim sheli
are very sore	כּוֹאֲבוֹת מְאֹד	koavot meod
are bleeding	מְדַמְּמוֹת	medamemot
I've broken my dentures.	הַתּוֹתָבוֹת שֶׁלִּי נִשְׁבְּרוּ.	hatotavot sheli nishberu
Can you repair my dentures?	תּוּכַל (תּוּכְלִי) לְתַקֵּן אֶת הַתּוֹתָבוֹת שֶׁלִּי?	tukhal (tukhli) letaken et hatotavot sheli
When will they be ready?	מָתַי הֵן תִּהְיֶינָה מוּכָנוֹת?	matay hen tihiyena mukhanot

Reference section

Where do you come from? ?מֵאֵיפֹה אַתָּה (אַתְּ)

Africa	אַפְרִיקָה	**afrika**
Asia	אַסְיָה	**asiya**
Australia	אוֹסְטְרַלְיָה	os**tra**liya
Europe	אֵירוֹפָּה	e**ro**pa
North America	צְפוֹן אָמֵרִיקָה	tzfon am**e**rika
South America	דְּרוֹם אָמֵרִיקָה	drom am**e**rika
Algeria	אַלְג'יר	al**jir**
Austria	אוֹסְטְרִיָה	**os**triya
Belgium	בֶּלְגְיָה	**bel**giya
Canada	קָנָדָה	**ka**nada
China	סִין	sin
Commonwealth of Independent States	מְדִינוֹת חֶבֶר הָעַמִּים	medi**not** **ḥe**ver haa**mim**
Denmark	דֶּנְמַרְק	**den**mark
England	אַנְגְלִיָה	**ang**liya
Egypt	מִצְרַיִם	mitz**ra**im
France	צָרְפַת	tzar**fat**
Germany	גֶּרְמַנְיָה	ger**ma**niya
Great Britain	בְּרִיטַנְיָה הַגְּדוֹלָה	bri**ta**niya hagdo**la**
Greece	יָוָן	ya**van**
India	הוֹדוּ	**ho**du
Ireland	אִירְלַנְד	**ir**land
Israel	יִשְׂרָאֵל	yisra**el**
Italy	אִיטַלְיָה	**i**talia
Japan	יַפָּן	ya**pan**
Jordan	יַרְדֵּן	yar**den**
Lebanon	לְבָנוֹן	leva**non**
Morocco	מָרוֹקוֹ	ma**ro**ko
Netherlands	הוֹלַנְד	**ho**land
New Zealand	נְיוּ זִילַנְד	nyu **zi**land
Norway	נוֹרְבֶגְיָה	nor**ve**giya
Portugal	פּוֹרְטוּגָל	portu**gal**
Russia	רוּסְיָה	**ru**siya
Scotland	סְקוֹטְלַנְד	**skot**land
South Africa	דְּרוֹם אַפְרִיקָה	drom **af**rika
Sweden	שְׁבֶדְיָה	**shve**diya
Switzerland	שְׁוַיצַרְיָה	shvi**tza**riya
Syria	סוּרְיָה	**su**ria
Tunisia	טוּנִיס	**tu**nis
Turkey	טוּרְקִיָה	**tur**kiya
United States	אַרְצוֹת הַבְּרִית	**ar**tzot hab**rit**

Numbers מִסְפָּרִים

0	אֶפֶס	**e**fes
1	אֶחָד	e**ḥad**
2	שְׁנַיִם	sh**na**yim
3	שְׁלֹשָׁה	shlo**sha**
4	אַרְבָּעָה	arba**a**
5	חֲמִשָּׁה	ḥami**sha**
6	שִׁשָּׁה	shi**sha**
7	שִׁבְעָה	shiv**a**
8	שְׁמוֹנָה	shmo**na**
9	תִּשְׁעָה	tish**a**
10	עֲשָׂרָה	asa**ra**
11	אַחַד־עָשָׂר	a**ḥad**-a**sar**
12	שְׁנֵים־עָשָׂר	shneym-a**sar**
13	שְׁלֹשָׁה־עָשָׂר	shlo**sha**-a**sar**
14	אַרְבָּעָה־עָשָׂר	arba**a**-a**sar**
15	חֲמִשָּׁה־עָשָׂר	ḥami**sha**-a**sar**
16	שִׁשָּׁה־עָשָׂר	shi**sha**-a**sar**
17	שִׁבְעָה־עָשָׂר	shiv**a**-a**sar**
18	שְׁמוֹנָה־עָשָׂר	shmo**na**-a**sar**
19	תִּשְׁעָה־עָשָׂר	tish**a**-a**sar**
20	עֶשְׂרִים	es**rim**
21	עֶשְׂרִים וְאֶחָד	es**rim** vee**ḥad**
22	עֶשְׂרִים וּשְׁנַיִם	es**rim** ush**na**yim
23	עֶשְׂרִים וּשְׁלֹשָׁה	es**rim** ushlo**sha**
24	עֶשְׂרִים וְאַרְבָּעָה	es**rim** vearba**a**
25	עֶשְׂרִים וַחֲמִשָּׁה	es**rim** veḥami**sha**
26	עֶשְׂרִים וְשִׁשָּׁה	es**rim** veshi**sha**
27	עֶשְׂרִים וְשִׁבְעָה	es**rim** veshiv**a**
28	עֶשְׂרִים וּשְׁמוֹנָה	es**rim** ushmo**na**
29	עֶשְׂרִים וְתִשְׁעָה	es**rim** vetish**a**
30	שְׁלֹשִׁים	shlo**shim**
31	שְׁלֹשִׁים וְאֶחָד	shlo**shim** vee**ḥad**
32	שְׁלֹשִׁים וּשְׁנַיִם	shlo**shim** ush**na**yim
33	שְׁלֹשִׁים וּשְׁלֹשָׁה	shlo**shim** ushlo**sha**
40	אַרְבָּעִים	arba**im**
41	אַרְבָּעִים וְאֶחָד	arba**im** vee**ḥad**
42	אַרְבָּעִים וּשְׁנַיִם	arba**im** ush**na**yim
43	אַרְבָּעִים וּשְׁלֹשָׁה	arba**im** ushlo**sha**
50	חֲמִשִּׁים	ḥami**shim**
51	חֲמִשִּׁים וְאֶחָד	ḥami**shim** vee**ḥad**
52	חֲמִשִּׁים וּשְׁנַיִם	ḥami**shim** ush**na**yim
53	חֲמִשִּׁים וּשְׁלֹשָׁה	ḥami**shim** ushlo**sha**
60	שִׁשִּׁים	shi**shim**
61	שִׁשִּׁים וְאֶחָד	shi**shim** vee**ḥad**
62	שִׁשִּׁים וּשְׁנַיִם	shi**shim** ush**na**yim

63	שִׁשִּׁים וּשְׁלֹשָׁה	shi**shim** ushlo**sha**
70	שִׁבְעִים	shiv**im**
71	שִׁבְעִים וְאֶחָד	shiv**im** vee**ḥad**
72	שִׁבְעִים וּשְׁנַיִם	shiv**im** ush**na**yim
73	שִׁבְעִים וּשְׁלֹשָׁה	shiv**im** ushlo**sha**
80	שְׁמוֹנִים	shmo**nim**
81	שְׁמוֹנִים וְאֶחָד	shmo**nim** vee**ḥad**
82	שְׁמוֹנִים וּשְׁנַיִם	shmo**nim** ush**na**yim
83	שְׁמוֹנִים וּשְׁלֹשָׁה	shmo**nim** ushlo**sha**
90	תִּשְׁעִים	tish**im**
91	תִּשְׁעִים וְאֶחָד	tish**im** vee**ḥad**
92	תִּשְׁעִים וּשְׁנַיִם	tish**im** ush**na**yim
93	תִּשְׁעִים וּשְׁלֹשָׁה	tish**im** ushlo**sha**
100	מֵאָה	me**a**
101	מֵאָה וְאֶחָד	me**a** vee**ḥad**
102	מֵאָה וּשְׁנַיִם	me**a** ush**na**yim
110	מֵאָה וַעֲשָׂרָה	me**a** vaasa**ra**
120	מֵאָה וְעֶשְׂרִים	me**a** vees**rim**
130	מֵאָה וּשְׁלֹשִׁים	me**a** ushlo**shim**
140	מֵאָה וְאַרְבָּעִים	me**a** vearba**im**
150	מֵאָה וַחֲמִשִּׁים	me**a** veḥami**shim**
160	מֵאָה וְשִׁשִּׁים	me**a** veshi**shim**
170	מֵאָה וְשִׁבְעִים	me**a** veshiv**im**
180	מֵאָה וּשְׁמוֹנִים	me**a** ushmo**nim**
190	מֵאָה וְתִשְׁעִים	me**a** vetish**im**
200	מָאתַיִם	ma**ta**yim
300	שְׁלֹשׁ מֵאוֹת	shlosh me**ot**
400	אַרְבַּע מֵאוֹת	**ar**ba me**ot**
500	חֲמֵשׁ מֵאוֹת	ḥa**mesh** me**ot**
600	שֵׁשׁ מֵאוֹת	shesh me**ot**
700	שְׁבַע מֵאוֹת	shva me**ot**
800	שְׁמוֹנֶה מֵאוֹת	shmo**ne** me**ot**
900	תְּשַׁע מֵאוֹת	tsha me**ot**
1000	אֶלֶף	**e**lef
1100	אֶלֶף וּמֵאָה	**e**lef ume**a**
1200	אֶלֶף וּמָאתַיִם	**e**lef uma**ta**yim
2000	אַלְפַּיִם	al**pa**yim
5000	חֲמֵשֶׁת אֲלָפִים	ḥa**me**shet ala**fim**
10,000	עֲשֶׂרֶת אֲלָפִים	a**se**ret ala**fim**
50,000	חֲמִשִּׁים אֶלֶף	ḥami**shim** **e**lef
100,000	מֵאָה אֶלֶף	me**a** **e**lef
1,000,000	מִלְיוֹן	mil**yon**
1,000,000,000	בִּלְיוֹן	bil**yon**

first	רִאשׁוֹן	ri**shon**
second	שֵׁנִי	she**ni**
third	שְׁלִישִׁי	shli**shi**
fourth	רְבִיעִי	rev**ii**
fifth	חֲמִישִׁי	ḥami**shi**
sixth	שִׁשִּׁי	shi**shi**
seventh	שְׁבִיעִי	shv**ii**
eighth	שְׁמִינִי	shmi**ni**
ninth	תְּשִׁיעִי	tsh**ii**
tenth	עֲשִׂירִי	asi**ri**
once/twice	פַּעַם/פַּעֲמַיִם	**pa**am/paa**ma**yim
three times	שָׁלֹשׁ פְּעָמִים	sha**losh** pea**mim**
a half	חֵצִי	**ḥe**tzi
half a ...	חֲצִי ...	ḥa**tzi**
half of ...	חֲצִי ...	ḥa**tzi**
half (adj.)	חֲצִי	ḥa**tzi**
a quarter/one third	רֶבַע/שְׁלִישׁ	**re**va/shlish
a pair of	זוּג	zug
a dozen	תְּרֵיסָר	trey**sar**
one per cent	אָחוּז אֶחָד	**aḥuz** e**ḥad**
3.4%	שְׁלֹשָׁה נְקוּדָה אַרְבָּעָה אֲחוּזִים – 3:4	shlo**sha** neku**da** arbaa aḥu**zim**

Date and Time תַּאֲרִיךְ וְשָׁעָה

Year and age שָׁנָה וְגִיל

1981	אֶלֶף תְּשַׁע מֵאוֹת שְׁמוֹנִים וְאֶחָד	elef tsha me**ot** shmo**nim** vee**ḥad**
1993	אֶלֶף תְּשַׁע מֵאוֹת תִּשְׁעִים וְשָׁלֹשׁ	elef tsha me**ot** tish**im** vesha**losh**
2005	אַלְפַּיִם וְחָמֵשׁ	al**pa**yim veḥa**mesh**
year	שָׁנָה	sha**na**
leap year	שָׁנָה מְעוּבֶּרֶת	sha**na** meu**be**ret
decade	עָשׂוֹר	a**sor**
century	מֵאָה	me**a**
this year	בְּשָׁנָה זוֹ	besha**na** zo
last year	בַּשָּׁנָה שֶׁעָבְרָה	basha**na** sheav**ra**
next year	בַּשָּׁנָה הַבָּאָה	basha**na** haba**a**
each year	כָּל שָׁנָה	kol sha**na**
2 years ago	לִפְנֵי שְׁנָתַיִם	lif**ney** shna**ta**yim
in one year	בְּעוֹד שָׁנָה	be**od** sha**na**
in the nineties	בִּשְׁנוֹת הַתִּשְׁעִים	bish**not** hatish**im**
the 16th century	בַּמֵּאָה הַשֵּׁשׁ עֶשְׂרֵה	bame**a** ha**shesh** es**re**
in the 20th century	בַּמֵּאָה הָעֶשְׂרִים	bame**a** haes**rim**
How old are you?	בֶּן (בַּת) כַּמָּה אַתָּה (אַתְּ)?	ben (bat) **kama ata** (at)

I'm 30 years old.	אֲנִי בֵּן (בַּת) שְׁלֹשִׁים.	**ani** ben (bat) shlo**shim**
He/She was born in 1960.	הוּא/הִיא נוֹלַד (נוֹלְדָה) בְּאֶלֶף תְּשַׁע מֵאוֹת שִׁשִּׁים.	hu/hi no**lad** (nol**da**) bee**lef** tsha me**ot** shi**shim**
What is his/her age?	מַה גִּילוֹ/גִּילָהּ?	ma gi**lo**/gi**la**
Children under 16 are not admitted.	אֵין כְּנִיסָה לִילָדִים מִתַּחַת לְגִיל שֵׁשׁ עֶשְׂרֵה.	eyn kni**sa** lila**dim** mita**ḥ**at le**gil** shesh es**re**

Seasons עונות

spring/summer	אָבִיב/קַיִץ	a**viv**/**ka**yitz
autumn/winter	סְתָיו/חֹרֶף	stav/**ḥo**ref
in spring	בְּאָבִיב	baa**viv**
during the summer	בְּמֶשֶׁךְ הַקַּיִץ	be**me**shekh ha**ka**yitz
in autumn	בִּסְתָיו	bas**tav**
during the winter	בְּמֶשֶׁךְ הַחֹרֶף	be**me**shekh ha**ḥo**ref
high season	בָּעוֹנָה	bao**na**
low season	מִחוּץ לָעוֹנָה	mi**ḥutz** lao**na**

Months חֳדָשִׁים

January	יָנוּאָר	**ya**nuar
February	פֶבְּרוּאָר	**feb**ruar
March	מֶרְץ	mertz
April	אַפְּרִיל	ap**ril**
May	מַאי	may
June	יוּנִי	**yu**ni
July	יוּלִי	**yu**li
August	אוֹגוּסְט	**o**gust
September	סֶפְּטֶמְבֶּר	sep**tem**ber
October	אוֹקְטוֹבֶּר	ok**to**ber
November	נוֹבֶמְבֶּר	no**vem**ber
December	דֶּצֶמְבֶּר	de**tzem**ber
in September	בִּסֶפְּטֶמְבֶּר	besep**tem**ber
since October	מֵאָז אוֹקְטוֹבֶּר	me**az** ok**to**ber
the beginning of January	תְּחִילַת יָנוּאָר	t**ḥ**i**lat** **ya**nuar
the middle of February	אֶמְצַע פֶבְּרוּאָר	**em**tza **feb**ruar
the end of March	סוֹף מֶרְץ	sof mertz

Days and Date יוֹם וְתַאֲרִיךְ

What day is it today?	אֵיזֶה יוֹם הַיּוֹם?	**ey**ze yom ha**yom**
Sunday	יוֹם רִאשׁוֹן	yom ri**shon**
Monday	יוֹם שֵׁנִי	yom she**ni**
Tuesday	יוֹם שְׁלִישִׁי	yom shli**shi**
Wednesday	יוֹם רְבִיעִי	yom re**vii**
Thursday	יוֹם חֲמִישִׁי	yom ḥami**shi**
Friday	יוֹם שִׁשִּׁי	yom shi**shi**
Saturday	שַׁבָּת	sha**bat**
It's ...	הַיּוֹם ...	ha**yom**
July 1	הָרִאשׁוֹן בְּיוּלִי	hari**shon** be**yu**li
March 10	הָעֲשִׂירִי בְּמֶרְץ	haasi**ri** be**mertz**
in the morning	בַּבֹּקֶר	ba**bo**ker
during the day	בְּמֶשֶׁךְ הַיּוֹם	be**me**shekh ha**yom**
in the afternoon	אַחֲרֵי הַצָּהֳרַיִם	aḥa**rey** hatzohor**a**yim
in the evening	בָּעֶרֶב	ba**e**rev
at night	בַּלַּיְלָה	ba**lay**la
the day before yesterday	שִׁלְשׁוֹם	shil**shom**
yesterday	אֶתְמוֹל	et**mol**
today	הַיּוֹם	ha**yom**
tomorrow	מָחָר	ma**ḥar**
the day after tomorrow	מָחֳרָתַיִם	moḥoro**ta**yim
the day before	הַיּוֹם הַקּוֹדֵם	ha**yom** hako**dem**
the next day	הַיּוֹם הַבָּא	ha**yom** ha**ba**
two days ago	לִפְנֵי יוֹמַיִם	lif**ney** yo**ma**yim
in three days' time	בְּעוֹד שְׁלֹשָׁה יָמִים	be**od** shlo**sha** ya**mim**
last week	בַּשָּׁבוּעַ שֶׁעָבַר	basha**vu**a shea**var**
next week	בַּשָּׁבוּעַ הַבָּא	basha**vu**a ha**ba**
for a fortnight (two weeks)	בְּמֶשֶׁךְ שְׁבוּעַיִם	be**me**shekh shvu**a**yim
birthday	יוֹם הוּלֶדֶת	yom hu**le**det
day off	יוֹם חֹפֶשׁ	yom **ḥo**fesh
holiday	חֻפְשָׁה	ḥuf**sha**
holidays/vacation	פַּגְרָה	pag**ra**
week	שָׁבוּעַ	sha**vu**a
weekend	סוֹף שָׁבוּעַ	sof sha**vu**a
working day	יוֹם חוֹל	yom ḥol

Public holidays חַגִים

Two kinds of calendar are in use in Israel. The Gregorian calendar is current in normal daily activities. However, newspapers, radio stations and official documents follow the Hebrew lunar calendar, and Jewish holidays fall on different Gregorian dates each year.

The months of the Hebrew calendar:

תִּשְׁרֵי **Tishrey** (September–October)	נִיסָן **Nisan** (March–April)
חֶשְׁוָן ḥesh**van** (October–November)	אִיָּר **Iyar** (April–May)
כִּסְלֵו Kis**lev** (November-December)	סִיוָן **Sivan** (May–June)
טֵבֵת **Tevet** (December–January)	תַּמּוּז **Tamuz** (June-July)
שְׁבָט Shvat (January–February)	אָב Av (July–August)
אֲדָר/אֲדָר בֵּית **Adar/Adar** bet (February–March)/in a leap year	אֱלוּל **Elul** (August–September)

The main festivals:

רֹאשׁ הַשָּׁנָה	**Rosh hashana**	New Year – 1st and 2nd Tishrey
יוֹם כִּפּוּר	**Yom Kipur**	Day of Atonement – 10th Tishrey
סֻכּוֹת	**Sukot**	Day of Tabernacles – 15th to 21st Tishrey
שִׂמְחַת תּוֹרָה	**Simḥ at Tora**	Festival of the Torah – in Tishrey
חֲנֻכָּה	**Ḥanuka**	Festival of Light/Festival of Maccabees – in Kislev
פֶּסַח	**Pesahi**	Passover or Festival of Freedom – 15th to 21st Nisan
יוֹם הָעַצְמָאוּת	**Yom Haatzmaut**	Day of Independence – 5th Iyar
שָׁבוּעוֹת	**Shavuot**	(Pentecost or Weeks - 6th Sivan)

There are many other feasts and days of remembrance — *Purim* (carnival commemorating deliverance in ancient Persia), *Tu Bishvat* (tree planting), *Tisha Beav* (Destruction of the temple), *Yom Hashoa* (Day of Rememberance of the Holocaust) and several minor religious fasts. Some of these are public holidays.

Greetings and wishes בְּרָכוֹת וְאִחוּלִים

Happy New Year!	שָׁנָה טוֹבָה!	sha**na** to**va**
Happy holiday!	חַג שָׂמֵחַ!	ḥag sa**meaḥ**
Have a peaceful Sabbath!	שַׁבָּת שָׁלוֹם	sha**bat** sha**lom**
Happy birthday!	יוֹם הוּלֶדֶת שָׂמֵחַ!	yom hu**le**det sa**meaḥ**
Best wishes!	בְּהַצְלָחָה!	behatzla**ḥa**
Congratulations!	מַזָּל טוֹב!	ma**zal** tov
Good luck/All the best!	בְּהַצְלָחָה!	behatzla**ḥa**
Have a good trip!	נְסִיעָה טוֹבָה!	nesi**a** to**va**
Have a good holiday!	חֹפֶשׁ נָעִים!	**ḥo**fesh na**im**
Best regards from …	אִחוּלִים מִ...	iḥu**lim** mi
My regards to …	אִחוּלִים לְ...	iḥu**lim** le

What time is it? מַה הַשָּׁעָה?

Official time uses the 24-hour clock, which means that, for example, 1.30 pm is expressed as 13.30. Israeli time is GMT + 2 hours (+ 3 in summer). The 24-hour clock is not used in everyday conversation.

Excuse me. Can you tell me the time?	סְלִיחָה , מַה הַשָּׁעָה?	sli**ḥa** ma hasha**a**
It's …	הַשָּׁעָה ...	hasha**a**
five past one	אַחַת וַחֲמִשָּׁה	a**ḥat** veḥami**sha**
ten past two	שְׁתַּיִם וַעֲשָׂרָה	sh**ta**yim veasa**ra**
a quarter past three	שָׁלֹשׁ וָרֶבַע	sha**losh** ve**re**va
twenty past four	אַרְבַּע וְעֶשְׂרִים	**ar**ba vees**rim**
twenty-five past five	חָמֵשׁ עֶשְׂרִים וְחָמֵשׁ	ha**mesh** es**rim** veḥa**mesh**
half past six	שֵׁשׁ וָחֵצִי	shesh ve**ḥe**tzi
twenty-five to seven	עֶשְׂרִים וַחֲמִשָּׁה לְשֶׁבַע	es**rim** veḥami**sha** le**she**va
twenty to eight	עֶשְׂרִים לִשְׁמוֹנֶה	es**rim** lishmo**ne**
a quarter to nine	רֶבַע לְתֵשַׁע	**re**va le**te**sha
ten to ten	עֲשָׂרָה לְעֶשֶׂר	asa**ra** le**e**ser
five to eleven	חֲמִשָּׁה לְאַחַת עֶשְׂרֵה	ḥami**sha** lea**ḥat** es**re**
twelve o'clock (noon/midnight)	שְׁתֵּים עֶשְׂרֵה (בַּצָּהֳרַיִם/בַּלַּיְלָה)	shteym es**re** (batzoho**ra**yim/ba**lay**la)

in the morning	בַּבֹּקֶר	ba**bo**ker
in the afternoon	אַחֲרֵי הַצָּהֳרַיִם	aḥa**rey** hatzoho**ra**yim
in the evening	בָּעֶרֶב	ba**e**rev
The train leaves at ...	הָרַכֶּבֶת יוֹצֵאת בְּ...	hara**ke**vet yo**tzet** be
13.04 (1.04 p.m.)	שְׁלֹשׁ עֶשְׂרֵה וְאַרְבַּע דַּקּוֹת (אַחַת וְאַרְבַּע דַּקּוֹת אַחֲרֵי הַצָּהֳרַיִם)	shlosh es**re** vear**ba** da**kot** (a**ḥat** vear**ba** da**kot** aḥa**rey** hatzoho**ra**yim)
0.40 (0.40 a.m.)	אֶפֶס וְאַרְבָּעִים (אַרְבָּעִים אַחֲרֵי חֲצוֹת)	**e**fes vearba**im** (arba**im** aḥa**rey** ḥa**tzot**)
in five minutes	בְּעוֹד חָמֵשׁ דַּקּוֹת	be**od** ḥa**mesh** da**kot**
in a quarter of an hour	בְּעוֹד רֶבַע שָׁעָה	be**od** **re**va sha**a**
half an hour ago	לִפְנֵי חֲצִי שָׁעָה	lif**ney** ḥa**tzi** sha**a**
about two hours	בְּעֵרֶךְ שְׁעָתַיִם	be**e**rekh shaa**ta**yim
more than 10 minutes	יוֹתֵר מֵעֶשֶׂר דַּקּוֹת	yo**ter** me**e**ser da**kot**
less than 30 seconds	פָּחוֹת מִשְּׁלֹשִׁים שְׁנִיּוֹת	pa**ḥot** mishlo**shim** shni**yot**
The clock is fast/slow.	הַשָּׁעוֹן מְמַהֵר/מְפַגֵּר.	hasha**on** mema**her**/mefa**ger**

Common abbreviations רָאשֵׁי תֵּבוֹת נְפוֹצִים

אדמו"ר	rabbi, sage
או"ם	UN
אחה"צ	p.m.
אי"ה	God willing
אעפ"כ	nevertheless
ארה"ב	USA
ב"ה	God willing
בי"ח	hospital
ביח"ר	factory
בימ"ש	law court
בי"ס	school
בכ"ז	nevertheless
בָּל"ל	Bank Le'umi Le-Israel
בְּעַ"מ	Ltd
ב"ש	Be'er Sheba
גב'	Mrs/Ms
דו"חַ	report
הַנַּ"ל	the a/m
ז'	masculine
ז"א	i.e.
חוה"מ	working days during Pessach and Succoth festivals

חו"ל	abroad
י-ם	Jerusalem
לכ'	to (salutation in letter)
לפה"צ	a.m.
מו"מ	negotiations
מַנְכָּ"ל	general manager
מַעַ"מ	VAT
מ"צ	Military Police
מתנ"ס	community centre
נ'	feminine
נ"ב	PS
נ"ת	airport
עו"ד	advocate
צַהַ"ל	Israel Defence Forces
צ"ל	should be
קק"ל	Jewish National Fund
ר"ת	acronym
ת"א	Tel Aviv
ת"ז	ID card

Signs and notices שְׁלָטִים וְהוֹדָעוֹת

Beware of the dog	זְהִירוּת כֶּלֶב נוֹשֵׁךְ
Cash desk	קֻפָּה
Caution	זְהִירוּת
Cold	קַר
Danger (of death)	סַכָּנָה (סַכָּנַת מָוֶת)
Do not block entrance	לֹא לַחֲסוֹם אֶת הַכְּנִיסָה
Do not disturb	לֹא לְהַפְרִיעַ
Do not touch	לֹא לָגַעַת
Down	לְמַטָּה
Emergency exit	יְצִיאַת חֵרוּם
Enter without knocking	הִכָּנֵס בְּלִי לִדְפּוֹק
Entrance	כְּנִיסָה
Exit	יְצִיאָה
For hire	לְהַשְׂכָּרָה
For sale	לִמְכִירָה
... forbidden	... אָסוּר
Free admittance	כְּנִיסָה חָפְשִׁית
Gentlemen	גְּבָרִים
Hot	חַם
Information	מוֹדִיעִין
Ladies	נָשִׁים
Lift	מַעֲלִית
No admittance	אֵין כְּנִיסָה
No littering	אֵין לְהַשְׁלִיךְ אַשְׁפָּה
No smoking	אָסוּר לְעַשֵּׁן
No vacancies	אֵין מְקוֹמוֹת פְּנוּיִים
Open	פָּתוּחַ
Occupied	תָּפוּס
Out of order	מְקוּלְקָל
Please ring	נָא לְצַלְצֵל
Please wait	נָא לְחַכּוֹת
Private road	דֶּרֶךְ פְּרָטִית
Pull	מְשׁוֹךְ
Push	דְּחוֹף
Reserved	תָּפוּס
Sale	מְכִירָה
Sold out	אָזַל
To let	לְהַשְׂכִּיר
Tresspassers will be prosecuted	מַסִּיגֵי גְּבוּל יִתְבָּעוּ לְדִין
Up	לְמַעְלָה
Vacant	פָּנוּי
Wet paint	צֶבַע טָרִי

Emergency לִשְׁעַת חֵרוּם

Call the police	קְרָא (קִרְאִי) לַמִּשְׁטָרָה	kra (kiri) lamishta**ra**
Consulate	קוֹנְסוּלְיָה	kon**su**liya
DANGER	סַכָּנָה	saka**na**
Embassy	שַׁגְרִירוּת	shagri**rut**
FIRE	שְׂרֵפָה	sre**fa**
Gas	גַּז	gaz
Get a doctor	קְרָא (קִרְאִי) לְרוֹפֵא	kra (kiri) lero**fe**
Go away	הִסְתַּלֵּק (הִסְתַּלְּקִי)	hista**lek** (histal**ki**)
HELP	הַצִּילוּ	ha**tzi**lu
Get help quickly	קְרָא (קִרְאִי) לְעֶזְרָה מַהֵר	kra (kiri) leez**ra** ma**her**
I'm ill	אֲנִי חוֹלֶה (חוֹלָה)	**ani** ḥo**le** (ḥo**la**)
I'm lost	תָּעִיתִי בַּדֶּרֶךְ	taiti ba**de**rekh
Leave me alone	עֲזוֹב (עִזְבִי) אוֹתִי	a**zov** (iz**vi**) **oti**
LOOK OUT	זְהִירוּת	zehi**rut**
Poison	רַעַל	**raal**
POLICE	מִשְׁטָרָה	mishta**ra**
Stop that man/ woman	עֲצוֹר (עִצְרִי) אֶת הָאִישׁ/ הָאִשָּׁה הַזֶּה (הַזּוֹ)	a**tzor** (itz**ri**) et ha**ish**/hai**sha** ha**ze** (ha**zo**)
STOP THIEF	עִצְרוּ אֶת הַגַּנָּב	itz**ru** et haga**nav**

Emergency telephone numbers מִסְפְּרֵי טֶלֶפוֹן לִשְׁעַת חֵרוּם

POLICE	**100**
AMBULANCE	**101**
FIRE	**102**

Lost property—Theft אֲבֵדוֹת—גְּנֵבָה

Where's the ...?	אֵיפֹה ...	**ey**fo
lost property (lost and found) office	מַחְלֶקֶת אֲבֵדוֹת	maḥ**le**ket ave**dot**
police station	תַּחֲנַת מִשְׁטָרָה	taḥa**nat** mishta**ra**
I want to report a theft.	אֲנִי רוֹצֶה (רוֹצָה) לְהוֹדִיעַ עַל גְּנֵבָה.	**ani** ro**tze** (ro**tza**) leho**di**a al gne**va**
My ... has been stolen.	הַ... שֶׁלִּי נִגְנַב.	ha... she**li** nig**nav**
I've lost my ...	אִבַּדְתִּי אֶת הַ... שֶׁלִּי.	i**bad**ti et ha... she**li**
handbag	תִּיק יָד	tik yad
passport	דַּרְכּוֹן	dar**kon**
wallet	אַרְנָק	ar**nak**

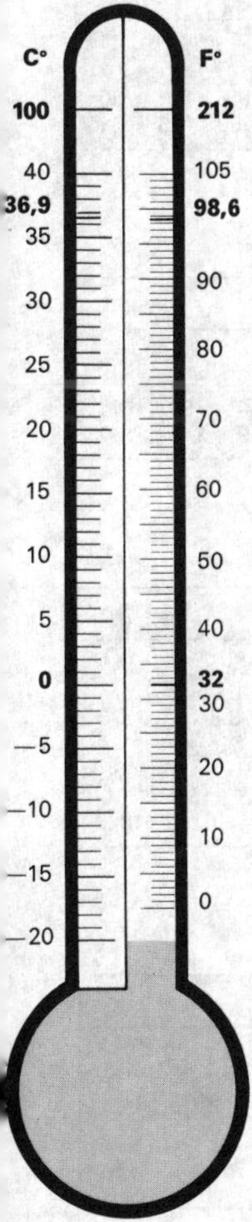

Conversion tables

Centimetres and inches

To change centimetres into inches, multiply by .39.

To change inches into centimetres, multiply by 2.54.

	in.	feet	yards
1 mm	0.039	0.003	0.001
1 cm	0.39	0.03	0.01
1 dm	3.94	0.32	0.10
1 m	39.40	3.28	1.09

	mm	cm	m
1 in.	25.4	2.54	0.025
1 ft.	304.8	30.48	0.304
1 yd.	914.4	91.44	0.914

(32 metres = 35 yards)

Temperature

To convert Centigrade into degrees Fahrenheit, multiply Centigrade by 1.8 and add 32.

To convert degrees Fahrenheit into Centigrade, subtract 32 from Fahrenheit and divide by 1.8.

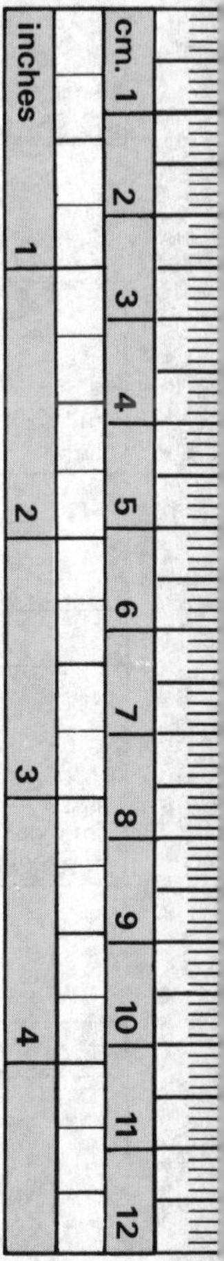

Kilometres into miles

1 kilometre (km.) = 0.62 miles

km.	10	20	30	40	50	60	70	80	90	100	110	120	130
miles	6	12	19	25	31	37	44	50	56	62	68	75	81

Miles into kilometres

1 mile = 1.609 kilometres (km.)

miles	10	20	30	40	50	60	70	80	90	100
km.	16	32	48	64	80	97	113	129	145	161

Fluid measures

1 litre (l.) = 0.88 imp. quart or 1.06 U.S. quart

1 imp. quart = 1.14 l. 1 U.S. quart = 0.95 l.

1 imp. gallon = 4.55 l. 1 U.S. gallon = 3.8 l.

litres	5	10	15	20	25	30	35	40	45	50
imp. gal.	1.1	2.2	3.3	4.4	5.5	6.6	7.7	8.8	9.9	11.0
U.S. gal.	1.3	2.6	3.9	5.2	6.5	7.8	9.1	10.4	11.7	13.0

Weights and measures

1 kilogram or kilo (kg.) = 1000 grams (g.)

100 g. = 3.5 oz. ½ kg. = 1.1 lb.

200 g. = 7.0 oz. 1 kg. = 2.2 lb.

1 oz. = 28.35 g.

1 lb. = 453.60 g.

CLOTHING SIZES, see page 115/YARDS AND INCHES, see page 112

Basic Grammar

Basic grammar guidelines

It is much easier to learn a language when you understand the basic structure and the thinking behind the words. Hebrew is written from right to left because the written language was originally carved on stone tablets with a hammer and chisel, and when right-handed people carve they are covering up with their left hand (which holds the chisel) what they have just written, if they work from left to right.

Hebrew word structure is very simple because, like all Semitic languages, the root of every word consists of only three letters. Prefix and suffix letters are added, which change the meaning.

All Hebrew letters are essentially consonants. A few letters are used intermittently to indicate vowels, though strictly speaking they are guttural or aspirate consonants: e.g. the letter ה (h) at the end of a word is often unvoiced and indicates the "a" sound, as in the final sound of "dahlia"; in Hebrew this word is written (from right to left!) as "hyld".

Pointing

Vowel signs consist of dots and dashes and they can also be used to change the meaning of the root word. For instance, the letters ספר will mean "book" when the word is given the vowels סֵפֶר, pronounced "**se**fer". But it will mean "he told" if given the vowels סִפֵּר, pronounced "si**per**". Adding the vowel signs is called "pointing". If the letters ספר have יה added to the end, they become the word סִפְרִיָּה (sifri**ya**), which means "library".

Standard modern Hebrew is written almost entirely without vowel signs. The only time pointing is used is when writing for people learning Hebrew, in prayer books and in poetry. Additionally, the letters י (y) and ו (v) are frequently inserted in modern unpointed Hebrew to make reading easier; this is called full pointing and gives rise to alternative spellings. Foreign words are often partially pointed to indicate the pronunciation. The rules of pointing are very strict and complicated. They were introduced in the early Middle Ages to aid pronunciation in a language that had largely died out in spoken form; the Hebrew of the Bible and the Talmud is not pointed, though the later commentaries are.

Modern Hebrew

Modern Hebrew is a direct descendent of talmudic Hebrew, which is itself descended from biblical Hebrew. A few words have changed their meaning slightly (for instance, the biblical word for "fever" now means "malaria") and words whose exact meaning in the Bible is not known have been adapted to modern use. One example is the word used to describe the aura which surrounds the Throne of God; it is the word used in modern Hebrew to mean "electricity"! Having evolved slowly over the millenia, modern Hebrew took a giant leap in the late 19th and early 20th century to adapt to modern needs. It is the only language of antiquity with a discontinuous history of everyday use which is a completely living language at the present time. Naturally, a large number of modern terms had to be coined, ranging from the Hebrew words for "police" and "orchestra" through "carbon dioxide" to "entrepreneur" and "recession".

Articles

The definite article (the) in Hebrew is -הַ (ha-) for both masculine and feminine genders in the singular and in the plural. It precedes—be careful—both noun and adjective, for example:

סֵפֶר	**se**fer	book
קָטָן	ka**tan**	small
הַסֵּפֶר	ha**se**fer	the book
הַסֵּפֶר הַקָּטָן	ha**se**fer haka**tan**	the small book

There is no indefinite article (a/an): the definite article is simply omitted to indicate an indefinite meaning.

Nouns

There are two genders: masculine and feminine. Nouns ending in a consonant are most frequently masculine, as are all nouns with a (human or zoological) masculine connotation. Nouns ending in **-a**, with the last syllable accented, are generally feminine, as are those denoting a feminine property and the names of towns and countries, for example:

	Masculine			Feminine	
חָתוּ	ḥa**tul**	(tom)cat	חֲתוּלָה	ḥatu**la**	female cat
פַּטִּישׁ	pa**tish**	hammer	עֲמָלָה	ama**la**	commission
אַבָּא	**a**ba	dad	סְפָרַד	sfa**rad**	Spain

Most plurals are formed by adding the suffix **-im** to masculine nouns (and also to adjectives—see below), and **-ot** to feminine ones. However, exceptions and irregular forms are so numerous that this is only a general rule of thumb, for example:

Regular

חָבֵר	ḥa**ver**	(boy)friend	חֲבֵרִים	ḥave**rim**	(male)friends
חֲבֵרָה	ḥave**ra**	girlfriend	חֲבֵרוֹת	ḥave**rot**	girlfriends

Irregular

(masc.)	שֻׁלְחָן	shul**ḥan**	table	שֻׁלְחָנוֹת	shulḥa**not**	tables
(femin.)	שָׁנָה	sha**na**	year	שָׁנִים	sha**nim**	years

Adjectives

In contrast to English, adjectives do not come before the noun in Hebrew but after it. They always agree with the noun in gender and in number, for example:

כִּסֵּא גָּדוֹל	ki**se** ga**dol**	large chair (m sing.)
חוּלְצוֹת גְּדוֹלוֹת	ḥul**tzot** gdo**lot**	large shirts (f pl.)

Possessive adjectives agree with the possessor, not with the object possessed. They also come after the noun:

Masculine			Feminine		
my/mine	שֶׁלִּי	she**li**	my/mine	שֶׁלִּי	she**li**
your/yours	שֶׁלְּךָ	shel**kha**	your/yours	שֶׁלָּךְ	she**lakh**
his	שֶׁלּוֹ	she**lo**	her/hers	שֶׁלָּה	she**la**
our/ours	שֶׁלָּנוּ	she**la**nu	our/ours	שֶׁלָּנוּ	she**la**nu
your/yours	שֶׁלָּכֶם	shela**khem**	your/yours	שֶׁלָּכֶן	shela**khen**
their/theirs	שֶׁלָּהֶם	shela**hem**	their/theirs	שֶׁלָּהֶן	shela**hen**

Verbs

The first thing to note about Hebrew verbs is that they change not only according to the tense, as in English (I wrote, I write ...), but also according to the subject (I, you, he, etc.) and whether the subject (person or noun) is masculine or feminine, singular or plural. As an example of a regular verb—there are many irregular ones—here is the conjugation of the verb "to write" in the past, present and future:

	Past tense wrote	**Present tense** write	**Future tense** will write
I (masc.)	ka**tav**ti	ko**tev**	ekh**tov**
I (femin.)	ka**tav**ti	ko**te**vet	ekh**tov**
you (masc.)	ka**tav**ta	ko**tev**	tikh**tov**
you (femin.)	ka**tavt**	ko**te**vet	tikhte**vi**
he	ka**tav**	ko**tev**	yikh**tov**
she	kat**va**	ko**te**vet	tikh**tov**
we (masc.)	ka**tav**nu	kot**vim**	nikh**tov**
we (femin.)	ka**tav**nu	kot**vot**	nikh**tov**
you (masc. pl.)	ketav**tem**	kot**vim**	tikhte**vu**
you (femin. pl.)	ketav**ten**	kot**vot**	tikh**tov**na
they (masc.)	kat**vu**	kot**vim**	yikhte**vu**
they (femin.)	kat**vu**	kot**vot**	tikh**tov**na

Pronouns

The indirect object (the dative case, like the English "I wrote **to him**"), and also the word אֶת ("et"), which is the sign of a direct object (accusative case), can be attached to personal pronouns; they then change their form with the gender and the number of the pronoun:

Sha**ma**ti et hatiz**mo**ret — I heard the orchestra

but

Sha**ma**ti **o**to — I heard him

Subject			Direct object		
I	אֲנִי	**ani**	me	אוֹתִי	**oti**
you (m.)	אַתָּה	**ata**	you (m.)	אוֹתְךָ	ot**kha**
you (f.)	אַתְּ	at	you (f.)	אוֹתָךְ	**otakh**
he	הוּא	hu	him	אוֹתוֹ	**oto**
she	הִיא	hi	her	אוֹתָהּ	**ota**
we	אֲנַחְנוּ	**ana**ḥnu	us	אוֹתָנוּ	**ota**nu
you (m. pl.)	אַתֶּם	**atem**	you (m. pl.)	אֶתְכֶם	et**khem**
you (f. pl.)	אַתֶּן	**aten**	you (f. pl.)	אֶתְכֶן	et**khen**
they (m. pl.)	הֵם	hem	they (m. pl.)	אוֹתָם	**otam**
they (f. pl.)	הֵן	hen	they (f. pl.)	אוֹתָן	**otan**

Indirect objects (to me, by you, on them) follow much the same pattern.

In this phrase book the feminine form of verbs, adjectives, etc. is given in parentheses.

Negation

The negative is formed by the word לֹא (lo), which means both "no" and "not". Where the pronoun in unambiguous, it is omitted unless needed for emphasis:

Past:	Present:	Future:
(אֲנִי) אָכַלְתִּי (**ani**) **akhal**ti I ate	אֲנִי אוֹכֶלֶת **ani** okh**e**let I (f.) eat	(אַתְּ) תֹּאכְלִי (at) tokhl**i** You (f. sing.) will eat
(אַתָּה) לֹא אָכַלְתָּ (**ata**) lo **akhal**ta You (m. sing.) didn't eat	הֵם לֹא אוֹכְלִים hem lo okh**lim** They (m.) do not eat	(אַתֶּם) לֹא תֹּאכְלוּ (atem) lo tokh**lu** You (m. pl.) will not eat

Dictionary
and alphabetical index

English–Hebrew

f feminine *m* masculine *pl* plural

A

abbreviations רָאשֵׁי תֵּיבוֹת *m/pl* rashey tevot 154
able, to be מְסוּגָל mesugal 163
about *(approximately)* בְּעֵרֶךְ beerekh 153
above מֵעַל meal 14
abscess מוּרְסָה *f* mursa 145
absorbent cotton צֶמֶר גֶּפֶן *m* tzemer gefen 108
accept, to לְקַבֵּל lekabel 59, 102
accessories אֲבִיזָרִים *m/pl* avizarim 115, 125
accident תְּאוּנָה *f* teuna 139
account חֶשְׁבּוֹן *m* ḥeshbon 130
ache כְּאֵב *m* keev 141
adaptor מַתְאֵם *m* matem 118
address כְּתֹבֶת *f* ktovet 21, 31, 76, 79, 102
adhesive דֶּבֶק *m* devek 104
adhesive tape נְיַר דֶּבֶק *m* neyar devek 104
admission כְּנִיסָה *f* knisa 82, 89, 155
Africa אַפְרִיקָה *f* afrika 146
after אַחֲרֵי aḥarey 14, 77
after-shave lotion מֵי גִּלּוּחַ *m/pl* mey giluaḥ 108
afternoon, in the אַחֲרֵי הַצָּהֳרַיִם aḥarey hatzohorayim 151, 153
again שׁוּב shuv 96, 135
against נֶגֶד neged 140
age גִּיל *m* gil 149, 150
ago לִפְנֵי lifney 149, 151
air bed מִזְרוֹן אֲוִיר *m* mizron avir 106
air conditioning מִזּוּג אֲוִיר *m* mizug avir 24, 28
airmail דֹּאַר אֲוִיר *m* doar avir 132
airplane מָטוֹס *m* matos 65
airport נְמַל תְּעוּפָה *m* nemal teufa 16, 21, 65
aisle seat מוֹשָׁב בַּמַּעֲבָר *m* moshav bamaavar 65
alarm clock שָׁעוֹן מְעוֹרֵר *m* shaon meorer 121
alcohol אַלְכּוֹהוֹל *m* alkohol 38, 55
alcoholic חָרִיף, אַלְכּוֹהוֹלִי ḥarif, alkoholi 55
all הַכֹּל hakol 103
allergic אַלֶרְגִּי alergi 141, 143
almond שָׁקֵד *m* shaked 51
alphabet אָלֶף-בֵּית *m* aef-bet 9
also גַּם gam 15
alter, to *(garment)* לְשַׁנּוֹת leshanot 114
altitude sickness מַחֲלַת גְּבָהִים *f* maḥalat gvahim 107
amazing מַפְלִיא mafli 84
amber עִנְבָּר *m* inbar 122
ambulance אַמְבּוּלַנְס *m* ambulans 79
American אֲמֶרִיקָאִי amerikai 93, 105, 126
amethyst אַחְלָמָה *f* aḥlama 122
amount סְכוּם *m* skhum 59, 131
amplifier מַגְבֵּר *m* magber 118
anaesthetic מְאַלְחֵשׁ *m* mealḥesh 144, 145
analgesic נֶגֶד כְּאֵבִים neged keevim 108
and ...וְ ve 14
animal חַיָּה *f* haiya 85
aniseed כַּמְנוּן *m* kamnun 50
ankle קַרְסֹל *m* karsol 139
anorak מְעִיל רוּחַ *m* meil ruaḥ 115
another אַחֵר aḥer 123
answer תְּשׁוּבָה *f* tshuva 136
antibiotic אַנְטִיבִּיוֹטִיקָה *f* antibiyotika 143
antidepressant תְּרוּפָה נֶגֶד דִּכָּאוֹן *f* trufa neged dikaon 143
antique shop חֲנוּת עַתִּיקוֹת *f* ḥanut atikot 98
antiques עַתִּיקוֹת *f/pl* atikot 83
antiseptic cream מִשְׁחָה אַנְטִיסֶפְּטִית *f* mishḥa antiseptit 107
any קְצָת ktzat 14
anyone מִישֶׁהוּ *m* mishehu 11, 16
anything מַשֶּׁהוּ *m* mashehu 17, 24, 25, 101, 103, 112
apartment דִּירָה *f* dira 23
aperitif אַפֶּרִיטִיב *m* aperitiv 55

appendicitis דַּלֶּקֶת תּוֹסֶפְתָן *f* daleket toseftan 142
appendix תּוֹסֶפְתָן *m* toseftan 138
appetizer מְתַאֲבֵן *m* metaaven 42
apple תַּפּוּחַ *m* tapuaḥ 51, 60, 64, 119
apple juice מִיץ תַּפּוּחִים *m* mitz tapuḥim 56
appliance מַכְשִׁיר *m* makhshir 118
appointment פְּגִישָׁה, תּוֹר *f* pgisha 131; *m* tor 137, 145
apricot מִשְׁמֵשׁ *m* mishmesh 51
April אַפְּרִיל *m* april 150
Arab עֲרָבִי aravi 57
archaeology אַרְכֵאוֹלוֹגְיָה *f* arkheologiya 83
architect אַדְרִיכָל *m* adrikhal 83
area code קוֹד חִיּוּג *m* kod ḥiyug 134
arm זְרוֹעַ *f* zroa 138, 139
around *(approximately)* בְּעֶרֶךְ beerekh 31
arrack עָרָק *m* arak 55
arrangement *(set price)* סִדּוּר *m* sidur 20
arrival בָּאִים baim 16, 65
arrive, to לְהַגִּיעַ lehagia 68, 70, 130
art אָמָנוּת *f* omanut 83
art gallery גָּלֶרְיָה לְאָמָנוּת *f* galeriya leomanut 81, 98
artichoke אַרְטִישׁוֹק *m* artishok 48
article סְחוֹרָה *f* sḥora 101
artificial מְלָאכוּתִי mlakhuti 124
artificial light אוֹר מְלָאכוּתִי *m* or mlakhuti 124
artist אָמָן *m* oman 81, 83
ashtray מַאֲפֵרָה *f* maafera 37
Asia אַסְיָה *f* asiya 146
ask for, to לְבַקֵּשׁ levakesh 25, 58, 136
asparagus אַסְפָּרָגוּס *m* asparagus 48
aspirin אַסְפִּירִין *m* aspirin 108
asthma אַסְתְּמָה *f* astma 140
astringent עוֹצֵר דִּמּוּם *m* otzer dimum 108
at ...בְּ be 14
at least לְפָחוֹת lefaḥot 25
at once מִיָּד miyad 31
aubergine חָצִיל *m* ḥatzil 48
August אוֹגוּסְט *m* ogust 150
aunt דּוֹדָה *f* doda 93
Australia אוֹסְטְרַלְיָה *f* ostraliya 146
automatic אוֹטוֹמָטִי otomati 20, 122, 124
autumn סְתָיו *m* stav 150
awful נוֹרָא nora 84, 94

B

baby תִּינוֹק *m* tinok 24, 110
baby food מָזוֹן לְתִינוֹק *m* mazon letinok 110
babysitter שְׁמַרְטַף *m* shmartaf 27
back גַּב *m* gav 138
back, to be/to get לַחֲזוֹר laḥazor 21, 80, 136
backache כְּאֵב גַּב *m* keev gav 140
backpack תַּרְמִיל גַּב *m* tarmil gav 106
bad רַע ra 13, 95
bag תִּיק *m* tik 18
bagel כַּעַךְ *m* kaakh 61
baggage *(luggage)* מִזְוָדוֹת *f/pl* mizvadot 26, 31, 71
baggage check שְׁמִירַת חֲפָצִים *f* shmirat ḥafatzim 68, 71
baggage locker תָּא שְׁמִירַת חֲפָצִים *m* ta shmirat ḥafatzim «tab»
baked אָפוּי afuy 46
baker's מַאֲפִיָּה *f* maafiya 98
balance *(finance)* מַאֲזָן *m* maazan 131
balcony מִרְפֶּסֶת *f* mirpeset 23
ball *(inflated)* כַּדּוּר *m* kadur 128
ball-point pen עֵט כַּדּוּרִי *m* et kaduri 104
ballet בַּלֶּט *m* balet 88
banana בָּנָנָה *f* banana 51, 60
Band-Aid פְּלַסְטֶר *m* plaster 107
bandage תַּחְבֹּשֶׁת *f* tahboshet 108
bangle צָמִיד *m* tzamid 121
bangs פּוֹנִי *m* poni 30
bank *(finance)* בַּנְק *m* bank 129, 130
banknote שְׁטָר *m* shtar 130
bar *(room)* בַּר *m* bar 33
barber's מִסְפָּרָה *f* mispara 30, 98
basketball כַּדּוּרְסַל *m* kadursal 89
bath אַמְבַּטְיָה *f* ambatya 23, 25, 27
bath salts מִלְחֵי אַמְבַּטְיָה *m/pl* milḥey ambatya 108
bath towel מַגֶּבֶת רַחֲצָה *f* magevet raḥatza 27
bathing cap כּוֹבַע יָם *m* kova yam 115
bathing hut סוּכָּה *f* suka 92
bathing suit בֶּגֶד יָם *m* beged yam 115
bathrobe חָלוּק רַחֲצָה *m* ḥaluk raḥatza 115
bathroom חֲדַר אַמְבַּטְיָה *m* ḥadar ambatya 27
battery סוֹלְלָה *f* solela 118, 125
bay leaf עֲלֵה דַּפְנָה *m* ale dafna 50
be, to לִהְיוֹת lihyot 162
beach חוֹף *m* ḥof 90
beach ball כַּדּוּר יָם *m* kadur yam 128
bean שְׁעוּעִית *f* sheuit 48
beard זָקָן *m* zakan 30
beautiful נֶהְדָּר nehedar 13, 84
beauty salon מְכוֹן יוֹפִי *m* mekhon yofi 30, 98
bed מִטָּה *f* mita 24, 28, 142, 144
bed and breakfast עִם אֲרוּחַת בֹּקֶר im aruḥat boker 24

bedpan סיר-מטה *m* sir mita 144
beef בקר *m* bakar 45
beer בירה *f* bira 53, 54
beet(root) סלק *m* selek 48
before *(time)* לפני lifney 14
begin, to להתחיל lehathil 87, 88
behind מאחורי meahorey 14, 77
Belgium בלגיה *f* belgiya 146
bell *(electric)* פעמון *m* paamon 144
below מתחת mitahat 14
belt חגורה *f* hagora 116
better יותר טוב yoter tov 14, 25, 101
between בין beyn 14
beverage משקה *m* mashke 57, 64
bicycle אופניים *m/pl* ofanayim 74
big גדול gadol 13, 101
bilberry אוכמנית *f* ukhmanit 51
bill חשבון *m* heshbon 28, 31, 59, 102; *(banknote)* שטר *m* shtar 130
billion *(Am.)* בליון *m* bilyon 148
binoculars משקפת *f* mishkefet 123
bird צפור *f* tzipor 85
birth הולדת *f* huledet 25
birthday יום הולדת *m* yom huledet 151
biscuit *(Br.)* ביסקויט *m* biskvit 60
bitter מר mar 58
black שחור shahor 112
black and white *(film)* שחור-לבן shahor lavan 124, 125
black coffee קפה שחור *m* kafe shahor 42, 57
blackcurrant דמדמנית שחורה *f* dumdemanit shehora 51
bladder שלפוחית *f* shalpuhit 138
blade *(razor)* סכין גלוח *f* sakin giluah 109
blanket שמיכה *f* smikha 27
bleach הבהרה *f* havhara 30
bleed, to לדמם ledamem 139, 145
blind *(window shade)* וילון *m* vilon 28
blister בועה *f* bua 139
blocked סתום satum 28
blood דם *m* dam 142
blood pressure לחץ דם *m* lahatz dam 141, 142
blood transfusion עירוי דם *m* iruy dam 144
blouse כתונת *f* kutonet 115
blow-dry יבוש עם אויר *m* yibush im avir 30
blue כחול kahol 112
blueberry אוכמנית *f* ukhmanit 51
blusher אודם *m* odem 108
boat סירה *f* sira 73
bobby pin סכת ראש *f* sikat rosh 110
body גוף *m* guf 138
boiled egg ביצה מבושלת *f* beytza mevushelet 41

bone עצם *f* etzem 138
book ספר *m* sefer 12, 104
booking office אשנב כרטיסים *m* eshnav kartisim 19, 68
booklet *(of tickets)* כרטיסיה *f* kartisiya 72
bookshop חנות ספרים *f* hanut sfarim 98, 104
boot נעל גבוהה *f* naal gvoha 117
born נולד nolad 150
borsht בורשט *m* borsht 43
botanical gardens גנים בוטניים *m/pl* ganim botaniyim 81
botany בוטניקה *f* botanika 83
bottle בקבוק *m* bakbuk 17, 54
bottle-opener פותחן בקבוקים *m* pothan bakbukim 120
bottom למטה lemata 145
bow tie עניבת פרפר *f* anivat parpar 115
bowel מעיים *m/pl* meayim 138
box קופסה *f* kufsa 119
boxing אגרוף *m* igruf 89
boy ילד *m* yeled 111, 128
boyfriend חבר *m* haver 93
bra חזיה *f* haziya 115
bracelet צמיד *m* tzamid 121
braces *(suspenders)* כתפיות *f/pl* ktefiyot 115
braised מאודה meude 46
brake בלמים *m/pl* blamim 78
brake fluid שמן בלמים *m* shemen blamim 75
brandy ברנדי *m* brendi 55
bread לחם *m* lehem 37, 39, 60
break down, to להתקלקל lehitkalkel 78
break, to לשבור lishbor 29, 118, 123, 139, 145
breakdown קלקול kilkul 78
breakdown van משאית גרר *f* masait grar 78
breakfast ארוחת בקר *f* aruhat boker 24, 27, 39
breast חזה *m* haze 138
breathe, to לנשום linshom 141, 142
bridge גשר *m* gesher 85
bring down, to להוריד lehorid 31
bring, to להביא lehavi 12, 54
British בריטי briti 93
broken שבור shavur 118, 123, 139, 140
brooch סכת נוי *f* sikat noy 121
brother אח *m* ah 93
brown חום hum 112
bruise חבורה *f* habura 139
Brussels sprouts כרוב ניצנים *m* kruv nitzanim 48
bubble bath סבון מקציף *m* sabon maktzif 108
bucket דלי *m* dli 128

buckle אַבְזָם *m* avzam 116
build, to לִבְנוֹת livnot 83
building בִּנְיָן *m* binyan 81, 83
bulb *(light)* נוּרָה *f* nura 28, 75, 119
bump *(lump)* תְּפִיחָה *f* tfiḥa 139
burn כְּוִיָּה *f* kviya 139
burn out, to *(bulb)* לְהִשָּׂרֵף lehisaref 28
bus אוֹטוֹבּוּס *m* otobus 18, 19, 65, 72, 80
bus stop תַּחֲנַת אוֹטוֹבּוּס *f* taḥanat otobus 71, 73
business עֵסֶק *m* esek 16, 131
business class מַחְלֶקֶת עֲסָקִים *f* maḥleket asakim 65
business district אֵזוֹר עֲסָקִים *m* ezor asakim 81
business trip נְסִיעַת עֲסָקִים *f* nesiat asakim 93
busy עָסוּק asuk 96
but אֲבָל aval 14
butane gas גָּז בִּשּׁוּל *m* gaz bishul 32, 106
butcher's אִטְלִיז *m* itliz 98
butter חֶמְאָה *f* ḥema 37, 60
button כַּפְתּוֹר *m* kaftor 29, 116
buy, to לִקְנוֹת liknot 82, 100, 104, 123

C

cabana סוּכָּה *f* suka 92
cabbage כְּרוּב *m* kruv 48
cabin *(ship)* תָּא *m* ta 73
cable מִבְרָק *m* mivrak 133
cable release מַחְשֵׂף גָּמִישׁ *m* maḥsef gamish 125
café בֵּית קָפֶה *m* beyt kafe 33
cake עוּגָה *f* uga 38, 40, 53, 60
calculator מַחְשֵׁב כִּיס *m* maḥshev kis 105
calendar לוּחַ שָׁנָה *m* luaḥ shana 104
call *(phone)* שִׂיחָה *f* siḥa 134, 136
call back, to לְצַלְצֵל letzaltzel 136
call, to *(give name)* לִקְרֹא likro 11
call, to *(phone)* לְצַלְצֵל letzaltzel 134, 136
call, to *(summon)* לִקְרֹא likro 156
calm שָׁקֵט shaket 90
cambric בָּטִיסְט *m* batist 113
camel-hair צֶמֶר גָּמָל *m* tzemer gamal 113
camera מַצְלֵמָה *f* matzlema 124, 125
camera case נַרְתִּיק מַצְלֵמָה *m* nartik matzlema 125
camera shop חֲנוּת צִלּוּם *f* ḥanut tzilum 98
camp site חַנְיוֹן *m* ḥanyon 32
camp, to לַעֲשׂוֹת קֶמְפִּינְג laasot kemping 32
campbed מִטַּת שָׂדֶה *f* mitat sade 106
camping קֶמְפִּינְג מַחֲנָאוּת *m* kemping, *f* maḥanaut 32
camping equipment צִיּוּד מַחֲנָאוּת *m* tziyud maḥanaut 106
can *(be able to)* יָכוֹל yakhol 12
can *(container)* פַּחִית *f* paḥit 119
can opener פּוֹתְחָן קוּפְסָאוֹת *m* potḥan kufsaot 120
Canada קָנָדָה kanada 146
Canadian קָנָדִי kanadi 93
cancel, to לְבַטֵּל levatel 65
candle נֵר *m* ner 120
candy סוּכָּרִיּוֹת *f/pl* sukariyot 126
change *(money)* כֶּסֶף קָטָן *m* kesef katan 77, 130
change, to לְהַחֲלִיף lehaḥalif 68, 72, 75, 123
cap כּוֹבַע מִצְחִיָּה *m* kova mitzḥiya 115
capers צָלָף *m* tzalaf 50
capital *(finance)* הוֹן *m* hon 131
car מְכוֹנִית *f* mekhonit 19, 20, 32, 75, 78
car hire שְׂכִירַת מְכוֹנִית *f* skhirat mekhonit 20
car park מִגְרַשׁ חֲנָיָה *m* migrash ḥanaya 77
car racing מֵרוֹץ מְכוֹנִיּוֹת *m* merotz mekhoniyot 89
car radio רַדְיוֹ לִמְכוֹנִית *m* radyo limkhonit 118
car rental שְׂכִירַת מְכוֹנִית *f* skhirat mekhonit 20
carafe קַנְקַן *m* kankan 54
carat קָרָט *m* karat 121
caravan קָרָוָן *m* karavan 32
caraway כַּרְוִיָּה *f* karviya 50
carbon paper נְיַר פֶּחָם *m* neyar peḥam 104
carbonated *(fizzy)* תּוֹסֵס toses 64, 57
carburettor מְאַיֵּד *m* meayed 78
card קְלָף, כַּרְטִיס *m* klaf, kartis 93, 131
card game מִשְׂחַק קְלָפִים *m* misḥak klafim 128
cardamom הֵל *m* hel«tab»
cardigan אֲפוּדַּת צֶמֶר *f* afudat tzemer 115
carp קַרְפִּיוֹן *m* karpiyon 44
carrot גֶּזֶר *m* gezer 48
cart עֲגָלָה *f* agala 18
carton *(of cigarettes)* קַרְטוֹן *m* karton 17, 126
cartridge *(camera)* קַסֶּטָה *f* kaseta 124
case נַרְתִּיק *m* nartik 121, 125
cash desk קֻפָּה *f* kupa 103, 155
cash, to לִפְדּוֹת lifdot 130, 133
cassette קַסֶּטָה *f* kaseta 118, 127
cassette recorder רְשַׁמְקוֹל קַסֶּטוֹת *m* reshamkol kasetot 118
castle טִירָה *f* tira 81
catacombs מְעָרוֹת קֶבֶר *f/pl* mearot kever 81
catalogue קָטָלוֹג *m* katalog 82
cathedral קָתֶדְרָלָה *f* katedrala 81
Catholic קָתוֹלִי katoli 84

cauliflower כְּרוּבִית *f* kruvit 48
caution זְהִירוּת *f* zehirut 155
cave מְעָרָה *f* meara 81
celery סֶלֶרִי *m* seleri 48
cemetery בֵּית קְבָרוֹת *m* beyt kvarot 81
centre מֶרְכָּז *m* merkaz 19, 21, 76, 81
century מֵאָה *f* mea 149
ceramics קֶרָמִיקָה *f* keramika 83
cereal דָּגָן *m* dagan 41
certificate תְּעוּדָה *f* teuda 144
chain *(jewellery)* שַׁרְשֶׁרֶת *f* sharsheret 121
chain bracelet צָמִיד שַׁרְשֶׁרֶת *m* tzamid sharsheret 121
chair כִּסֵּא *m* kise 106
chamber music מוּסִיקָה קָמֶרִית *f* musika kamerit 128
change, to *(money)* לְהַחֲלִיף lehahalif 18, 130
chapel קָפֶּלָה *f* kapela 81
charcoal פֶּחָמִים *m/pl* pehamim 106
charge מְחִיר *m* mehir 20, 32, 89, 136
charm *(trinket)* קָמֵעַ *m* kamea 121
charm bracelet צָמִיד עִם קָמֵעַ *m* tzamid im kamea 121
cheap זוֹל zol 13, 24, 25, 101
check הַמְחָאָה *f* hamhaa; *(restaurant)* חֶשְׁבּוֹן *m* heshbon 59
check, to לִבְדּוֹק livdok 75, 123
check in, to *(airport)* לְהַגִּיעַ לִנְמַל הַתְּעוּפָה lehagia linmal hateufa 65
check out, to לַעֲזוֹב laazov 31
check-up *(medical)* בְּדִיקָה רְפוּאִית *f* bedika refuit 142
cheese גְּבִינָה *f* gvina 51, 60
chemist's בֵּית מִרְקַחַת *m* beyt mirkahat 98, 107
cheque הַמְחָאָה *f* hamhaa 130, 131
cherry דּוּבְדְּבָן *m* duvdevan 51
chess שַׁחְמָט *m* shahmat 93
chess set מַעֲרֶכֶת שַׁחְמָט *f* maarekhet shahmat 128
chest חָזֶה *m* haze 138, 141
chestnut עַרְמוֹן *m* armon 51
chewing gum מַסְטִיק *m* mastik 126
chewing tobacco טַבַּק לְעִיסָה *m* tabak leisa 126
chicken עוֹף *m* of 47, 63
chicken breast חֲזֵה עוֹף *m* haze of 47
chicory עֹלֶשׁ *m* olesh 49
chiffon שִׁיפוֹן *m* shifon 113
child יֶלֶד, יַלְדָּה *m, f* yeled, yalda 24, 58, 82, 93, 139, 150
children's doctor רוֹפֵא יְלָדִים *m* rofe yeladim 137
China סִין *f* sin 146
chips פְּרִיכִים *m/pl* perikhim 47
chives בְּצַלְצָל *m* betzaltzal 50
chocolate שׁוֹקוֹלָד *m* shokolad 60, 119, 126; *(hot)* קָקָאוֹ *f* kakao 41, 56
chocolate bar טַבְלַת שׁוֹקוֹלָד *f* tavlat shokolad 60
cholent חַמִּין *m* hamin 46
chop *(meat)* צֶלַע *f* tzela 45
choice בְּחִירָה *f* behira 40
chromium כְּרוֹם *m* krom 122
church כְּנֵסִיָּה *f* knesiya 81, 84
cigar סִיגָר *m* sigar 126
cigarette סִיגַרְיָה *f* sigariya 17, 95, 126
cigarette case נַרְתִּיק לְסִיגַרְיוֹת *m* nartik lesigariyot 121, 126
cigarette holder פּוּמִית *f* pumit 126
cigarette lighter מַצִּית *m* matzit 121, 126
cine camera מַצְלֵמַת קוֹלְנוֹעַ *f* matzlemat kolnoa 124
cinema קוֹלְנוֹעַ *m* kolnoa 86
cinnamon קִינָמוֹן *m* kinamon 50
circle *(theatre)* יָצִיעַ *m* yatzia 87
city עִיר *f* ir 81
city centre מֶרְכַּז הָעִיר *m* merkaz hair 81
classical קְלָסִי klasi 128
clean נָקִי naki 58
clean, to לְנַקּוֹת lenakot 29, 75
cleansing cream קְרֶם נִקּוּי *m* krem nikuy 109
cliff צוּק *m* tzuk 85
clip סִכָּה לַעֲנִיבָה *f* sika leaniva 121
cloakroom מֶלְתָּחָה *f* meltaha 87
clock שְׁעוֹן קִיר *m* sheon kir 121, 153
clock-radio שְׁעוֹן-רַדְיוֹ *m* shaon radyo 118
close, to לִסְגּוֹר lisgor 11, 82, 107, 132
closed סָגוּר sagur 155
cloth בַּד *m* bad 117
clothes בְּגָדִים *m/pl* begadim 29, 115
clothes peg/pin אֶטְבֵי כְּבִיסָה *m* itvey kvisa 120
clothing בְּגָדִים *m/pl* begadim 111
cloud עָנָן *m* anan 94
clove צִפֹּרֶן *m* tziporen 50
coach *(bus)* אוֹטוֹבּוּס *m* otobus 72
coat מְעִיל *m* meil 115
coconut אֱגוֹז קוֹקוֹס *m* egoz kokos 51
cod בַּקָּלָה *f* bakala 44
coffee קָפֶה *m* kafe 42, 60
coin מַטְבֵּעַ *f* matbea 83
cold קַר kar 14, 25, 60, 94, 155
cold *(illness)* הִצְטַנְּנוּת *f* hitztanenut 107, 140
cold cuts בָּשָׂר קַר *m* basar kar 60
collar צַוָּארוֹן *m* tzavaron 116
collect call שִׂיחַת גּוּבַיְנָא *f* sihat guvayna«tab»
colour צֶבַע *m* tzeva 103, 111, 124, 125
colour chart קָטָלוֹג צְבָעִים *m* katalog

tzvaim 30
colour rinse שטיפת צבע *f* shtifat tzeva 30
colour shampoo שמפו צובע *m* shampu tzovea 110
colour slide שקופית צבע *f* shkufit tzeva 124
colourfast צבע עמיד *m* tzeva amid 113
comb מסרק *m* masrek 110
come, to לבוא lavo 16, 36, 95, 137, 144, 146
comedy קומדיה *f* komediya 86
commission *(fee)* עמלה *f* amala 130
common *(frequent)* נפוץ nafotz 154
compact disc תקליטון סי-די *m* takliton si di 127
compass מצפן *m* matzpen 106
complaint תלונה *f* tluna 58
concert קונצרט *m* kontzert 88
concert hall אולם קונצרטים *m* ulam kontzertim 81, 88
condom אמצעי מניעה *m* emtzai menia 108
conductor *(orchestra)* מנצח *m* menatzeaḥ 88
conference room אולם ישיבות *m* ulam yeshivot 24
confirm, to לאשר leasher 65
confirmation אשור *m* ishur 23
congratulation מזל טוב *m* mazal tov 152
connection *(transport)* קשר *m* kesher 65, 68
constipation עצירות *f* atzirut 140
contact lens עדשת מגע *f* adshat maga 123
contagious מדבק midabek 142
contain, to להכיל lehakhil 38
contraceptive אמצעי מניעה *m* emtzai menia 108
contract חוזה *m* ḥoze 131
control בקרת *f* bikoret 16
convent מנזר *m* minzar 81
cookie עוגיה *f* ugit 60
cool box ארגז קלקר *m* argaz kalkar 106
copper נחשת *f* neḥoshet 122
coral אלמוג *m* almog 122
corduroy קורדרוי korderoy 113
corkscrew חולץ פקקים *m* ḥoletz pkakim 106
corn *(Am.)* תירס *m* tiras 48
corn plaster פלסטר ליבלות *m* plaster leyabalot 108
corner פנה *f* pina 21, 36, 77
cost מחיר *m* meḥir 131
cost, to לעלות laalot 11, 80, 133
cot מיטה מתקפלת *f* mita mitkapelet 24
cotton כותנה *f* kutna 113
cotton wool צמר גפן *m* tzemer gefen 108
cough שעול *m* shiul 107, 141
cough drops טבליות נגד שעול *f/pl* tavliyot neged shiul 108
cough, to להשתעל lehishtael 142
counter אשנב, דלפק *m* eshnav, delpek 133
country ארץ *f* eretz 92
countryside מחוץ לעיר miḥutz lair 85
courgette קשוא *m* kishu 48
court house בית משפט *m* beyt mishpat 81
cover charge תשלום מינימום *m* tashlum minimum 59
crayon עפרון *m* iparon 104
cramp התכווצות *f* hitkavtzut 140
cream שמנת *f* shamenet; *(toiletry)* קרם *m* krem 109
crease resistant בלתי מתקמט bilti mitkamet 113
credit אשראי *m* ashray 130
credit card כרטיס אשראי *m* kartis ashray 20, 31, 59, 102, 130
crepe קרפ *m* krep 113
crockery חרס *m* ḥeres 120
cross צלב *m* tzlav 121
crossing *(maritime)* הפלגה *f* haflaga 73
crossroads הצטלבות *f* hitztalvut 77
cruise שיט *m* shayit 73
crystal בדלח *m* bedolaḥ 122
cucumber מלפפון *m* melafefon 48
cuff link כפתור חפתים *m* kaftor ḥofatim 121
cuisine מטבח *m* mitbaḥ 34
cup ספל *m* sefel 120
curler גלגל *m* galgal 110
currency מטבע *m* matbea 129
currency exchange office החלפת מטבע חוץ *f* haḥlafat matbea ḥutz 18, 68, 129
current זרם *m* zerem 90
curtain וילון *m* vilon 28
curve *(road)* עקומה *f* akuma 79
customs מכס *m* mekhes 16, 102
cut *(wound)* חתך *m* ḥatakh 139
cut glass זכוכית מלוטשת *f* zekhukhit meluteshet 122
cut off, to *(interrupt)* לנתק lenatek 135
cut, to *(with scissors)* לחתוך laḥatokh 30
cuticle remover מספרי צפרנים *m/pl* misperey tzipornayim 109
cutlery סכום *m* sakum 120
cutlet צלע *f* tzela 45
cycling רכיבה באופנים *f* rekhiva beofanayim 89
cystitis דלקת שלפוחית השתן *f* daleket shalpuḥit hasheten 142

D

dairy חֲנוּת לְמוּצְרֵי חָלָב f ḥanut lemutzrey ḥalav 98

dance רִקוּד m rikud 88, 95

dance, to לִרְקוֹד lirkod 88, 95

danger סַכָּנָה f sakana 155, 156

dangerous מְסֻכָּן mesukan 90

dark חָשׁוּךְ, כֵּהֶה ḥashukh, kehe 25, 101, 111, 112

date (appointment) פְּגִישָׁה f pegisha 95; (day) תַּאֲרִיךְ m taarikh 25, 151; (fruit) תָּמָר m tamar 51

daughter בַּת f bat 93

day יוֹם m yom 20, 24, 32, 80, 94, 151

day off יוֹם חֹפֶשׁ m yom ḥofesh 151

daylight אוֹר יוֹם m or yom 124

decade עָשׂוֹר m asor 149

decaffeinated נְטוּל קָאפֵין netul kafein 42, 57

December דְּצֶמְבֶּר m detzember 150

decision הַחְלָטָה f haḥlata 25, 102

deck (ship) סִפּוּן m sipun 73

deck chair כִּסֵּא נֹחַ m kise noaḥ 92, 106

declare, to (customs) לְהַצְהִיר lehatzhir 17

deep עָמֹק amok 142

degree (temperature) מַעֲלָה f maala 140

delay אִחוּר m iḥur 69

delicatessen מַעֲדָנִיָּה f maadaniya 98

delicious מְצֻיָּן metzuyan 59

deliver, to לִשְׁלֹחַ lishloaḥ 102

delivery מִשְׁלוֹחַ m mishloaḥ 102

denim דֶּנִים m denim 113

Denmark דֶּנְמַרְק denmark 146

dentist רוֹפֵא שִׁנַּיִם m rofe shinayim 98, 145

denture שִׁנַּיִם תּוֹתָבוֹת f/pl shinayim totavot 145

deodorant דֵּאוֹדוֹרַנְט m deodorant 109

department store חֲנוּת כָּל־בּוֹ f ḥanut kolbo 98

deposit הַפְקָדָה f hafkada 130; (down payment) פִּקָּדוֹן m pikadon 20

dessert מָנָה אַחֲרוֹנָה f mana aḥarona 38, 53

diabetic חוֹלֵה סֻכֶּרֶת m ḥole sakeret 38, 141

dialling code קוֹד חִיּוּג m kod ḥiyug 134

diamond יַהֲלוֹם m yahalom 122, 127

diaper חִתּוּל m ḥitul 110

diarrhoea שִׁלְשׁוּל m shilshul 140

dictionary מִלּוֹן m milon 104

diesel סוֹלָר m solar 75

diet דִּיאֵטָה f dieta 38

difficult קָשֶׁה kashe 13

difficulty בְּעָיָה f beaya 28, 102

digital דִּיגִיטָלִי digitali 122

dill שֶׁבֶת f shevet 50

dine, to לֶאֱכֹל leekhol 94

dining car מָזְנוֹן m miznon 68, 70

dining room חֲדַר אֹכֶל m hadar okhel 27

dinner אֲרוּחַת עֶרֶב f faruḥat erev 34, 94

direct יָשִׁיר yashir 65

direct, to לְהַדְרִיךְ lehadrikh 12

direction כִּוּוּן m kivun 76

director (theatre) בִּימַאי m bimay 87

directory (phone) מַדְרִיךְ m madrikh 134

disabled נֶכֶה nekhe 82

disc דִּיסְק m disk 127

discotheque דִּיסְקוֹטֶק m diskotek 88, 96

discount הֲנָחָה f hanaḥa 131

disease מַחֲלָה f maḥala 142

dish מַאֲכָל m maakhal 36

dishwashing detergent תַּכְשִׁיר נִקּוּי לְכֵלִים m takhshir nikuy lekhelim 120

disinfectant חֹמֶר חִטּוּי m ḥomer ḥituy 108

dislocated נָקוּעַ nakua 140

display case אָרוֹן m aron 100

dissatisfied מִתְלוֹנֵן mitlonen 103

disturb, to לְהַפְרִיעַ lehafria 16

dizziness סְחַרְחֹרֶת f seharḥoret 140

do, to לַעֲשׂוֹת laasot 162

doctor רוֹפֵא m rofe 79, 137, 144

doctor's office מִרְפָּאָה f mirpaa 137

dog כֶּלֶב m kelev 92

doll בֻּבָּה f buba 128

dollar דּוֹלָר m dolar 18, 102, 130

double bed מִטָּה זוּגִית f mita zugit 23

double room חֶדֶר זוּגִי m ḥeder zugi 19, 23

down לְמַטָּה lemata 14

downtown מֶרְכַּז הָעִיר m merkaz hair 81

dozen תְּרֵיסָר m treysar 149

drawing paper נְיַר צִיּוּר m neyar tziyur 104

drawing pins נְעָצִים m/pl neatzim 104

dress שִׂמְלָה f simla 115

dressing gown חָלוּק m haluk 115

drink מַשְׁקֶה m mashke 53, 55, 56, 58, 64

drink, to לִשְׁתּוֹת lishtot 35, 36, 38

drinking water מֵי שְׁתִיָּה m/pl mey shtiya 32

drip, to לְטַפְטֵף letatef 28

drive, to לִנְהוֹג linhog 76

driving licence רִשְׁיוֹן נְהִיגָה m rishyon nehiga 20, 79

drop (liquid) טִפָּה f tipa 108

drugstore בֵּית מִרְקַחַת m beyt mirkaḥat 98, 107

dry יָבֵשׁ yavesh 30, 55, 108, 110

dry cleaner's מִכְבָּסָה לְנִקּוּי יָבֵשׁ f mikhbasa lenikuy yavesh 29, 98

dry shampoo שַׁמְפּוּ יָבֵשׁ m shampu yavesh 110

duck בַּרְוָז *m* barvaz 47
dummy *(baby's)* מוֹצֵץ *m* motzetz 110
during בְּמֶשֶׁךְ bemeshekh 14, 150, 151
duty *(customs)* מֶכֶס *m* mekhes 16
duty-free shop חֲנוּת לְלֹא מֶכֶס *f* ḥanut lelo mekhes 19
dye צֶבַע *m* tzeva 30, 110

E

each כָּל kol 149
ear אֹזֶן *f* ozen 138
ear drops טִפּוֹת אָזְנַיִים *f/pl* tipot oznayim 108
earache כְּאֵב אָזְנַיִים *m* keev oznayim 141
early מוּקְדָם mukdam 13, 31
earring עָגִיל *m* agil 121
east מִזְרָח *m* mizraḥ 77
easy קַל kal 14
eat, to לֶאֱכוֹל leekhol 36, 38, 144
egg בֵּיצָה *f* beytza 40, 41, 60
eggplant חָצִיל *m* hiatzil 48
Egypt מִצְרַיִם«tab» *m* mitzraim 146
eight שְׁמוֹנָה shmona 147
eighteen שְׁמוֹנָה-עָשָׂר shmona asar 147
eighth שְׁמִינִי shmini 149
eighty שְׁמוֹנִים shmonim 148
elastic אֶלַסְטִי elasti 107
elastic bandage תַּחְבּוֹשֶׁת אֶלַסְטִית *f* taḥboshet elastit 107
electric(al) חַשְׁמַלִּי ḥashmali 118
electrical appliance מַכְשִׁיר חַשְׁמַלִּי *m* makhshir ḥashmali 118
electrical goods shop חֲנוּת לְמַכְשִׁירֵי חַשְׁמַל *f* ḥanut lemakhshrey ḥashmal 98
electricity חַשְׁמַל *m* ḥashmal 32
electronic אֶלֶקְטְרוֹנִי elektroni 128
elevator מַעֲלִית *f* maalit 27, 100
eleven אַחַד-עָשָׂר aḥad asar 147
embassy שַׁגְרִירוּת *f* shagrirut 156
embroidery רִקְמָה *f* rikma 127
emerald בָּרֶקֶת *f* bareket 122
emergency חֵרוּם *m* ḥerum 156
emergency exit יְצִיאַת חֵרוּם *f* yetziat ḥerum 27, 99
emery board נְיַר לֶטֶשׁ *m* neyar letesh 109
empty רֵיק rek 14
enamel אֶמָאיל *m* emayl 122
end סוֹף *m* sof 150
engaged *(phone)* תָּפוּס tafus 136
engagement ring טַבַּעַת אֵרוּסִים *f* tabaat erusim 122
engine *(car)* מָנוֹעַ *m* manoa 78
England אַנְגְלִיָה *f* angliya 134, 146
English אַנְגְלִי angli 93; *(language)* אַנְגְלִית *f* anglit 11, 16, 80, 82, 84, 104, 105, 126
enjoy oneself, to לֵהָנוֹת lehanot 96
enjoyable נָעִים naim 31
enlarge, to לְהַגְדִיל lehagdil 125
enough מַסְפִּיק maspik 14
entrance כְּנִיסָה *f* knisa 67, 99, 155
envelope מַעֲטָפָה *f* maatafa 104
equipment צִיּוּד *m* tziyud 91, 106
eraser מַחַק *m* maḥak 104
escalator מַדְרֵגוֹת נָעוֹת *f/pl* madregot naot 100
estimate *(cost)* הַעֲרָכָה *f* haarakha 78, 131
Eurocheque יוּרוֹצֶ'ק *m* yurotshek 130
Europe אֵירוֹפָּה *f* eropa 146
evening עֶרֶב *m* erev 95, 96
evening, in the בָּעֶרֶב baerev 151, 153
evening dress תִּלְבֹּשֶׁת עֶרֶב *f* tilboshet erev 88; *(woman's)* שִׂמְלַת עֶרֶב *f* simlat erev 115
every כָּל kol 143
everything הַכֹּל hakol 31, 59
exchange rate שַׁעַר *m* shaar 18, 130
exchange, to לְהַחֲלִיף lehaḥalif 103
excursion טִיוּל קָצָר *m* tiyul katzar 80
excuse, to לִסְלוֹחַ lisloaḥ 10
exercise book מַחְבֶּרֶת *f* maḥberet 105
exhaust pipe צִנּוֹר מַפְלֵט *m* tzinor maflet 78
exhibition תַּעֲרוּכָה *f* taarukha 81
exit יְצִיאָה *f* yetzia 67, 99, 155
expect, to לְצַפּוֹת letzapot 130
expenses הוֹצָאוֹת *f/pl* hotzaot 131
expensive יָקָר yakar 13, 19, 24, 101
exposure *(photography)* חֲשִׂיפָה *f* ḥasifa 124
exposure counter סוֹפֵר חֲשִׂיפוֹת *m* sofer ḥasifot 125
express אֶקְסְפְּרֶס ekspres 132
expression בִּטּוּי *m* bituy 10, 100
expressway דֶּרֶךְ מְהִירָה *f* derekh mehira 76
extension *(phone)* שְׁלוּחָה *f* shluḥa 135
extension cord/lead כֶּבֶל הַאֲרָכָה *m* kevel haarakha 118
extra נוֹסָף nosaf 27
eye עַיִן *f* ayin 138, 139
eye drops טִפּוֹת עֵינַיִים *f/pl* tipot eynayim 108
eye shadow צֶבַע לְעַפְעַפַּיִים *m* tzeva leafapayim 109
eye specialist רוֹפֵא עֵינַיִים *m* rofe eynayim 137
eyebrow pencil עִפָּרוֹן לְגַבּוֹת *m* iparon legabot 109
eyesight רְאִיָּה *f* reiya 123

F

fabric *(cloth)* בַּד *m* bad 112
face פָּנִים *m/pl* panim 138
face pack מַסֵיכַת פָּנִים *f* masekhat panim 30
face powder פּוּדְרָה לְפָנִים *f* pudra lepanim 109
factory בֵּית חֲרֹשֶׁת *m* beyt ḥaroshet 81
fair יָרִיד *m* yarid 81
fall *(autumn)* סְתָיו *m* stav 150
fall, to לִפּוֹל lipol 139
family מִשְׁפָּחָה *f* mishpaḥa 93, 144
fan belt חֲגוֹרַת מְאַוְרֵר *f* ḥagorat meavrer 75
far רָחוֹק raḥok 14, 100
fare *(ticket)* מְחִיר *m* meḥir«tab»
farm מֶשֶׁק *m* meshek 85
fast מָהִיר mahir 124
fat *(meat)* שׁוּמָן *m* shuman 38
father אָב *m* av 93
faucet בֶּרֶז *m* berez 28
fax פַקְס *m* faks 133
February פֶבְּרוּאָר *m* februar 150
fee *(doctor's)* תַּשְׁלוּם *m* tashlum 144
feeding bottle בַּקְבּוּק לְתִינוֹק *m* bakbuk letinok 110
feel, to *(physical state)* לְהַרְגִּישׁ lehargish 140, 142
felafel פָלָפֶל *m* falafel 61
felt לֶבֶד *m* leved 113
felt-tip pen עֵט לוֹרְד *m* et lord 105
ferry מַעְבֹּרֶת *f* maaboret 73
fever חֹם *m* ḥom 140
few כַּמָּה kama 14
field שָׂדֶה *m* sade 85
fifteen חֲמִשָּׁה-עָשָׂר ḥamisha asar 147
fifth חֲמִישִׁי ḥamishi 149
fifty חֲמִשִּׁים ḥamishim 147
fig תְּאֵנָה *f* teena 51
file *(tool)* פְּצִירָה *f* ptzira 109
fill in, to לְמַלֵּא lemale 26, 144
filling *(tooth)* מִלּוּי *m* miluy 145
filling station תַּחֲנַת דֶּלֶק *f* taḥanat delek 75
film סֶרֶט *m* seret 86, 124, 125
film winder קִדּוּם הַסֶּרֶט *m* kidum haseret 125
filter מַסְנֵן *m* masnen 125
filter-tipped עִם פִילְטֶר im filter 126
find, to לִמְצֹא limtzo 11, 12, 76, 84, 100
fine *(OK)* בְּסֵדֶר beseder 10, 25, 92
fine arts אָמָּנוּת יָפָה *f* omanut yafa 83
finger אֶצְבַּע *f* etzba 138
fire שְׂרֵפָה *f* srefa 156
first רִאשׁוֹן rishon 68, 72, 77, 149
first course מָנָה רִאשׁוֹנָה *f* mana rishona 42
first name שֵׁם פְּרָטִי *m* shem prati 25
first-aid kit עֶרְכַּת עֶזְרָה רִאשׁוֹנָה *f* erkat ezra rishona 108
fish דָּג *m* dag 44
fishing דַּיִג *m* dayig 90
fishing tackle צִיּוּד דַּיִג *m* tziyud dayig 106
fishmonger's חֲנוּת דָּגִים *f* ḥanut dagim 98
fit, to לְהַתְאִים lehatim 114
fitting room חֲדַר הַלְבָּשָׁה *m* ḥadar halbasha 114
five חֲמִשָּׁה ḥamisha 147
fix, to לְסַדֵּר lesader 145
fizzy *(mineral water)* תּוֹסֵס toses 57
flannel פְלָנֶל *m* flanel 113
flash *(photography)* מַבְזֵק *m* mavzek 125
flash attachment חִבּוּר לְמַבְזֵק *m* ḥibur lemavzek 125
flashlight פָּנָס יָד *m* panas yad 106
flat *(apartment)* דִּירָה *f* dira 23
flat tyre תֶּקֶר *m* teker 75, 78
flea market שׁוּק פִּשְׁפְּשִׁים *m* shuk pishpeshim 81
flight טִיסָה *f* tisa 65
floor קוֹמָה *f* koma 27
floor show הוֹפָעָה *f* hofaa 88
florist's חֲנוּת פְּרָחִים *f* ḥanut praḥim 98
flour קֶמַח *m* kemaḥ 38
flower פֶּרַח *m* peraḥ 85
flu שַׁפַּעַת *f* shapaat 142
fluid נוֹזֵל *m* nozel 123
foam rubber mattress מִזְרוֹן גּוּמָאֲוִיר *m* mizron gumavir 106
fog עֲרָפֶל *m* arafel 94
folding chair כִּסֵּא מִתְקַפֵּל *m* kise mitkapel 106
folding table שֻׁלְחָן מִתְקַפֵּל *m* shulḥan mitkapel 106
folk music שִׁירֵי עַם *m/pl* shirey am 128
follow, to לִנְסֹעַ לְפִי linsoa lefi 77
food אֹכֶל, מָזוֹן *m* okhel, mazon 38, 58, 110
food poisoning הַרְעָלַת קֵיבָה *f* haralat keva 142
foot כַּף רֶגֶל *f* kaf regel 138
foot cream מִשְׁחָה לְרַגְלַיִם *f* mishḥa leraglayim 109
football כַּדּוּרֶגֶל *m* kaduregel 89
footpath שְׁבִיל *m* shvil 85
for בִּשְׁבִיל bishvil 14
forbid, to לֶאֱסֹר leesor 155
forbidden אָסוּר asur 155
forecast תַּחֲזִית *f* taḥazit 94
foreign זָר zar 56
forest יַעַר *m* yaar 85
forget, to לִשְׁכֹּחַ lishkoaḥ 58

fork מזלג *m* maz**leg** 37, 58, 120
form *(document)* טופס *m* **to**fes 25, 26, 133, 144
fortnight שבועיים *m/pl* shvu**a**yim 151
fortress מבצר *m* miv**tzar** **81**
forty ארבעים arba**im** 147
foundation cream קרם בסיס *m* krem **ba**sis 109
fountain מזרקה *f* mizra**ka** 81
fountain pen עט נובע *m* et no**vea** 105
four ארבעה arba**a** 147
fourteen ארבעה-עשר arba**a** a**sar** 147
fourth רביעי re**vi**i 149
frame *(glasses)* מסגרת *f* mis**ge**ret 123
France צרפת *f* tzar**fat** 146
fresh טרי ta**ri** 51, 58
Friday יום ששי *m* yom shi**shi** **151**
fried מטוגן metu**gan** 44
fried egg ביצה מטוגנת *f* beyt**za** metu**ge**net 41
friend חבר *m* ḥa**ver**; *f* חברה ḥave**ra** 93
fringe פוני *m* **po**ni 30
from ...מ mi... 14
frost כפור *m* kfor 94
fruit פרי *m* pri 51
fruit cocktail קוקטיל פירות *m* **kok**teyl pe**rot** 51
fruit juice מיץ פירות *m* mitz pe**rot** 38, 41
fruit salad סלט פירות *m* sa**lat** pe**rot** 52
frying pan מחבת *f* maḥ**vat** 120
full מלא ma**le** 13
full board פנסיון מלא *m* pensi**yon** ma**le** 24
full insurance בטוח מקיף *m* bitu**aḥ** ma**kif** 20
furniture רהיטים *m/pl* rahi**tim** 83
furrier's חנות פרוות *f* ḥa**nut** par**vot** 98

G

gabardine גברדין *m* gabar**din** 113
gallery גלריה *f* gale**ri**ya 81, 98
game משחק *m* mis**ḥak** 128
garage מוסך *m* mu**sakh** 26, 78
garden גן *m* gan 85
gardens גנים *m/pl* ga**nim** 81
garlic שום *m* 50
gas גז *m* gaz 156
gasoline בנזין *m* ben**zin** 75, 78
gastritis דלקת קיבה *f* da**le**ket **ke**va 142
gauze גזה *f* **ga**za 108
gem אבן יקרה *f* **e**ven yeka**ra** 121
general כללי kla**li** 27, 100, 137
general delivery דואר שמור *m* **do**ar sha**mur** 133
general practitioner רופא כללי *m* ro**fe** kla**li** 137
genitals אברי מין *m/pl* ev**rey** min 138
gentleman גבר *m* **ge**ver 155
genuine אמיתי ami**ti** 118
geology גאולוגיה *f* geo**lo**giya 83
Germany גרמניה *f* ger**ma**niya 146
get, to *(obtain)* להשיג leha**sig** 90,134
get off, to לרדת la**re**det 72
get past, to לעבור laa**vor** 70
get to, to להגיע leha**gia** 19, 76
get up, to לקום la**kum** 144
gherkin מלפפון כבוש *m* melafe**fon** **kavush** 50
gift מתנה *f* mata**na** 17
gin ג׳ין *m* jin 55
gin and tonic ג׳ין וטוניק *m* jin ve**to**nik 56
ginger זנגביל *m* **zang**vil 50
girdle מחוך *m* ma**ḥokh** 115
girl ילדה *f* yal**da** 111, 128
girlfriend חברה *f* ḥave**ra** 93
give, to לתת la**tet** 12, 75, 123, 126, 130,135
give way, to *(traffic)* לתת זכות קדימה **latet** ze**khut** kdi**ma** 79
gland בלוטה *f* balu**ta** 138
glass כוס *f* kos 37, 54, 58,143
glasses משקפיים *m/pl* mishka**fa**yim 123
gloomy קודר ko**der** 84
glove כפפה *f* kfa**fa** 115
glue דבק *m* **de**vek 105
go away! הסתלק hista**lek** 156
go back, to לחזור laḥa**zor** 77
go out, to לצאת la**tzet** 95
go, to ללכת, לנסוע la**le**khet, lin**soa** 21, 72, 77, 96, 163
gold זהב *m* za**hav** 121, 122
gold plated מצופה זהב metzu**pe** za**hav** 122
golden זהב za**hov** 112
golf גולף *m* golf 89
good טוב tov 13, 86, 101
good afternoon שלום sha**lom** 10
goodbye שלום sha**lom** 10
good evening ערב טוב **e**rev tov 10
good morning בקר טוב **bo**ker tov 10
good night לילה טוב **lay**la tov 10
goose אווז *m* a**vaz** 47
gooseberry דומדמנית *f* dumde**ma**nit 51
gram גרם *m* gram 119
grammar דקדוק *m* dik**duk** 159
grammar book ספר דקדוק *m* **se**fer dik**duk** 105
grape ענב *m* e**nav** 51, 61
grapefruit אשכולית *f* eshko**lit** 51
grapefruit juice מיץ אשכוליות *m* mitz eshkoli**yot** 41
graze שפשוף *m* shif**shuf** 139
greasy שמן sha**men** 30, 110

great *(excellent)* נֶהְדָר nehe**dar** 95
Great Britain בְּרִיטַנְיָה הַגְּדוֹלָה *f* bri**ta**niya hagdo**la** 146
Greece יָוָן *f* ya**van** 146
green יָרוֹק ya**rok** 112
green bean שְׁעוּעִית יְרוּקָה *f* sheu**it** yeru**ka** 48
greengrocer's יַרְקָן *m* yar**kan** 98
greeting בְּרָכָה *f* bra**kha** 10, 152
grey אָפוֹר a**for** 112
grilled בַּגְּרִיל bi**gril** 46
grocer's חֲנוּת מַכֹּלֶת *f* ḥa**nut** ma**ko**let 98
groundsheet יְרִיעַת בִּדּוּד *f* yeri**at** bi**dud** 106
group קְבוּצָה *f* kvu**tza** 82
guesthouse בֵּית הַאֲרָחָה *m* beyt haara**ḥa** 19, 22
guide מַדְרִיךְ *m* madri**kh** 80
gum *(teeth)* חֲנִיכַיִם *m/pl* ḥani**kha**yim 145
gynaecologist רוֹפֵא נָשִׁים *m* ro**fe** na**shim** 137

H
hair שֵׂעָר *m* se**ar** 30, 110
hair dryer מְיַבֵּשׁ שֵׂעָר *m* meya**besh** se**ar** 118
hair gel גֵּל שֵׂעָר *m* jel se**ar** 30, 110
hair lotion קְרֶם לַשֵּׂעָר *m* krem lese**ar** 110
hairbrush מִבְרֶשֶׁת שֵׂעָר *f* miv**re**shet se**ar** 110
haircut תִּסְפֹּרֶת *f* tis**po**ret 30
hairdresser מִסְפָּרָה *f* mispa**ra** 30, 98
hairgrip מִצְבָּטִים לַשֵּׂעָר *m/pl* mitzba**tim** lese**ar** 110
hairpin סִכַּת רֹאשׁ *f* si**kat** rosh 110
half חֲצִי *m* **ḥe**tzi 149
half an hour חֲצִי שָׁעָה **ḥa**tzi sha**a** 153
half board חֲצִי פֶּנְסִיּוֹן **ḥatz** pensi**yon** 24
half price הֲנָחָה *f* hana**ḥa** 69
hall *(large room)* אוּלָם *m* u**lam** 81, 88
hall porter שׁוֹעֵר *m* sho**er** 26
hammer פַּטִּישׁ *m* pa**tish** 120
hammock עַרְסָל *m* ar**sal** 106
hand יָד *f* yad 138
hand cream מִשְׁחָה לְיָדַיִם *f* mish**ḥa** leya**da**yim 109
hand washable כָּבִיס בַּיָּד ka**vis** ba**yad** 113
handbag תִּיק יָד *m* tik yad 115, 156
handball כַּדּוּר יָד *m* ka**dur** yad 89
handicrafts מְלֶאכֶת יָד *f* **mle**khet yad 83
handkerchief מִמְחָטָה *f* mimḥa**ta** 115
handmade עֲבוֹדַת יָד *f* avo**dat** yad 112
hanger קוֹלָב *m* ko**lav** 27
happy שָׂמֵחַ same**aḥ** 152
harbour נָמָל *m* na**mal** 73, 81
hard קָשֶׁה ka**she** 123
hard-boiled *(egg)* בֵּיצָה קָשָׁה *f* **bey**tza ka**sha** 41
hardware store חֲנוּת לְחָמְרֵי בִּנְיָן *f* ḥa**nut** leḥom**rey** bin**yan** 99
hat כּוֹבַע *m* **ko**va 115
hay fever קַדַּחַת הַשַּׁחַת *f* ka**da**ḥat ha**sha**ḥat 107, 141
hazelnut אִלְסָר *m* il**sar** 51
head רֹאשׁ *m* rosh 138, 139
head waiter מֶלְצָר רָאשִׁי *m* mel**tzar** ra**shi** 58
headache כְּאֵב רֹאשׁ *m* ke**ev** rosh 107, 141
headphones אָזְנִיּוֹת *f/pl* ozni**yot** 118
health food shop חֲנוּת לְמָזוֹן טִבְעוֹנִי *f* ḥa**nut** lema**zon** tivo**ni** 99
health insurance *(company)* בִּטּוּחַ בְּרִיאוּת *m* bitu**aḥ** bri**ut** 144
Hebrew עִבְרִית *m* iv**rit** 11, 95
health insurance form טֹפֶס בִּטּוּחַ בְּרִיאוּת *m* **to**fes bitu**aḥ** bri**ut** 144«tab»«tab»
heart לֵב *m* lev 138
heart attack הֶתְקֵף לֵב *m* het**kef** lev 141
heat, to לְחַמֵּם leḥa**mem** 90
heavy כָּבֵד ka**ved** 13, 101
heel עָקֵב *m* a**kev** 117
helicopter מַסּוֹק *m* ma**sok** 74
hello שָׁלוֹם sha**lom** 10
help עֶזְרָה *f* ez**ra** 156
help! הַצִּילוּ hatzi**lu** 156
help, to לַעֲזוֹר laa**zor** 12, 21, 70, 100,134
herb tea תֵּה צְמָחִים *m* te zma**ḥim** 56
herbs תַּבְלִינִים *m/pl* tavli**nim** 50
here פֹּה, הִנֵּה hi**ne**, po 13
herring דָּג מָלוּחַ *m* dag malu**aḥ** 44
hi שָׁלוֹם sha**lom** 10
high גָּבוֹהַ gavo**ha** 85, 141
high season בָּעוֹנָה bao**na** 150
hill גִּבְעָה *f* giv**a** 85
hire שְׂכִירָה *f* skhi**ra** 20, 74
hire, to לִשְׂכּוֹר lis**kor** 19, 20, 74, 89, 91, 119, 155
history הִסְטוֹרְיָה *f* his**to**riya 83
hitchhike, to לָקַחַת טְרֶמְפּ la**ka**ḥat tremp 74
hold on! *(phone)* חַכֵּה ḥa**ke** 136
hole חוֹר *m* ḥor 29
holiday חֻפְשָׁה *f* ḥuf**sha** 151, 152
holidays פַּגְרָה *f* pag**ra** 151
home הַבַּיְתָה ha**bay**ta 96
home address כְּתֹבֶת הַבַּיִת *f* **kto**vet ha**ba**yit 31
home town עִיר מְגוּרִים *f* ir megu**rim** 25
honey דְּבַשׁ *m* dvash 42
hope, to לְקַוּוֹת leka**vot** 96
horse racing מֵרוֹץ סוּסִים *m* me**rotz** su**sim** 89

horseback riding רְכִיבָה עַל סוּס f rekhiva al sus 89
horseradish צְנוֹן m tznon 50
hospital בֵּית חוֹלִים m beyt ḥolim 99, 142, 144
hot חַם ḥam 14, 25, 37, 94
hot water מַיִם חַמִּים m/pl mayim ḥamim 24, 28
hot-water bottle בַּקְבּוּק חַם m bakbuk ḥam 27
hotel מָלוֹן m malon 19, 21, 22, 26, 30, 80, 96, 102
hotel directory/guide רְשִׁימַת בָּתֵּי מָלוֹן f reshimat batey malon 19
hotel reservation הַזְמָנַת מָלוֹן f hazmanat malon 19
hour שָׁעָה f shaa 80, 143, 153
house בַּיִת m bayit 83, 85
household article מוּצַר לַבַּיִת m mutzar labayit 120
how אֵיךְ eykh 11
how far זֶה רָחוֹק ze raḥok 11, 76, 100
how long כַּמָּה זְמַן kama zman 11, 26
how many כַּמָּה kama 11
how much כַּמָּה kama 11, 24
humus חוּמוּס m ḥumus 61
hundred מֵאָה mea 148
hungry רָעֵב raev 13, 35
hunting צַיִד m tzayid 90
hurry, to be in a לְמַהֵר lemaher 21
hurt (to be) לְהִפָּגַע lehipaga 139
hurt, to לִכְאוֹב likhov 139, 140, 142, 145
husband בַּעַל m baal 93
hydrofoil רַחֶפֶת f raḥefet 73

I

I אֲנִי ani 162
ice קֶרַח m keraḥ 94
ice cream גְּלִידָה f glida 53
ice cube קוּבִּיַּת קֶרַח f kubiyat keraḥ 27
ice pack רְטִיַּת קֶרַח f retiyat keraḥ 106
iced tea תֶּה קַר m te kar 57
if אִם im 143
ill חוֹלֶה hole 140
illness מַחֲלָה f maḥala 140
important חָשׁוּב ḥashuv 13
imported מְיוּבָּא meyuva 112
impressive מַרְשִׁים marshim 84
in בְּ... be... 15
include, to לִכְלוֹל likhlol 24, 31, 32, 59, 80
included כּוֹלֵל kolel 20, 31, 32, 40, 59, 80
India הוֹדוּ hodu 146
indigestion קִלְקוּל קֵיבָה m kilkul keva 141
indoor סָגוּר sagur 90
inflammation דַּלֶּקֶת f daleket 142

inflation אִינְפְלַצְיָה f inflatziya 131
inflation rate שַׁעַר הָאִינְפְלַצְיָה m shaar hainflatziya 131
information מוֹדִיעִין m modiin 67, 155
injection זְרִיקָה f zrika 142, 143, 144
injure, to לִפְצוֹעַ liftzoa 139
injured נִפְצָע niftza 79, 139
injury פְּצִיעָה f petzia 139
ink דְּיוֹ m dyo 105
insect bite עֲקִיצַת חֶרֶק f akitzat ḥarak 107, 139
insect repellent תַּכְשִׁיר דּוֹחֶה חֲרָקִים m takhshir doḥe ḥarakim 108
inside בִּפְנִים bifnim 14
instant coffee קָפֶה נָמֵס m kafe names 57
instrument (musical) כְּלִי m kli 127
insurance בִּטּוּחַ m bituaḥ 20, 144
insurance company חֶבְרַת בִּטּוּחַ f ḥevrat bituaḥ 79
interest (finance) רִבִּית f ribit 120
interested, to be לְהִתְעַנְיֵן lehitanyen 83, 96
interesting מְעַנְיֵן meanyen 84
international בֵּינְלְאוּמִי beynleumi 133, 134
interpreter תּוּרְגְּמָן m turgeman 131
intersection הִצְטַלְּבוּת f hitztalvut 77
introduce, to לְהַכִּיר lehakir 92
investment הַשְׁקָעָה f hashkaa 131
invitation הַזְמָנָה f hazmana 94
invite, to לְהַזְמִין lehazmin 94
invoice חֶשְׁבּוֹן m ḥeshbon 131
iodine יוֹד m yod 108
Ireland אִירְלַנְד f irland 146
Irish אִירִי iri 93
iron (for laundry) מַגְהֵץ m maghetz 118
iron, to לְגַהֵץ legahetz 29
ironmonger's חֲנוּת לַחוֹמְרֵי בִּנְיָן f ḥanut leḥomrey binyan 99
Israel יִשְׂרָאֵל f Israel 146
it זֶה ze 161
Italy אִיטַלְיָה f italiya 146
ivory שֶׁנְהָב m shenhav 122

J

jacket זָקֵט m jaket 115
jade יַרְקָן m yarkan 122
jam (preserves) רִיבָּה f riba 41
jam, to לְהִתְקַע lehitaka 28, 125
January יָנוּאָר yanuar 150
Japan יָפָן f yapan 146
jar (container) צִנְצֶנֶת f tzintzenet 119
jaundice צַהֶבֶת f tzahevet 142
jaw לֶסֶת f leset 138
jazz גָּז m jaz 128
jeans גִּינְס m/pl jins 115

jersey חֻלְצַת טְרִיקוֹ *f* ḥultzat triko 115
jewel box קוּפְסַת תַּכְשִׁיטִים *f* kufsat takhshitim 121
jeweller's צוֹרֵף *m* tzoref 99, 121
joint מִפְרָק *m* mifrak 138
journey נְסִיעָה *f* nesia 71
Jordan יַרְדֵּן *f* yarden 146
juice מִיץ *m* mitz 38, 56
July יוּלִי *m* yuli 150
jumper סוּדָר *m* sudar 115
June יוּנִי *m* yuni 150
just *(only)* רַק rak 12, 16, 38, 100

K

keep, to לִשְׁמֹר lishmor 59
kerosene נֵפְט *m* neft 106
key מַפְתֵּחַ *m* mafteaḥ 27
kidney כִּלְיָה *f* kilya 138
kilo(gram) קִילוֹ(גְרָם) *m* kilo(gram) 119
kilometre קִילוֹמֶטֶר *m* kilometer 20
kind נֶחְמָד neḥmad 95; *(type)* מִין *m* min 85, 140
knee בֶּרֶךְ *f* berekh 138
kneesocks גַּרְבַּיִם אֲרוּכּוֹת *f/pl* garbayim arukot 115
knife סַכִּין *f* sakin 37, 58, 120
knock, to לִדְפּוֹק lidpok 155
know, to לָדַעַת ladaat 16
kosher כָּשֵׁר kosher 34

L

label תָּוִית *f* tavit 105
lace תַּחֲרָה *f* taḥara 113
lady אִשָּׁה *f* isha 155
lake אֲגַם *m* agam 81, 85, 90
lamb *(meat)* טָלֶה *m* tale 45
lamp מְנוֹרָה *f* menora 28, 118
landscape נוֹף *m* nof 92
language שָׂפָה *f* safa 104
lantern פָּנָס *m* panas 106
large גָּדוֹל gadol 20, 101, 130
last אַחֲרוֹן aḥaron 14, 68
late מְאוּחָר meuḥar 13
later יוֹתֵר מְאוּחָר yoter meuḥar 135
laugh, to לִצְחוֹק litzḥok 95
laundry *(clothes)* כְּבִיסָה *f* kvisa 29; *(place)* מִכְבָּסָה *f* mokhbasa 29, 99
laundry service מִכְבָּסָה *f* mikhbasa 24
laxative חֹמֶר מְשַׁלְשֵׁל *m* ḥomer meshalshel 108
lead *(theatre)* תַּפְקִיד רָאשִׁי *m* tafkid rashi 87
leap year שָׁנָה מְעוּבֶּרֶת *f* shana meuberet 149
leather עוֹר *m* or 113, 117

leave, to *(deposit)* לִשְׁמוֹר lishmor 26; *(leave behind)* לְהַשְׁאִיר lehashir 20, 71
leeks כְּרֵישָׁה *f* krisha 49
left שְׂמֹאל smol 21, 69, 77
left-luggage office שְׁמִירַת חֲפָצִים *f* shmirat ḥafatzim 68, 71
leg רֶגֶל *f* regel 138
lemon לִימוֹן *m* limon 37, 51, 57, 64
lemonade לִימוֹנָדָה *f* limonada 56
lens עֲדָשָׁה *f* adasha 123, 125
lentils עֲדָשִׁים *f/pl* adashim 49
less פָּחוֹת paḥot 14
lesson שִׁעוּר *m* shiur 91
let, to *(hire out)* לְהַשְׂכִּיר lehaskir 155
letter מִכְתָּב *m* mikhtav 132
letter box תֵּיבַת דֹּאַר *f* teyvat doar 132
letter of credit כְּתַב אַשְׁרַאי *m* ktav ashray 130
lettuce חַסָּה *f* ḥasa 49
level crossing מַעֲבַר רַכֶּבֶת *m* maavar rakevet 79
library סִפְרִיָּה *f* sifriya 81, 99
licence *(driving)* רִשָּׁיוֹן *m* rishayon 20, 79
lie down, to לִשְׁכַּב lishkav 142
life belt חֲגוֹרַת הַצָּלָה *f* ḥagorat hatzala 73
life boat סִירַת הַצָּלָה *f* sirat hatzala 73
life guard *(beach)* מַצִּיל *m* matzil 90
lift *(elevator)* מַעֲלִית *f* maalit 27, 100
light קַל kal 13, 56, 101; *(colour)* בָּהִיר bahir 101, 111, 112; *(lamp)* תְּאוּרָה teura 28
light meter מַדְאוֹר *m* mador 125
lighter מַצִּית *m* matzit 126
lighter fluid/gas נוֹזֵל/גַּז לְמַצִּית *m* nozel/gaz lematzit 126
lightning בָּרָק *m* barak 94
like, to לְבַקֵּשׁ לִרְצוֹת levakesh, lirtzot 13, 20, 23, 60, 96, 111
like, to *(please)* לִמְצֹא חֵן limtzo ḥen 25, 92, 102
linen *(cloth)* פִּשְׁתָּן *m* pishtan 113
lip שָׂפָה *f* safa 138
lipsalve מִשְׁחָה לִשְׂפָתַיִם *f* mishḥa lisfatayim 109
lipstick שְׂפָתוֹן *m* sifton 109
liqueur לִיקֶר *m* liker 55
listen, to לְהַקְשִׁיב lehakshiv 128
litre לִיטֶר *m* liter 75, 119
little *(a little)* קְצָת ktzat 14
liver כָּבֵד *m* kaved 138
local מְקוֹמִי mekomi 36, 69
long אָרוֹךְ arokh 115
long-sighted מַרְחִיק רְאוּת marḥik reut 123
look, to לְהִסְתַּכֵּל lehistakel 100; 123, 139
look for, to לְחַפֵּשׂ lehapes 13
look out! זְהִירוּת zehirut 156

loose *(clothes)* חָפְשִׁי hof**shi** 114
lose, to לְאַבֵּד lea**bed** 123, 156
loss הֶפְסֵד *m* hef**sed** 131
lost אָבוּד a**vud** 13
lost and found office/lost property office מַחְלֶקֶת אֲבֵדוֹת *f* ma**ḥle**ket ave**dot** 67, 156
lot *(a lot)* הַרְבֵּה har**be** 14
loud *(voice)* רָם ram 135
love, to לֶאֱהוֹב lee**hov** 95
lovely יָפֶה ya**fe** 94
low נָמוּךְ na**mukh** 141
low season מְחוּץ לָעוֹנָה mi**hutz** lao**na** 150
luggage מִזְוָדוֹת *f/pl* mizva**dot** 17, 18, 21, 26, 31
luggage locker תָּא שְׁמִירַת חֲפָצִים *m* ta shmi**rat** ḥafa**tzim** 18, 68, 70
luggage trolley עֲגָלָה *f* aga**la** 18, 70
lump *(bump)* תְּפִיחָה *f* tfi**ḥa** 139
lung רֵיאָה *f* re**a** 138

M

machine *(washable)* מְכוֹנָה *f* mekho**na** 113
magazine מַגָזִין *m* maga**zin** 105
magnificent נִפְלָא nif**la** 84
maid חַדְרָנִית *f* ḥadra**nit** 26
mail דֹּאַר *m* **do**ar 28, 132
mailbox תֵּיבַת דֹּאַר *f* te**vat do**ar 132
main רָאשִׁי, עִיקָּרִי, מֶרְכָּזִי ra**shi**, ika**ri**, merka**zi** 67, 100
make up, to *(prepare bed)* לְהַצִּיעַ lehatzi**a** 28
make, to לַעֲשׂוֹת laa**sot** 131
make-up remover pad סְפוֹגִית לְהוֹרָדַת אִפּוּר *f* sfo**git** lehora**dat** i**pur** 109
mallet פַּטִּישׁ *m* pa**tish** 106
malt beer בִּירָה שְׁחוֹרָה *f* **bi**ra shḥo**ra** 54
man אִישׁ, גֶּבֶר *m* ish, **ge**ver 114, 156
manager מְנַהֵל *m* mena**hel** 26
manicure מָנִיקוּר *m* mani**kur** 30
many הַרְבֵּה har**be** 14
map מַפָּה *f* ma**pa** 76, 105
March מֶרְץ *m* mertz 150
marinated כָּבוּשׁ ka**vush** 44
marjoram אֵזוֹבִית *f* ezo**vit** 50
market שׁוּק *m* shuk 81, 99
marmalade מַרְמֶלָדָה *f* marme**la**da 41
married נָשׂוּי na**suy** 93
mass *(church)* מִיסָה *f* **mi**sa 84
match *(matchstick)* גַּפְרוּר *m* gafru**rim** 106, 126
match *(sport)* תַּחֲרוּת *f* taḥa**rut** 89
match, to *(colour)* מַשֶּׁהוּ דּוֹמֶה **ma**shehu 112
matinée הַצָּגָה יוֹמִית *f* hatza**ga** yo**mit** 87

matt *(finish)* מַט mat 125
mattress מִזְרוֹן *m* miz**ron** 106
May מַאי *m* may 150
may *(can)* אֶפְשָׁר ef**shar** 12, 37
meadow אָחוּ *m* a**ḥu** 85
meal אֲרוּחָה *f* aru**ḥa** 24, 34, 143
mean, to לוֹמַר lo**mar**«tab»
means אֶמְצָעִים *m/pl* emtza**im** 73
measles חַצֶּבֶת *f* ha**tze**vet 142
measure, to לִמְדּוֹד lim**dod** 113
meat בָּשָׂר *m* ba**sar** 35, 39, 58
meatball כַּדּוּר בָּשָׂר *m* ka**dur** ba**sar** 45
mechanic מְכוֹנַאי *m* mekho**nay** 78
mechanical pencil עִפָּרוֹן מֵכָנִי ipa**ron** mekha**ni** 105, 121
medical certificate תְּעוּדָה רְפוּאִית *f* teu**da** refu**it** 144
medicine רְפוּאָה *f* refu**a** 83; *(drug)* תְּרוּפָה *f* tru**fa** 143
medium *(meat)* בֵּינוֹנִי beyno**ni** 46
medium-sized בֵּינוֹנִי beyno**ni** 20
meet, to לְהִפָּגֵשׁ lehipa**gesh** 96
melon מֶלוֹן *m* me**lon** 52
memorial אַנְדַּרְטָה *f* andar**ta** 81
mend, to לְתַקֵּן leta**ken** 76
mend, to *(clothes)* לְתַקֵּן leta**ken** 29
menthol *(cigarettes)* מֶנְטוֹל men**tol** 126
menu תַּפְרִיט *m* taf**rit** 36, 39, 40
message הוֹדָעָה *f* hoda**a** 28, 136
metre מֶטֶר *m* **me**ter 111
mezzanine (theatre) יָצִיעַ *m* ya**tzia** 87
middle אֶמְצַע *m* **em**tza 150
Middle Eastern מִזְרָחִי mizra**ḥi** 37
mild (light) עָדִין a**din** 126
mileage קִילוֹמֶטְרָז' *m* kilome**traj** 20
milk חָלָב *m* ḥa**lav** 42, 60, 64
milkshake מִילְקְשֵׁיְק *m* **milk**sheyk 56
milliard בִּלְיוֹן *m* bil**yon** 148
million מִלְיוֹן *m* mil**yon** 148
mineral water מַיִם מִינֶרָלִיִּים *m/pl* **ma**yim minerali**yim** 57
minister *(religion)* כֹּמֶר *m* **ko**mer 84
mint נַעֲנָע *f* **naa**na 50
minute דַּקָּה *f* da**ka** 21, 69, 153
mirror רְאִי *m* re**i** 114, 123
miscellaneous שׁוֹנוֹת *f/pl* sho**not** 127
Miss גְּבֶרֶת *f* **gve**ret 10
miss, to חָסֵר ḥa**ser** 18, 29, 58
mistake טָעוּת *f* ta**ut** 31, 58, 59, 102
moccasin מוֹקַסִּין *m* moka**sin** 117
moisturizing cream קְרֶם לַחוּת *m* krem la**ḥut** 109
moment רֶגַע *m* **re**ga 12, 136
monastery מִנְזָר *m* min**zar** 81
Monday יוֹם שֵׁנִי *m* yom she**ni** 151
money כֶּסֶף *m* **ke**sef 18, 129, 130
money order הַמְחָאַת דֹּאַר *f* hamḥa**at do**ar

133
month חֹדֶשׁ *m* **ḥo**desh 16, 150
monument אַנְדַּרְטָה *f* andar**ta** 81
moon יָרֵחַ *m* ya**re**aḥ 94
moped אוֹפַנַּיִם עִם מָנוֹעַ *m/pl* ofa**na**yim im ma**no**a 74
more יוֹתֵר yo**ter** 14, 11
morning, in the בַּבֹּקֶר ba**bo**ker 143, 151, 153
mortgage מַשְׁכַּנְתָּא *f* mash**kan**ta 131
mosque מִסְגָּד *m* mis**gad** 84
mosquito net כִּלָּה *f* ki**la** 106
mother אֵם *f* em 93
motorbike אוֹפַנּוֹעַ *m* ofa**no**a 74
motorboat סִירַת מָנוֹעַ *f* si**rat** ma**no**a 92
motorway דֶּרֶךְ מְהִירָה *f* **de**rekh mehi**ra** 76
mountain הַר *m* har 85
mountaineering טִפּוּס בֶּהָרִים *m* ti**pus** beha**rim** 89
moustache שָׂפָם *m* sa**fam** 30
mouth פֶּה *m* pe 138, 142
mouthwash תַּשְׁטִיף פֶּה *m* tash**tif** pe 108
move, to לְהָזִיז leha**ziz** 139
movie camera מַצְלֵמַת קוֹלְנוֹעַ *f* matzle**mat** kol**no**a 124
movies קוֹלְנוֹעַ *m* kol**no**a 86, 96
Mr. מַר *m* mar 10
Mrs. גְּבֶרֶת *f* g**ve**ret 10
much הַרְבֵּה har**be** 14
mug סֵפֶל גָּדוֹל *m* se**fal** ge**dol** 120
muscle שְׁרִיר *m* shrir 138
museum מוּזֵאוֹן *m* muze**on** 81
mushroom פִּטְרִיָּה *f* pitri**ya** 49
music מוּסִיקָה *f* **mu**sika 83, 128
musical מַחֲזֶמֶר *m* maḥa**ze**mer 86
mustard חַרְדָּל *m* ḥar**dal** 50, 60
myself בְּעַצְמִי beatz**mi** 119

N

nail *(human)* צִפֹּרֶן *f* tzi**po**ren 109
nail brush מִבְרֶשֶׁת לְצִפָּרְנַיִם *f* miv**re**shet letzipor**na**yim 109
nail clippers גּוֹזֵז צִפָּרְנַיִם *m* go**zez** tzipor**na**yim 109
nail polish remover תַּכְשִׁיר לְהוֹרָדַת לַכָּה *m* takh**shir** lehora**dat la**ka 109
nail scissors מִסְפָּרַיִם לְצִפָּרְנַיִם *m/pl* mispa**ra**yim letzipor**na**yim 109
name שֵׁם *m* shem 23, 25, 79, 92, 133, 136
napkin מַפִּית *f* ma**pit** 37, 105, 108
nappy חִתּוּל *m* ḥi**tul** 110
narrow צַר tzar 117
nationality אֶזְרָחוּת *f* ezra**ḥut** 25, 92
natural history טֶבַע *m* **te**va 83
nausea בְּחִילָה *f* beḥi**la** 140
near קָרוֹב ka**rov** 14
nearby בַּסְּבִיבָה basvi**va** 32, 77
nearest הַקָּרוֹב haka**rov** 75, 78, 98
neat *(drink)* לֹא מָהוּל lo ma**hul** 56
neck צַוָּאר *m* tza**var** 30, 138
necklace מַחֲרֹזֶת *f* maḥa**ro**zet 121
need, to לְהִזְדַּקֵּק lehizda**kek** 29, 137
needle מַחַט *f* **ma**ḥat 27
negative נֶגָטִיב *m* nega**tiv** 125
nephew אַחְיָן *m* aḥ**yan** 93
nerve עָצָב *m* a**tzav** 138
nervous system מַעֲרֶכֶת עֲצַבִּים *f* maa**re**khet atza**bim** 138
never אַף פַּעַם לֹא af **pa**am lo 15
new חָדָשׁ ḥa**dash** 14
New Year רֹאשׁ הַשָּׁנָה *m* rosh hasha**na** 152
New Zealand נְיוּ זִילַנְד *f* nyu **zi**land 146
newsagent's חֲנוּת עִתּוֹנִים *f* ḥa**nut** ito**nim** 99
newspaper עִתּוֹן *m* **i**ton 104, 105
newsstand דּוּכַן עִתּוֹנִים *m* du**khan** ito**nim** 19, 68, 99, 104
next הַבָּא ha**ba** 14, 65, 68, 73, 76, 149, 151
next time בַּפַּעַם הַבָּאָה ba**pa**am haba**a** 95
next to ...סָמוּךְ לְ sa**mukh** le 15, 77
nice *(beautiful)* יָפֶה ya**fe** 94
niece אַחְיָנִית *f* aḥya**nit** 93
night לַיְלָה *m* **lay**la 10, 25, 151
night cream קְרֶם לַיְלָה *m* krem **lay**la 109
night, at בַּלַּיְלָה ba**lay**la 151
nightclub מוֹעֲדוֹן לַיְלָה *m* moa**don lay**la 88
nightdress/-gown כֻּתֹּנֶת לַיְלָה *f* ku**to**net **lay**la 115
nine תִּשְׁעָה tish**a** 147
nineteen תִּשְׁעָה-עָשָׂר tish**a a**sar 147
ninety תִּשְׁעִים tish**im** 148
ninth תְּשִׁיעִי tshi**i** 149
no לֹא lo 10
noisy רוֹעֵשׁ ro**esh** 25
nonalcoholic לֹא אַלְכּוֹהוֹלִי, קַל lo alko**ho**li, kal 56
none לֹא כְּלוּם lo khlum 15
nonsmoker לֹא מְעַשְּׁנִים lo measch**nim** 36, 70
noodle אִטְרִית *f* i**trit** 48
noon צָהֳרַיִם *m/pl* tzoho**ra**yim 31, 153
normal רָגִיל ra**gil** 30
north צָפוֹן *m* tza**fon** 77
North America צְפוֹן אָמֶרִיקָה *f* tzfon a**me**rika 146
Norway נוֹרְבֶגְיָה *f* nor**ve**giya 146
nose אַף *m* af 138
nose drops טִפּוֹת אַף *f/pl* ti**pot** af 108
nosebleed דִּמּוּם מֵהָאַף *m* di**mum** meha**af** 141

not לא lo 15, 163
note *(banknote)* שְטָר *m* shtar 130
note paper נְיַר כְּתִיבָה *m* neyar ktiva 105
notebook פִּנְקָס *m* pinkas 105
nothing שׁוּם דָּבָר shum davar 15
notice *(sign)* הוֹדָעָה *f* hodaa 155
notify, to לְהוֹדִיעַ lehodia 144
November נוֹבֶמְבֶּר *m* november 150
now עַכְשָׁו akhshav 15
number מִסְפָּר *m* mispar 25, 26, 65, 135, 136, 147
nurse אָחוֹת *f* aḥot 144
nutmeg אֱגוֹז מוּסְקָט *m* egoz muskat 50

O

occupied תָּפוּס tafus 13, 155
October אוֹקְטוֹבֶּר *m* oktober 150
oil שֶׁמֶן *m* shemen 37, 75, 110
oily *(greasy)* שָׁמֵן shamen 30, 110
old זָקֵן, יָשָׁן zaken, yashan 14
old town עִיר עַתִּיקָה *f* ir atika 81
olive זַיִת *m* zeyit 61
on עַל al 15
one-way *(traffic)* חַד סִטְרִי ḥad sitri 77, 79
on foot בָּרֶגֶל baregel 76
on time בַּזְּמַן bazman 68
once פַּעַם *f* paam 149
one אֶחָד eḥad 147
onion בָּצָל *m* batzal 49
only רַק, בִּלְבַד rak, bilvad 15, 25, 80, 87, 108
onyx שֹׁהַם *m* shoham 122
open פָּתוּחַ patuaḥ 14, 82, 155
open, to לִפְתּוֹחַ liftoaḥ 11, 17, 82, 107, 130, 132, 142
open-air פָּתוּחַ patuaḥ 90
opera אוֹפֶּרָה *f* opera 88
opera house בֵּית אוֹפֶּרָה *m* beyt opera 81, 88
operation נִתּוּחַ *m* nituaḥ 144
operator מֶרְכָּזִיָּה *f* merkaziya 134
operetta אוֹפֶּרֶטָה *f* opereta 88
opposite מוּל mul 77
optician אוֹפְּטִיקַאי *m* optikay 99, 123
or אוֹ o 15
orange תַּפּוּז *m* tapuz 52, 61
orange *(colour)* כָּתוֹם katom 112
orange juice מִיץ תַּפּוּזִים *m* mitz tapuzim 41
orangeade אוֹרַנְזָ'דָה *f* oranjada 57
orchestra תִּזְמֹרֶת *f* tizmoret 88
orchestra *(seats)* שׁוּרוֹת קִדְמִיּוֹת *f/pl* shurot kidmiyot 87
order, to *(goods, meal)* לְהַזְמִין lehazmin 58, 102, 103
ornithology צִפֳּרִים *f/pl* tziporim 83
other אַחֵר aḥer 73, 101
out of order מְקוּלְקָל mekulkal 136, 155
out of stock אָזַל azal 103
outlet *(electric)* שֶׁקַע *m* sheka 27
outside בַּחוּץ baḥutz 15, 36
oval אֶלִיפְּטִי elipti 101
overalls סַרְבָּל *m* sarbal 115
overdone *(meat)* יוֹתֵר מִדַּי מְבוּשָׁל yoter miday mevushal 58
overheat, to *(engine)* לְהִתְחַמֵּם lehithamem 78
overtake, to לַעֲקוֹף laakof 79

P

pacifier *(baby's)* מוֹצֵץ *m* motzetz 110
packet חֲפִיסָה *f* ḥafisa 126
pail דְּלִי *m* dli 128
pain כְּאֵב *m* keev 140, 141, 144
painkiller תְּרוּפָה נֶגֶד כְּאֵבִים *f* trufa neged keevim 140
paint צֶבַע *m* tzeva 155
paint, to לְצַיֵּר letzayer 83
paintbox קֻפְסַת צְבָעִים *f* kufsat tzvaim 105
painter צַיָּר *m* tzayar 83
painting צִיּוּר *m* tziyur 83
pair זוּג *m* zug 115, 117, 149
palace אַרְמוֹן *m* armon 81
palpitations רְעִידוֹת לֵב *f/pl* reidot lev 141
pancake לְבִיבָה *f* leviva 47
panties תַּחְתּוֹנִים *m/pl* taḥtonim 115
pants *(trousers)* מִכְנָסַיִם *m/pl* mikhnasayim 115
panty girdle מָחוֹךְ גַּרְבּוֹנִים *m* meḥokh garbonim 115
panty hose גַּרְבּוֹנִים *m/pl* garbonim 115
paper נְיָר *m* neyar 105
paper napkin מַפִּית נְיָר *f* mapit negar 105, 120
paperback סֵפֶר כִּיס *m* sefer kis 105
paperclip מְהַדֵּק *m* mehadek 105
paraffin *(fuel)* נֵפְט *m* neft 106
parcel חֲבִילָה *f* ḥavila 132, 133
pardon, I beg your סְלִיחָה *f* sliḥa 10
parents הוֹרִים *m/pl* horim 93
park פָּארְק *m* park 81
park, to לַחֲנוֹת laḥanot 26, 77
parka מְעִיל רוּחַ *m* meil ruaḥ 115
parking חֲנָיָה *f* ḥanaya 77, 79
parking meter מַדְחָן *m* madḥan 78
parliament building כְּנֶסֶת *f* kneset 81
parsley פֶּטְרוֹסִילְיָה *f* petrosilya 50
part חֵלֶק *m* ḥelek 138
partridge חָגְלָה *f* ḥogla 47
party *(social gathering)* מְסִבָּה *f* mesiba 95
parve פַּרְוֶה parve 35

DICTIONARY מילון

pass *(mountain)* מַעֲבַר הָרִים *m* maavar harim 85
pass through, to לִהְיוֹת בְּמַעֲבָר lihyot bemaavar 16
pass, to *(driving)* לַעֲקוֹף laakof 79
passport דַּרְכּוֹן *m* darkon 16, 17, 26, 156
passport photo תְּמוּנַת דַּרְכּוֹן *f* tmunat darkon 124
pasta פַּסְטָה *f* pasta 48
paste *(glue)* דֶּבֶק *m* devek 105
pastry עוּגוֹת *f/pl* ugot 53
pastry shop חֲנוּת עוּגוֹת *f* ḥanut ugot 99
patch, to *(clothes)* לְהַטְלִיא lehatli 29
path שְׁבִיל *m* shvil 85
patient חוֹלֶה *m* ḥole 144
pay, to לְשַׁלֵּם leshalem 17, 31, 59, 102, 136
payment תַּשְׁלוּם *m* tashlum 102, 131
pea אֲפוּנָה *f* afuna 49
peach אֲפַרְסֵק *m* afarsek 52
peak פִּסְגָּה *f* pisga 85
peanut בֹּטֶן *m* boten 52
pear אַגָּס *m* agas 52
pearl פְּנִינָה *f* pnina 122
peg *(tent)* יָתֵד *f* yated 106
pen עֵט *m* et 105
pencil עִפָּרוֹן *m* iparon 105
pencil sharpener מְחַדֵּד *m* meḥaded 105
pendant תִּלְיוֹן *m* tilyon 121
penicilline פֶּנִיצִילִין *m* penitzilin 143
penknife אוֹלָר *m* olar 120
pensioner גִּימְלַאי *m* gimlay 82
people אֲנָשִׁים *m/pl* anashim 92
pepper פִּלְפֵּל *m* pilpel 37, 50, 60
per cent אָחוּז *m* aḥuz 149
per day לְיוֹם leyom 20, 32, 89
per hour לְשָׁעָה leshaa 78, 89
per person לְאִישׁ leish 32
per week לְשָׁבוּעַ leshavua 20, 24
percentage אָחוּז *m* aḥuz 131
perform, to *(theater)* לְהַצִּיג lehatzig 87
perfume בֹּשֶׂם *m* bosem 109
perhaps אוּלַי ulay 15
period *(monthly)* מַחֲזוֹר *m* maḥazor 141
period pains כְּאֵבֵי מַחֲזוֹר *m/pl* keevey maḥazor 141
permanent wave סִלְסוּל תְּמִידִי *m* silsul tmidi 30
permit רִשָּׁיוֹן *m* rishayon 90
person אִישׁ *m* ish 32
personal אִישִׁי ishi 130
personal call/person-to-person call שִׂיחָה אִישִׁית *f* siḥa ishit 134
personal cheque הַמְחָאָה אִישִׁית *f* hamḥaa ishit 130
petrol בֶּנְזִין *m* benzin 75, 78
pewter בְּדִיל-עוֹפֶרֶת *m* bdil-oferet 122
pheasant פַּסְיוֹן *m* pasyon 47
photo תַּצְלוּם *m* tatzlum 82, 124, 125
photocopy הֶעְתֵּק *m* heetek 131
photograph, to לְצַלֵּם letzalem 82
photographer צַלָּם *m* tzalam 99
photography צִלּוּם *m* tzilum 124
phrase בִּטּוּי *m* bituy 12
pick up, to *(person)* לֶאֱסוֹף leesof 80, 96
pickle חָמוּץ *m* kavḥamutz 50
picnic פִּיקְנִיק *m* piknik 60
picnic basket אַרְגָּז לְפִּיקְנִיק *m* argaz lepiknik 106
picture *(painting)* תְּמוּנָה *f* tmuna 83
piece פְּרוּסָה *f* prusa 119
pigeon יוֹנָה *f* yona 47
pill כַּדּוּר *m* kadur 143; *(contraceptive)* גְּלוּלָה *f* glula 141
pillow כַּר *m* kar 27
pin סִכָּה *f* sika 110, 109, 121
pineapple אֲנָנָס *m* ananas 52
pink וָרוֹד varod 112
pipe מִקְטֶרֶת *f* mikteret 126
pipe cleaner כְּלִי נִקּוּי לְמִקְטֶרֶת *m* kli nikuy lemikteret 126
pipe tobacco טַבָּק לְמִקְטֶרֶת *m* tabak lemikteret 126
pipe tool מַכְשִׁיר נִקּוּי לְמִקְטֶרֶת *m* makhshir nikuy lemikteret 126
place מָקוֹם *m* makom 25
place of birth מְקוֹם הוּלֶדֶת *m* mekom huledet 25
place, to לְהַזְמִין lehazmin 134
plain *(colour)* אָחִיד aḥid 112
plane מָטוֹס *m* matos 65
planetarium פְּלָנֶטַרְיוּם *m* planetariyum 81
plaster גֶּבֶס *m* geves 140
plate צַלַּחַת *f* tzalaḥat 37, 58, 120
platform *(station)* רָצִיף *m* ratzif 67, 68, 69, 70
platinum פְּלָטִינָה *f* platina 122
play *(theatre)* מַחֲזֶה *m* maḥaze 86
play, to לְשַׂחֵק lesaḥek 89, 93
playground מִגְרַשׁ מִשְׂחָקִים *m* migrash misḥakim 32
playing card קְלָף *m* klaf 105, 128
please בְּבַקָּשָׁה bevakasha 10
plimsolls נַעֲלֵי סְפּוֹרְט *f/pl* naaley sport 117
plug *(electric)* תֶּקַע *m* teka 29, 118
plum שָׁזִיף *m* shazif 52
pneumonia דַּלֶּקֶת רֵאוֹת *f* daleket reot 142
poached שָׁלוּק shaluk 44
pocket כִּיס *m* kis 116
pocket calculator מַחְשֵׁב כִּיס *m* maḥshev kis 105
pocket watch שְׁעוֹן כִּיס *m* sheon kis 121

point of interest *(sight)* מַרְאֶה *m* mare 80
point, to לְהַרְאוֹת leharot 12
poison רַעַל *m* raal 108, 156
poisoning הַרְעָלָה *f* harala 142
pole *(ski)* מוֹט *m* mot 91; *(tent)* מוֹט *m* mot 106
police מִשְׁטָרָה *f* mishtara 79, 156
police station תַּחֲנַת מִשְׁטָרָה *f* tahanat mishtara 99, 156
pond בְּרֵיכָה *f* brekha 85
poplin כּוּתְנַת פּוֹפְּלִין *f* kutnat poplin 113
poppyseed פֶּרֶג *m* pereg 53
porcelain חַרְסִינָה *f* harsina 127
port נָמָל *m* namal 73
portable נַיָּד nayad 118
porter סַבָּל *m* sabal 18
portion מָנָה *f* mana 38, 53, 58
Portugal פּוֹרְטוּגָל *f* portugal 146
possible, *(as soon as)* אֶפְשָׁרִי efshari 137
post *(mail)* דֹּאַר *m* doar 28, 132
post office דֹּאַר *m* doar 99, 132
post, to לִשְׁלוֹחַ lishloah 28
postage stamp בּוּל *m* bul 28, 126, 132, 133
postcard גְּלוּיָה *f* gluya 105, 126
poste restante דֹּאַר שָׁמוּר *m* doar shamur 133
potato תַּפּוּחַ אֲדָמָה *m* tapuah adama 49
pot roast בָּקָר צָלוּי *m* bakar tzaluy 45
pottery קַדָּרוּת *f* kadarut 83
poultry עוֹף *m* of 47
pound לִירָה *f* lira 18, 102, 130
powder פּוּדְרָה *f* pudra 109
powder compact פּוּדְרִיָּה *f* pudriya 121
powder puff פּוּדְרִיָּה *f* pudriya 109
pregnant בְּהֵרָיוֹן beherayon 141
premium *(gasoline)* סוּפֶּר super 75
prescribe, to לִרְשׁוֹם lirshom 143
prescription מִרְשָׁם *m* mirsham 107, 143
present מַתָּנָה *f* matana«tab»
press stud לַחְצָנִית *f* lahtzanit 116
press, to *(iron)* לְגַהֵץ legahetz 29
pressure לַחַץ *m* lahatz 75, 141
pretty יָפֶה yafe 84
price מְחִיר *m* mehir 24
priest כֹּמֶר *m* komer 84
print *(photo)* תְּמוּנָה *f* tmuna 124
private פְּרָטִי prati 24, 80, 91, 155
processing *(photo)* פִּתּוּחַ *m* pituah 124
profit רֶוַח *m* revah 131
programme תָּכְנִיָּה *f* tokhniya 87
pronounce, to לְבַטֵּא levate 12
pronunciation מִבְטָא *m* mivta 6
propelling pencil עִפָּרוֹן מֵכָנִי miparon mekhani 105, 121
Protestant פְּרוֹטֶסְטַנְטִי protestanti 84

provide, to לְסַדֵּר lesader 131
prune שָׁזִיף מְיֻבָּשׁ *m* shazif meyubash 52
public holiday חַג *m* hag 152
pull, to לִמְשׁוֹךְ limshokh 155
pull, to *(tooth)* לַעֲקוֹר laakor 145
pullover סוּדָר *m* sudar 115
pump מַשְׁאֵבָה *f* masheva 106
pumpkin דְּלַעַת *f* dlaat 49
puncture תֶּקֶר *m* teker 75
purchase קְנִיָּה *f* kniya 131
pure נָקִי naki 113
purple אַרְגָּמָן argaman 112
push, to לִדְחוֹף lidhof 155
put, to לָשִׂים lasim 24
pyjamas פִּיגָ'מָה *f* pijama 116

Q

quail שְׂלָו *m* slav 47
quality אֵיכוּת *f* ekhut 103, 112
quantity כַּמּוּת *f* kamut 14
quarter רֶבַע *m* reva 149
quarter of an hour רֶבַע שָׁעָה *m* reva shaa 153
quartz קְוַרְץ *m* kvartz 122
question שְׁאֵלָה *f* sheela 11
quick(ly) מָהִיר (מַהֵר) mahir (maher) 14, 79, 137, 156
quiet שָׁקֵט shaket 23, 25

R

rabbi רַב *m* rav 84
race מֵרוֹץ *m* merotz 89
race course/track מַסְלוּל מֵרוֹצִים *m* maslul merotzim 89
racket *(sport)* מַחְבֵּט *m* mahbet 89
radiator *(car)* מַקְרֵן *m* makren 78
radio רַדְיוֹ *m* radyo 24, 118
radish צְנוֹנִית *f* tznonit 49
railway רַכֶּבֶת *f* rakevet 67
railway station תַּחֲנַת רַכֶּבֶת *f* tahanat rakevet 19, 21, 67, 70
rain גֶּשֶׁם *m* geshem 94
raincoat מְעִיל גֶּשֶׁם meil geshem 116
raisin צִמּוּק *m* tzimuk 52
rangefinder מַד מֶרְחָק *m* mad merhak 125
rare *(meat)* נָא na 46
rash פְּרִיחָה *f* priha 139
raspberry פֶּטֶל *m* petel 52
rate *(inflation)* שַׁעַר *m* shaar 131
rate *(of exchange)* שַׁעַר *m* shaar 19, 130; *(price)* תַּעֲרִיף *m* taarif 20
razor תַּעַר *m* taar 109
razor blades סַכִּינֵי גִּלּוּחַ *m/pl* sakiney giluah 109
reading lamp מְנוֹרַת לַיְלָה *f* menorat layla

27
ready מוּכָן mu**khan** 29, 117, 123, 125, 145
real *(genuine)* אֲמִתִּי ami**ti** 117, 121
rear אֲחוֹרִי aḥo**ri** 75
receipt קַבָּלָה *f* kaba**la** 103, 144
reception קַבָּלָה *f* kaba**la** 23
receptionist פְּקִיד קַבָּלָה *m* pe**kid** kaba**la** 26
recommend, to לְהַמְלִיץ leham**litz** 35, 37, 80, 86, 88, 137, 145
record *(disc)* תַּקְלִיט *m* tak**lit** 127, 128
record player פָּטֵפוֹן *m* pate**fon** 118
recorder רַשְׁמְקוֹל *m* resham**kol** 118
rectangular מַלְבֵּנִי malbe**ni** 101
red אָדוֹם a**dom** 55, 105, 112
reduction הֲנָחָה *f* hana**ḥa** 24, 82
refill *(pen)* מִלּוּי (לְעֵט) *m* mi**luy** 105
refund *(to get a)* הֶחְזֵר *m* heḥ**zer** 103
regards אִחוּלִים *m/pl* iḥu**lim** 152
registered mail דֹּאַר רָשׁוּם *m* **doar** ra**shum** 132
registration form טֹפֶס רִשּׁוּם *m* **to**fes ri**shum** 25, 26
religion דָּת *f* dat 83
religious service תְּפִלָּה *f* tfi**la** 84
rent, to לִשְׂכּוֹר lis**kor** 19, 20, 89, 91, 155
rental שְׂכִירָה *f* skhi**ra** 20
repair תִּקּוּן *m* ti**kun** 125
repair, to לְתַקֵּן leta**ken** 29, 118, 117, 121, 123, 125, 145
repeat, to לוֹמַר שֵׁנִית lo**mar** she**nit** 11
report, to *(a theft)* לְהוֹדִיעַ leho**dia** 156
required הֶכְרֵחִי hekhre**hi** 88
requirement בַּקָּשָׁה *f* baka**sha** 27
reservation הַזְמָנָה *f* hazma**na** 19, 23, 66, 69
reservations office אֶשְׁנָב כַּרְטִיסִים *m* esh**nav** karti**sim** 67
reserve, to לְהַזְמִין lehaz**min** 19, 23, 36, 87
reserved תָּפוּס ta**fus** 155
rest שְׁאָר *m* she**ar** 130
restaurant מִסְעָדָה *f* misa**da** 19, 32, 35, 67
return ticket כַּרְטִיס הָלוֹךְ וָשׁוֹב *m* **kar**tis ha**lokh** va**shov** 65, 69
return, to *(come back)* לַחֲזוֹר laḥa**zor** 21, 80; *(give back)* לְהַחֲזִיר lehaḥa**zir** 103
rheumatism שִׁגָּרוֹן *m* shiga**ron** 141
rib צֵלָע *f* **ze**la 138
ribbon סֶרֶט *m* **se**ret 105
rice אֹרֶז *m* **o**rez 48
right *(correct)* נָכוֹן na**khon** 14; *(direction)* יָמִין ya**min** 21, 68, 77
ring *(jewellery)* טַבַּעַת *f* ta**baat** 121
ring, to *(doorbell)* לְצַלְצֵל letzal**tzel** 155
river נָהָר *m* na**har** 85, 90
road assistance עֶזְרָה בַּדֶּרֶךְ *f* **ez**ra ba**de**rekh 78
road map מַפַּת דְּרָכִים *f* ma**pat** dra**khim** 105
road sign תַּמְרוּר *m* tam**rur** 79
roasted צָלוּי tza**luy** 46
roll לַחְמָנִיָּה *f* laḥmani**ya** 42, 60
roll film סֶרֶט מְגוּלְגָּל *m* **se**ret megul**gal** 124
roller skate סְקֶט *m* sket 128
room חֶדֶר *m* **ḥe**der 19, 23, 24, 25, 27; *(space)* מָקוֹם *m* ma**kom** 32
room service שֵׁרוּת חֲדָרִים *m* she**rut** ḥada**rim** 24
rope חֶבֶל *m* **ḥe**vel 106
rosary מַחֲרֹזֶת תְּפִלָּה *f* maḥa**ro**zet tfi**la** 121
rosemary רוֹזְמָרִין *m* rozma**rin** 50
rouge אֹדֶם *m* **o**dem 109
round עָגוֹל a**gol** 101
round up, to לְעַגֵּל lea**gel** 59
round-neck עִם צַוָּארוֹן עָגוֹל im tzava**ron** a**gol** 115
round-trip ticket כַּרְטִיס הָלוֹךְ וָשׁוֹב *m* **kar**tis ha**lokh** va**shov** 65, 69
route דֶּרֶךְ *f* **de**rekh 85
rowing boat סִירַת חֲתִירָה *f* si**rat** ḥati**ra** 91
royal מַלְכוּתִי malkhu**ti** 81
rubber *(eraser)* מַחַק *m* **ma**hak 105; *(material)* גּוּמִי *m* **gu**mi 117
ruby אֹדֶם *m* **o**dem 122
rucksack תַּרְמִיל גַּב *m* tar**mil** gav 106
ruin חֻרְבָּה *f* ḥor**va** 81
ruler *(for measuring)* סַרְגֵּל *m* sar**gel** 105
rum רוּם *m* rum 55
running water מַיִם זוֹרְמִים *m/pl* **ma**yim zor**mim** 24
Russia רוּסְיָה *f* **ru**siya 146

S

safe כַּסֶּפֶת *f* ka**se**fet 26
safe *(free from danger)* בָּטוּחַ *m* ba**tuaḥ** 90
safety pin סִכַּת בִּטָּחוֹן *f* si**kat** bita**ḥon** 109
saffron כַּרְכֹּם *m* kar**kom** 50
sage מַרְוָה *f* mar**va** 50
sailing boat סִירַת מִפְרָשׂ *f* si**rat** mif**ras** 91
salad סָלָט *m* sa**lat** 42
sale מְכִירָה *f* mekhi**ra** 100, 131
salt מֶלַח *m* **me**laḥ 37, 38, 50, 60
salty מָלוּחַ ma**luaḥ** 58
same כָּזֶה ka**ze** 117
sand חוֹל *m* ḥol 90
sandal סַנְדָּל *m* san**dal** 117
sandwich כָּרִיךְ *m* ka**rikh** 60
sanitary napkin/towel תַּחְבֹּשֶׁת הִגְיֵנִית *f* taḥ**bo**shet hig**ye**nit 108

sapphire ספיר *m* sapir 122
satin סטין *m* satin 113
Saturday שבת *f* shabat 151
sauce רטב *m* rotev 48
saucepan סיר בשול *m* sir bishul 120
saucer תחתית *f* tahtit 120
sausage נקניקיה *f* naknikiya 45, 61
scarf צעיף *m* tzaif 116
scarlet שני shani 112
scenery נוף *m* nof 92
scenic route דרך נופית *f* derekh nofit 85
school בית ספר *m* beyt sefer 79
scissors מספריים *m/pl* misparayim 120, 109
scooter קטנוע *m* katnoa 74
Scotland סקוטלנד *f* scotland 146
scrambled eggs ביצה מקושקשת *f* beytza mekushkeshet 41
screwdriver מברג *m* mavreg 107
sculptor פסל *m* pasal 83
sculpture פסול *m* pisul 83
sea ים *m* yam 85, 90
seafood מאכלי ים *m/pl* maakhley yam 44
season עונה *f* ona 150
seasoning תבול *m* tibul 37
seat belt חגורת בטיחות *f* ḥagorat betiḥut 75
second שני sheni 149
second שניה *f* shniya 153
second-hand shop חנות מציאות *f* ḥanut metziot 99
secretary מזכיר *m* mazkir 27
see, to לראות lirot 12, 25, 26, 87, 89, 96, 121
sell, to למכור limkor 100
send, to לשלוח lishloaḥ 78, 102, 103, 132, 133
sentence משפט *m* mishpat 12
separately לחוד leḥud 59
September ספטמבר *m* september 150
seriously קשה kashe 139
service שרות *m* sherut 24, 59, 98, 100
service *(church)* תפילה *f* tfila 84
serviette מפית *f* mapit 37
set *(hair)* סדור *m* sidur 30
set menu תפריט קבוע *m* tafrit kavua 36, 40
setting lotion מייצב *m* meyatzev 30, 110
seven שבעה shiva 147
seventeen שבעה-עשר shiva asar 147
seventh שביעי shvii 149
seventy שבעים shivim 148
sew, to לתפור litpor 29
shade *(colour)* גוון *m* gavan 111
shampoo שמפו *m* shampu 30, 110
shampoo and set שמפו וסדור *m* shampu vesidur 30
shape צורה *f* tzura 103
share *(finance)* מניה *f* mnaya 131
sharp *(pain)* חד ḥad 140
shave גלוח *m* giluaḥ 30
shaver מכונת גלוח *f* mekhonat giluaḥ 27, 118
shaving brush מברשת גלוח *f* mivreshet giluaḥ 109
shaving cream משחת גלוח *f* mishhiat giluaḥ 109
shelf מדף *m* madaf 119
ship אניה *f* oniya 73
shirt חולצה *f* ḥultza 116
shivery מרגיש צמרמורת margish tzemarmoret 140
shoe נעל *m* naal 117
shoe polish משחת נעליים *f* mishḥat naalayim 117
shoe shop חנות נעליים *f* ḥanut naalayim 99
shoelace שרוך *m* srokh 117
shoemaker's סנדלר *m* sandlar 99
shop חנות *f* ḥanut 98
shop window חלון ראוה *m* ḥalon raava 100, 111
shopping קניות *f/pl* kniyot 97
shopping area אזור קניות *m* ezor kniyot 82, 100
shopping centre מרכז קניות *m* merkaz kniyot 99
short קצר katzar 30, 115, 114
short-sighted קצר ראיה ktzar reiya 123
shorts מכנסיים קצרים *m/pl* mikhnasayim ktzarim 116
shoulder כתף *f* katef 138
show הצגה , הופעה *f* hatzaga, hofaa 87; 88
show, to להראות leharot 12, 13, 76, 100, 101, 119, 124
shower מקלחת *f* miklaḥat 23, 32
shrink, to להתכווץ lehitkavetz 113
shut סגור sagur 14
shutter *(window)* תריס *m* tris 29; *(camera)* תריס *m* tris 125
sick *(ill)* חולה ḥole 140
sickness *(illness)* מחלה *f* maḥala 140
side צד *m* tzad 30
sideboards/-burns פאות *f/pl* peot 31
sightseeing טיול *m* tiyul 80
sightseeing tour טיול מאורגן *m* tiyul meurgan 80
sign *(notice)* שלט *m* shelet 77, 155
sign, to לחתום laḥatom 26, 130
signature חתימה *f* ḥatima 25
signet ring טבעת חותם *f* tabaat ḥotam 121
silk משי *m* meshi 113

silver כֶּסֶף *m* kesef 121, 122
silver *(colour)* כֶּסֶף **ke**sef 112
silver plated מְצֻפֶּה כֶּסֶף metzu**pe ke**sef 122
silverware כְּלֵי כֶּסֶף *m/pl* kley **ke**sef 121, 127
simple פָּשׁוּט pa**shut** 124
since מֵאָז me**az** 15, 150
sing, to לָשִׁיר la**shir** 88
single *(unmarried)* רַוָּק *m* ra**vak** 93
single cabin תָּא לְיָחִיד *m* ta leya**ḥid** 73
single room חֶדֶר לְיָחִיד *m* **hie**der leya**ḥid** 19, 23
sister אָחוֹת *f* a**ḥot** 93
sit down, to לָשֶׁבֶת la**she**vet 95
six שִׁשָּׁה shi**sha** 147
sixteen שִׁשָּׁה-עָשָׂר shi**sha** a**sar** 147
sixth שִׁשִּׁי shi**shi** 149
sixty שִׁשִּׁים shi**shim** 147
size גֹּדֶל *m* **go**del 124
size *(clothes)* מִדָּה *f* mi**da** 113, 117
ski מִגְלָשׁ סְקִי *m* mig**lash** ski 91
ski boot נַעַל סְקִי *f* **na**al ski 91
ski, to לַעֲשׂוֹת סְקִי laa**sot** ski 91
skiing סְקִי *m* ski 89, 91
skiing equipment צִיּוּד סְקִי *m* tziyud ski 91
skin עוֹר *m* or 138
skin-diving צְלִילָה *f* tzli**la** 91
skin-diving equipment צִיּוּד צְלִילָה *m* tzi**yud** tzli**la** 91, 106
skirt חֲצָאִית *f* ḥatza**it** 116
sky שָׁמַיִם *m/pl* sha**ma**yim 94
sleep, to לִישׁוֹן li**shon** 144
sleeping bag שַׂק שֵׁינָה *m* sak she**na** 106
sleeve שַׁרְווּל *m* shar**vul** 115, 142
sleeveless בְּלִי שַׁרְווּלִים bli sharvu**lim** 115
slice פְּרוּסָה *f* pru**sa** 120
slide *(photo)* שְׁקוּפִית *f* shku**fit** 124
slip *(underwear)* שִׂמְלָה תַּחְתּוֹנִית *f* sim**la** taḥto**nit** 116
slipper נַעַל בַּיִת *f* **na**al **ba**yit 117
slow down, to לְהָאֵט leha**it** 79
slow(ly) אִטִּי (לְאַט) **i**ti (le**at**) 14, 21, 135
small קָטָן ka**tan** 13, 20, 25, 101, 117, 130
smoke, to לְעַשֵּׁן lea**shen** 95
smoked מְעוּשָּׁן meu**shan** 44
smoker מְעַשְּׁנִים measḥ**nim** 70
snack חֲטִיף *m* ḥa**tif** 60
snack bar מִזְנוֹן *m* miz**non** 67
snap fastener לַחְצָנִית *f* laḥtza**nit** 116
sneaker נַעַל סְפּוֹרְט *f* **na**al sport 117
snorkel שְׁנוֹרְקֶל *m* shnor**kel** 128
snow שֶׁלֶג *m* **she**leg 94
snuff טַבַּק הֲרָחָה *m* ta**bak** hara**ḥa** 126
soap סַבּוֹן *m* sa**bon** 27, 109
soccer כַּדּוּרֶגֶל *m* kadu**re**gel 89

sock גֶּרֶב *f* **ge**rev 116
socket *(electric)* שֶׁקַע *m* **she**ka 27
soft רַךְ rakh 123
soft drink מַשְׁקֶה קַל *m* mash**ke** kal 61
soft-boiled *(egg)* בֵּיצָה רַכָּה *f* bey**tza** ra**ka** 41
sole *(shoe)* סוּלְיָה *f* sul**ya** 117
soloist סוֹלָן *m* so**lan** 88
some קְצָת ktzat 14
someone מִישֶׁהוּ *m* mishe**hu** 95
something מַשֶּׁהוּ *m* mashe**hu** 29, 36, 53, 107, 111, 113, 125, 139
son בֵּן *m* ben 93
song שִׁיר *m* shir 128
soon בְּקָרוֹב beka**rov** 15
sore *(painful)* כּוֹאֵב ko**ev** 145
sore throat כְּאֵב גָּרוֹן *m* ke**ev** ga**ron** 141
sorry סְלִיחָה sli**ḥa** 10, 16
soup מָרָק *m* ma**rak** 43
south דָּרוֹם *m* da**rom** 77
South Africa דְּרוֹם אַפְרִיקָה *f* drom **af**rika 146
South America דְּרוֹם אָמֶרִיקָה *f* drom a**me**rika 146
souvenir מַזְכֶּרֶת *f* maz**ke**ret 127
souvenir shop חֲנוּת מַזְכָּרוֹת *f* ḥa**nut** mazka**rot** 99
spade אֵת *f* et 128
Spain סְפָרַד *f* sfa**rad** 146
spare tyre צְמִיג רֶזֶרְבִי *m* tz**mig** re**zer**vi 75
spark(ing) plug מַצָּת *m* ma**tzat** 76
sparkling *(wine)* נָתֵז **ne**tez 55
speak, to לְדַבֵּר leda**ber** 11, 16, 84, 135
speaker *(loudspeaker)* רַמְקוֹל *m* ram**kol** 118
special מְיוּחָד meyu**ḥad** 20; 37
special delivery אֶקְסְפְּרֶס eks**pres** 132
specialist מוּמְחֶה *m* mum**ḥe** 142
speciality מַאֲכָל מְיוּחָד *m* maa**khal** meyu**ḥad** 40
specimen *(medical)* דּוּגְמָה *f* dug**ma** 142
spectacle case נַרְתִּיק לְמִשְׁקָפַיִים *m* nar**tik** lemishka**fa**yim 123
speed מְהִירוּת *f* mehi**rut** 79
spell, to לְאַיֵּת lea**yet** 11
spend, to לְהוֹצִיא lehot**zi** 101
spice תַּבְלִין *m* tav**lin** 50
spinach תֶּרֶד *m* **te**red 49
spine עַמּוּד שִׁדְרָה *m* a**mud** shid**ra** 138
sponge סְפוֹג *m* sfog 109
spoon כַּף *m* kaf 37, 58, 120
sport סְפּוֹרְט *m* sport 89
sporting goods shop חֲנוּת לְדִבְרֵי סְפּוֹרְט *f* ḥa**nut** lediv**rey** sport 99
sprained נָקוּעַ na**kua** 140
spring *(water)* מַעְיָן *m* maa**yan** 85; *(season)* אָבִיב *m* a**viv** 150

square מְרוּבָּע meruba 101
square *(town)* כִּכָּר *f* kikar 82
stadium אִצְטַדְיוֹן *m* itztadyon 82
staff *(personnel)* עוֹבְדִים *m/pl* ovdim 26
stain כֶּתֶם *m* ketem 29
stainless steel פְּלָדָה אַלְחֶלֶד *f* pildat alheled 120, 122
stamp *(postage)* בּוּל *m* bul 28, 126, 132, 133
staple סִכָּה לְשַׁדְכָן *f* sika leshadkhan 105
star כּוֹכָב *m* kokhav 94
start, to לְהַתְנִיעַ לְהַתְחִיל mlehathil; lehatnia 80, 87, 88; *(car)* 78
starter *(meal)* מָנָה רִאשׁוֹנָה *f* mana rishona 42
station *(railway)* תַּחֲנָה *f* tahana 19, 21, 67, 70
station *(underground/subway)* תַּחֲנָה *f* tahana 71, 72
stationer's חֲנוּת לְמַכְשִׁירֵי כְּתִיבָה hanut lemakhshirey ktiva 99, 104
statue פֶּסֶל *m* pesel 82
stay, to לְהִשָּׁאֵר lehishaer 16, 24, 26, 142; *(reside)* לִשְׁהוֹת lishhot 93
steal, to לִגְנוֹב lignov 156
steamed מְאוּיָּד meuyad 44
stewed מְבוּשָּׁל mevushal 46
stiff neck עֹרֶף נוּקְשֶׁה *m* oref nukshe 141
still *(mineral water)* לֹא תּוֹסֵס lo toses 57
sting עֲקִיצָה *f* akitza 139
sting, to לַעֲקוֹץ laakotz 139
stitch, to לִתְפּוֹר litpor 29, 117
stock exchange בּוּרְסַת מְנָיוֹת *f* bursat menayot 82
stocking גֶּרֶב נָשִׁים *f* gerev nashim 116
stomach ache כְּאֵב קֵיבָה *m* keev keva 141
stools צוֹאָה *f* tzoa 142
stop *(bus)* תַּחֲנָה *f* tahana 72, 73
stop! עֲצוֹר atzor 156
stop, to לַעֲצוֹר laatzor 21, 68, 71
stop thief! עִצְרוּ אֶת הַגַּנָּב itzru et haganav 156
store *(shop)* חֲנוּת *f* hanut 98
straight *(drink)* לֹא מָהוּל lo mahul 56
straight ahead יָשָׁר קָדִימָה yashar kadima 21, 77
strange מוּזָר muzar 84
strawberry תּוּת שָׂדֶה *m* tut sade 52
street רְחוֹב *m* rehov 25, 77
street map מַפַּת רְחוֹבוֹת *f* mapat rehovot 19, 105
string חוּט מְשִׁיחָה *m* hut meshiha 105
strong חָזָק hazak 126, 143
student סְטוּדֶנְט תַּלְמִיד *m* student, talmid 82, 93
study, to לִלְמוֹד lilmod 93
stuffed מְמוּלָּא memula 49
sturdy חָזָק hazak 101
suede זַמְשׁ *m* zamsh 113, 117
sugar סוּכָּר *m* sukar 37, 38, 60, 64
suit *(man's)* חֲלִיפָה *f* halifa 116; *(woman's)* חֲלִיפַת נָשִׁים halifat nashim 116
suitcase מִזְוָדָה *f* mizvada 18
summer קַיִץ *m* kayitz 150
sun שֶׁמֶשׁ *m* shemesh 94
sun-tan cream מִשְׁחַת שִׁזּוּף *f* mishhat shizuf 109
sun-tan oil שֶׁמֶן שִׁזּוּף *m* shemen shizuf 109
sunburn כְּוִיַּת שֶׁמֶשׁ *f* kviyat shemesh 107
Sunday יוֹם רִאשׁוֹן *m* yom rishon 151
sunglasses מִשְׁקְפֵי שֶׁמֶשׁ *m/pl* mishkefey shemesh 123
sunshade *(beach)* סוֹכֵךְ *m* sokhekh 91
sunstroke מַכַּת שֶׁמֶשׁ *f* makat shemesh 141
super *(petrol)* סוּפֶּר super 75
superb נִפְלָא nifla 84
supermarket סוּפֶּרְמַרְקֶט *m* supermarket 99
supplement תּוֹסֶפֶת *f* tosefet 40
suppository נֵר *m* ner 108
surgery *(consulting room)* מִרְפָּאָה *f* mirpaa 137
surname שֵׁם מִשְׁפָּחָה *m* shem mishpaha 25
suspenders *(Am.)* כְּתֵפִיּוֹת *f/pl* ktefiyot 116
swallow, to לִבְלוֹעַ livloa 143
sweater סוּדָר *m* sudar 116
sweatshirt חוּלְצַת מֵיזָע *f* hultzat meyza 116
Sweden שְׁבֶדְיָה *m/f* shvediya 146
sweet מָתוֹק matok 55, 58
sweet *(confectionery)* מַמְתָּק *m* mamtak 126
sweet corn תִּירָס *m* tiras 49
sweet shop מִגְדָּנִיָּה *f* migdaniya 99
sweetener מַמְתִּיק *m* mamtik 38
swell, to לְהִתְנַפֵּחַ lehnapeahi 139
swelling נְפִיחוּת *f* nefihut 139
swim, to לִשְׂחוֹת lishot 90
swimming שְׂחִיָּה *f* shiya 89, 91
swimming pool בְּרֵיכַת שְׂחִיָּה *f* brekhat shiya 32, 90
swimming trunks/swimsuit בֶּגֶד יָם *m* beged yam 116
switch *(electric)* מַפְסֵק *m* mafsek 29
switchboard operator מֶרְכָּזָנִית *f* merkazanit 26
Switzerland שְׁוַיְצַרְיָה *f* shvitzariya 146
swollen נָפוּחַ nafuah 139
synagogue בֵּית כְּנֶסֶת *m* beyt kneset 84

synthetic סִנְתֶּטִי sin**te**ti 113
system מַעֲרֶכֶת *f* maa**re**khet 138

T

T-shirt חוּלְצַת-טִי *f* hul**tzat** ti 116
table שֻׁלְחָן *m* shul**ḥan** 36, 106
tablet *(medical)* טַבְלִית *f* tav**lit** 108
tahina טְחִינָה *f* te**ḥi**na 61
tailor's חַיָּט *m* ḥa**yat** 99
take, to לָקַחַת la**ka**ḥat 18, 25, 73, 102, 143
take away, to לָקַחַת la**ka**ḥat 60, 102
take to, to ...לָקַחַת לְ la**ka**ḥat le... 67
taken *(occupied)* תָּפוּס ta**fus** 69
talcum powder טַלְק *m* talk 109
tampon טַמְפּוֹן *m* tam**pon** 108
tangerine מַנְדָּרִינָה *f* manda**ri**na 52
tap *(water)* בֶּרֶז *m* **be**rez 28
tape recorder רְשַׁמְקוֹל *m* resham**kol** 118
tarragon טַרְגּוֹן *m* **ta**ragon 50
tax מַס *m* mas 102
taxi מוֹנִית *f* mo**nit** 19, 21, 67
tea תֵּה *m* te 42, 60, 64
team קְבוּצָה *f* kvu**tza** 89
tear, to לִקְרוֹעַ lik**ro**a 140
teaspoon כַּפִּית *f* ka**pit** 120, 143
telegram מִבְרָק *m* miv**rak** 133
telegraph office מִבְרָקִיָה *f* mivraki**ya** 99
telephone טֶלֶפוֹן *m* **te**lefon 28, 78, 134
telephone booth תָּא טֶלֶפוֹן *m* ta **te**lefon 134
telephone call שִׂיחַת טֶלֶפוֹן *f* si**ḥat te**lefon 134, 136
telephone directory מַדְרִיךְ טֶלֶפוֹן *m* mad**rikh te**lefon 134
telephone number מִסְפַּר טֶלֶפוֹן *m* **mis**par **te**lefon 134, 135, 156
telephone, to *(call)* לְטַלְפֵּן letal**pen** 134
telephoto lens עֲדָשַׁת טֶלֶפוֹטוֹ *f* ad**shat** tele**fo**to 125
television טֶלֶוִיזְיָה *f* tele**vi**zya 24, 118
telex טֶלֶקְס *m* **te**leks 133
telex, to לִשְׁלוֹחַ טֶלֶקְס mish**lo**aḥ **te**leks 130
tell, to לוֹמַר lo**mar** 12, 72, 76, 136, 153
temperature חֹם *m* hom 142
temporary זְמַנִּי zma**ni** 145
ten עֲשָׂרָה asa**ra** 147
tendon גִּיד *m* gid 138
tennis טֶנִיס *m* **te**nis 89
tennis court מִגְרַשׁ טֶנִיס *m* mig**rash te**nis 89
tent אֹהֶל *m* **o**hel 32
tent peg יָתֵד *m* ya**ted** 106
tent pole מוֹט לְאֹהֶל *m* mot le**o**hel 106
tenth עֲשִׂירִי asi**ri** 149

terrace מִרְפֶּסֶת *f* mir**pe**set 36
terrifying מַפְחִיד maf**ḥid** 84
tetanus טֶטָנוּס *m* **te**tanus 140
than מֵאֲשֶׁר mea**sher** 14
thank you תּוֹדָה to**da** 10
thank, to לְהוֹדוֹת leho**dot** 10, 96
that הַהוּא ha**hu** 11, 100,
theatre תֵּיאַטְרוֹן *m* tea**tron** 82, 86
theft גְּנֵבָה *f* gne**va** 156
their שֶׁלָּהֶם shela**hem** 161
then אָז az 15
there שָׁם sham 14
thermometer מַדְחוֹם *m* mad**ḥom** 108, 144
they הֵם hem 162
thief גַּנָּב *m* ga**nav** 156
thigh יָרֵךְ *f* ya**rekh** 138
thin דַּק dak 112
think, to *(believe)* לַחְשׁוֹב laḥa**shov** 94, 102
third שְׁלִישִׁי shli**shi** 149
thirsty, to be צָמֵא tza**me** 13, 35
thirteen שְׁלוֹשָׁה-עָשָׂר shlo**sha** a**sar** 147
thirty שְׁלוֹשִׁים shlo**shim** 147
this זֶה ze 11, 100
thousand אֶלֶף **e**lef 148
thread חוּט *m* ḥut 27
three שְׁלוֹשָׁה shlo**sha** 147
throat גָּרוֹן *m* ga**ron** 138, 141
throat lozenge טַבְלִית לִכְאֵב גָּרוֹן *f* tav**lit** likhev garon 108
through דֶּרֶךְ **de**rekh 15
through train רַכֶּבֶת יְשִׁירָה *f* ra**ke**vet yeshi**ra** 68
thumb בֹּהֶן *f* **bo**hen 138
thumbtack נַעַץ *m* **na**atz 105
thunder רַעַם *m* **ra**am 94
thunderstorm סוּפַת רְעָמִים *f* su**fat** rea**mim** 94
Thursday יוֹם חֲמִישִׁי *m* yom ḥami**shi** 151
thyme קוֹרָנִית *f* kora**nit** 50
ticket כַּרְטִיס *m* kar**tis** 69, 72, 87, 89
ticket office אֶשְׁנָב כַּרְטִיסִים *m* esh**nav** karti**sim** 67
tie עֲנִיבָה *f* ani**va** 116
tie clip/pin סִכָּה לַעֲנִיבָה *f* si**ka** leani**va** 122
tight *(close-fitting)* הָדוּק ha**duk** 114
tights גַּרְבּוֹנִים *m/pl* garbo**nim** 116
time זְמַן *m* zman 68, 80
time *(occasion)* פַּעַם *f* **pa**am 95, 142, 143
timetable *(trains)* לוּחַ זְמַנִּים *m* **lu**aḥ zma**nim** 68
tin *(container)* קוּפְסָא *f* **kuf**sa 120
tint צֶבַע *m* **tze**va 110
tinted כֵּהֶה ke**he** 123
tire צְמִיג *m* tza**mig** 75, 76
tired עָיֵף a**yef** 13

tissue (handkerchief) מִמְפַּחַת נְיָר f mitpaḥat neyar 109

to ...לְ 15

toast טוֹסְט m tost 41

tobacco טַבַּק m tabak 126

tobacconist's חֲנוּת טַבַּק f ḥanut tabak 99, 126

today הַיּוֹם hayom 29, 151

toe אֶצְבַּע הָרֶגֶל f etzba haregel 138

toilet paper נְיָר טוֹאָלֶט m neyar toalet 109

toilet water מֵי פָּנִים m/pl mey panim 109

toiletry תַּמְרוּקִים m/pl tamrukim 108

toilets שֵׁרוּתִים sherutim 24, 27, 32, 37, 67

tomato עַגְבָנִיּוֹת f agvaniyot 49

tomato juice מִיץ עַגְבָנִיּוֹת m mitz agvaniyot 57

tomb קֶבֶר m kever 82

tomorrow מָחָר maḥar 29, 96, 151

tongue לָשׁוֹן f lashon 138

tonic water טוֹנִיק m tonik 57

tonight הָעֶרֶב haerev 29, 86, 87, 95

tonsils שְׁקֵדִים m/pl shkedim 138

too (also) גַּם gam 15

too much מִדַּי יוֹתֵר yoter miday 14

tools כֵּלִים m/pl kelim 120

tooth שֵׁן f shen 145

toothache כְּאֵב שִׁנַּיִם m keev shinayim 145

toothbrush מִבְרֶשֶׁת שִׁנַּיִם f mivreshet shinayim 109, 118

toothpaste מִשְׁחַת שִׁנַּיִם f mishḥat shinayim 109

top, at the לְמַעְלָה lemala 30, 145

torch (flashlight) פָּנָס יָד m panas yad 106

torn קָרוּעַ karua 140

touch, to לָגַעַת lagaat 155

tough (meat) קָשֶׁה kashe 58

tour טִיּוּל m tiyul 80

tourist office לִשְׁכַּת תַּיָּרוּת f lishkat tayarut 22, 80

tow truck מְכוֹנִית גְּרָר f masait grar 78

towards לִקְרַאת likrat 15

towel מַגֶּבֶת f magevet 27, 109

towelling (terrycloth) בַּד מַגֶּבֶת m bad magevet 113

tower מִגְדָּל m migdal 82

town עִיר ir 19, 76, 88

town center מֶרְכַּז הָעִיר m merkaz hair 21, 72, 76

town hall עִירִיָּה f iriya 82

toy צַעֲצוּעַ m tzaatzua 128

toy shop חֲנוּת צַעֲצוּעִים f ḥanut tzaatzuim 99

traffic light רַמְזוֹר m ramzor 77

trailer קָרָוָן m karavan 32

train רַכֶּבֶת f rakevet 68, 69, 70, 153

transfer (finance) הַעֲבָרָה f haavara 131

transformer שַׁנַּאי m shanay 118

translate, to לְתַרְגֵּם letargem 12

transport, means of אֶמְצָעֵי תַּחְבּוּרָה m/pl emtzeey taḥbura 73

travel agency סוֹכְנוּת נְסִיעוֹת f sokhnut nesiot 99

travel guide מַדְרִיךְ טִיּוּלִים m madrikh tiyulim 105

travel sickness מַחֲלַת נְסִיעָה f maḥalat nesia 107

travel, to לִנְסוֹעַ linsoa 93

traveller's cheque הַמְחָאַת נוֹסְעִים f hamḥaat nosim 18, 59, 102, 130

travelling bag תִּיק נְסִיעָה m tik nesiot 18

treatment טִפּוּל m tipul 143

tree עֵץ m etz 85

tremendous עֲצוּם atzum 84

trim, to (a beard) לְיַשֵּׁר leyasher 31

trip נְסִיעָה f nesia 72, 152

trolley עֲגָלָה f agala 18, 70

trousers מִכְנָסַיִם m/pl mikhnasayim 116

truck מַשָּׂאִית f masait 79

try on, to לִמְדּוֹד limdod 114

tube שְׁפוֹפֶרֶת f shfoferet 119

Tuesday יוֹם שְׁלִישִׁי m yom shlishi 151

tumbler כּוֹס גְּדוֹלָה f kos gedola 120

tuna טוּנָה f tuna 44

turkey תַּרְנְגוֹל הוֹדוּ m tarnegol hodu 47

Turkey טוּרְקִיָּה f turkiya 146

turkish טוּרְקִי turki 57

turn, to (change direction) לִפְנוֹת lifnot 21, 77

turnip לֶפֶת f lefet 49

turquoise (colour) טוּרְקִיז turkiz 112

turtleneck סְוֶדֶר פּוֹלוֹ m sudar polo 115

tweezers מַלְקָחַיִת f melkaḥit 109

twelve שְׁנֵים-עָשָׂר shneym asar 147

twenty עֶשְׂרִים esrim 147

twice פַּעֲמַיִם f/pl paamayim 149

twin beds שְׁתֵּי מִטּוֹת f/pl shtey mitot 23

two שְׁנַיִם shnayim 147

typewriter מְכוֹנַת כְּתִיבָה f mekhonat ktiva 27

typing paper נְיָר לִמְכוֹנַת כְּתִיבָה m neyar limkhonat ktiva 105

tyre צָמִיג m tzamig 75, 76

U

ugly מְכוֹעָר mekhoar 13, 84

umbrella מִטְרִיָּה f mitriya 116

umbrella (beach) סוֹכֵךְ m sokhekh 91

uncle דּוֹד m dod 93

unconscious חֲסַר הַכָּרָה ḥasar hakara 139

מִלּוֹן

under מתחת mitaḥat 15
underdone *(meat)* נא na 46
underpants תחתונים *m/pl* taḥtonim 116
undershirt גופיה *f* gufiya 116
understand, to להבין lehavin 12, 16
undress, to להתפשט lehitpashet 142
United States ארצות הברית *f/pl* artzot habrit 146
university אוניברסיטה *f* universita 82
unleaded נטול עופרת netul oferet 75
until עד ad 15
up למעלה lemala 15
upset stomach קלקול קיבה *m* kilkul keva 107
upstairs למעלה lemala 15
urgent דחוף daḥuf 13, 145
urine שתן *m* sheten 142
use שמוש *m* shimush 17, 108
use, to להשתמש lehishtamesh 134
usually בדרך כלל bederekh klal«tab»

V

V-neck צווארון וי *m* tzavaron vi 115
vacancy חדר פנוי *m* ḥeder panuy
vacant פנוי panuy 13, 155
vacation פגרה *f* pagra 151
vaccinate, to לחסן leḥasen 140
vacuum flask תרמוס *m* termos 120
valley עמק *m* emek 85
value ערך *m* erekh 131
vanilla וניל *m* vanil 50
VAT *(sales tax)* מעמ *m* maam 24
vegetable ירק *m* yarak 48
vegetable store ירקן *m* yarkan 99
vegetarian צמחוני zimḥoni 38
vein וריד *m* varid 138
velvet קטיפה *f* ktifa 113
velveteen חקוי קטיפה *m* ḥikuy ktifa 113
venereal disease מחלת מין *f* maḥalat min 142
venison בשר צבי *m* besar tzvi 45
vermouth ורמוט *m* vermut 55
very מאד meod 15
vest גופיה *f* gufiya 116
vest *(Am.)* וסט *m* vest 116
veterinarian רופא חיות *m* rofe ḥayot 99
video camera מצלמת וידאו *f* matzlemat video 124
video cassette קסטת וידאו *f* kasetat video 118, 124, 127
video recorder מכונת הקלטה וידאו *f* mekhonat haklata video 118
view *(panorama)* נוף *m* nof 23, 25
village כפר *m* kfar 85
vinegar חמץ *m* hiometz 37
vineyard כרם *m* kerem 85
visit בקור *m* bikur 92
visit, to לבקר levaker 95
visiting hours שעות בקור *f/pl* sheot bikur 144
vitamin pill גלולת ויטמינים *f* glulat vitaminim 108
vodka וודקה *f* vodka 56
volleyball כדורעף *m* kaduraf 89
voltage מתח *m* metaḥ 27, 118
vomit, to להקיא lehaki 140

W

waist מתן *m* moten 142
waistcoat וסט *m* vest 116
wait, to לחכות leḥakot 21, 95, 108
waiter מלצר *m* meltzar 26, 36
waiting room חדר המתנה *m* ḥadar hamtana 67
waitress מלצרית *f* meltzarit 26, 36
wake, to להעיר lehair 27
Wales וילס *f* veyls 146
walk, to ללכת lalekhet 74, 85
wall חומה *f* ḥoma 85
wallet ארנק *m* arnak 156
walnut אגוז המלך *m* egoz hamelekh 52
want, to לרצות lirtzot 12, 101, 103
warm חם ḥam 94
washable כביס kavis 113
washbasin כיור *m* kiyor 28
washing powder אבקת כביסה *f* avkat kvisa 120
washing-up liquid תכשיר נקוי לכלים *m* takhshir nikuy lekhelim 120
watch שעון *m* shaon 121, 122
watchmaker's שען *m* shean 99, 121
watchstrap רצועה לשעון *f* retzua leshaon 122
water מים *m/pl* mayim 24, 28, 32, 75, 90
water flask מימיה *f* meymiya 106
water-skis מגלשים לסקי מים *m/pl* miglashim liski mayim 91
waterfall מפל מים *m* mapal mayim 85
waterproof נגד מים neged mayim 122
wave גל *m* gal 90
we אנחנו anaḥnu 162
weather מזג אויר *m* mezeg avir 94
weather forecast תחזית מזג אויר *f* taḥazit mezeg avir 94
wedding ring טבעת נשואים *f* tabaat nisuim 121
Wednesday יום רביעי *m* yom revii 151
week שבוע *m* shavua 16, 20, 24, 80, 92, 151
weekend סופשבוע *m* sofshavua 20
well טוב tov 10, 140
well-done *(meat)* מבושל היטב mevushal

hey**tev** 46
west מערב *m* maa**rav** 77
what מה ma 11
wheel גלגל *m* gal**gal** 78
when מתי ma**tay** 11
where איפה **ey**fo 11
where from מאיפה me**ey**fo 92, 146
which איזה **ey**zo 11
whisky מ ויסקי **vis**ki 17, 56
white לבן la**van** 55, 112
who מי mi 11
why מדוע ma**du**a 11
wick פתילה *f* pti**la** 126
wide רחב ra**ḥav** 117
wide-angle lens עדשה רחבת זוית *f* ada**sha** reḥa**vat** za**vit** 125
wife אשה *f* i**sha** 93
wig פאה נכרית *f* pe**a** nokh**rit** 110
wind רוח *f* **ru**aḥ 94
window חלון *m* ḥa**lon** 28, 36, 65, 69
window *(shop)* חלון ראוה *m* ḥa**lon** raa**va** 100, 111
windscreen/shield חלון קדמי *m* ḥa**lon** kid**mi** 76
windsurfer גלשן רוח *m* gal**shan** **ru**aḥ 91
wine יין *m* **ya**yin 17, 54, 58
wine list רשימת יינות *f* reshi**mat** yey**not** 54
wine merchant's חנות משקאות *f* ḥa**nut** mashka**ot** 99
winter חורף *m* **ho**ref 150
winter sports ספורט חורף *m* sport **ho**ref 91
wiper *(car)* מגב *m* ma**gav** 76
wish איחול *m* i**ḥul** 152
with עם im 15
withdraw, to *(from account)* למשוך lim**shokh 130**
withdrawal משיכה *f* meshi**kha** 130
without בלי bli 15
wonderful נהדר nehe**dar** 96
wood חורשה *f* ḥur**sha** 85
wool צמר *m* **tze**mer 113
word מלה *f* mi**la** 12, 14, 133
working day יום חול *m* yom ḥol 151
worse יותר גרוע yo**ter** ga**ru**a 13
worsted צמר סרוק *m* **tze**mer sa**ruk** 13
wound פצע *m* **pe**tza 139
wrap up, to לעטוף laa**tof** 103
write, to לכתוב likh**tov** 12, 101, 162
wristwatch שעון יד *m* she**on** yad 122
writing pad בלוק לכתיבה *m* blok likhti**va** 105
writing paper נייר לכתיבה *m* ne**yar** likhti**va** 27, 105
wrong לא נכון lo na**khon** 14, 77, 135

Y

year שנה *f* sha**na** 149
yellow צהוב tza**hov** 112
yes כן ken 10
yesterday אתמול et**mol** 151
yet עדיין a**da**yin 15, 16; אולם u**lam** 15
yield, to *(traffic)* לתת זכות קדימה la**tet** ze**khut** kdi**ma** 79
yoghurt יוגורט *m* **yo**gurt 41, 60
young צעיר tza**ir** 14
youth hostel אכסנית נוער *f* akhsani**yat** **no**ar 22, 32

Z

zero אפס *m* **e**fes 147
zip(per) רוכסן *m* rokh**san** 116
zoo גן חיות *m* gan ḥa**yot** 82
zoology זואולוגיה *f* zoo**lo**giya 83
zucchini קישוא *m* ki**shu** 48

מַפְתֵּחַ עִבְרִי

מַפְתֵּחַ עִבְרִי

LEBANON
SYRIA
Nahariya
Isefat
Acre
Capernaum
Sea of Galilee
Haifa
MEDITERRANEAN SEA
Tiberias
Nazareth
Caesarea
Beit-Shean
Hadera
Jordan
Shekhem (Nabulus)
Netanya
Herzliya
TEL AVIV-JAFFA
Bat Yam
Jericho
AMMAN
Jerusalem
Ashdod
Qumran
Bethlehem
Ashqelon
Hebron
Dead Sea
Gaza
Masada
Beersheba
ISRAEL
NEGEV
Avdat
JORDAN
EGYPT
Yorvata
Ovda
Eilat
Aqaba
Gulf of Aqaba